Boxing in Atlantic City

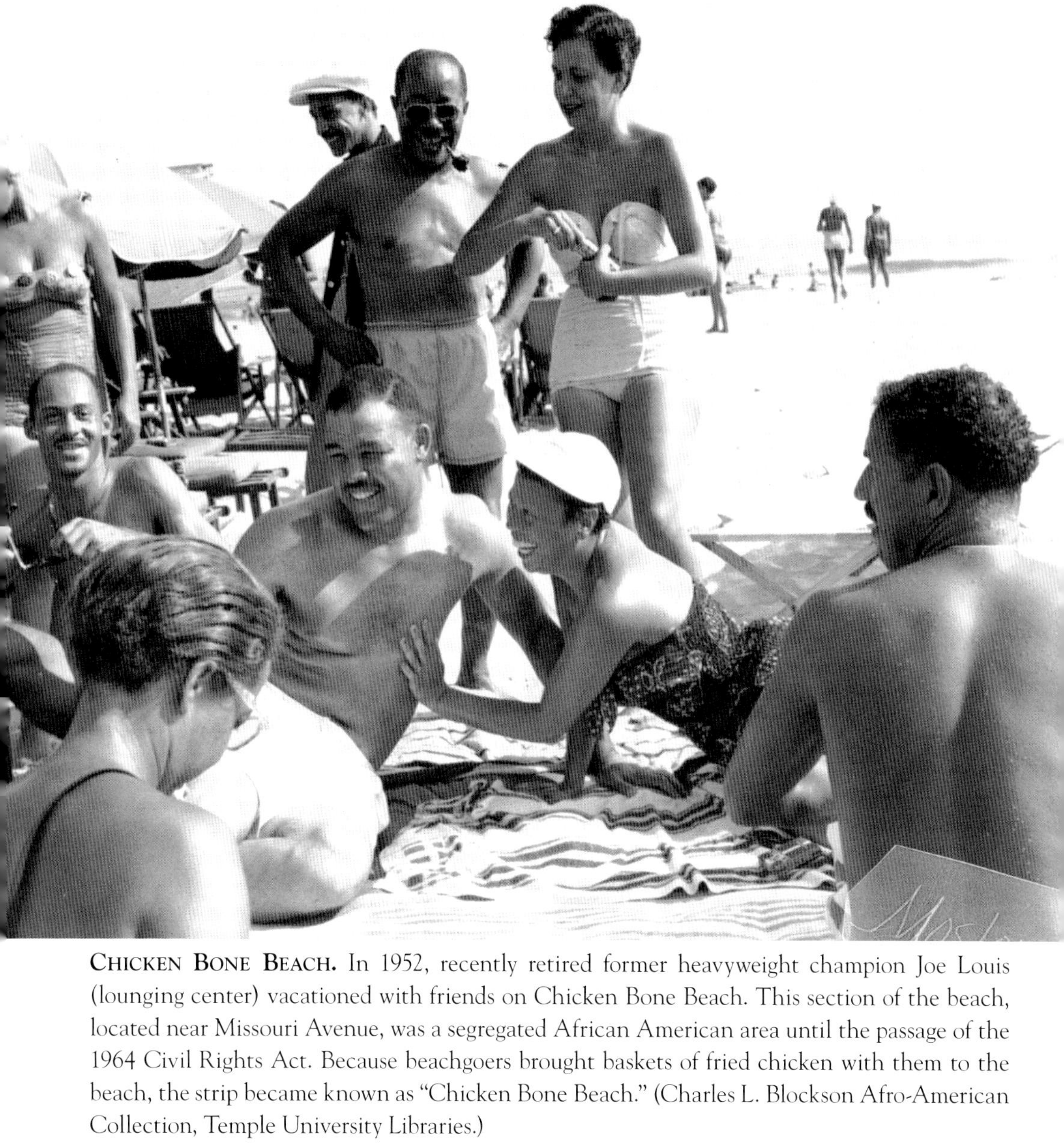

CHICKEN BONE BEACH. In 1952, recently retired former heavyweight champion Joe Louis (lounging center) vacationed with friends on Chicken Bone Beach. This section of the beach, located near Missouri Avenue, was a segregated African American area until the passage of the 1964 Civil Rights Act. Because beachgoers brought baskets of fried chicken with them to the beach, the strip became known as "Chicken Bone Beach." (Charles L. Blockson Afro-American Collection, Temple University Libraries.)

FRONT COVER: Arturo Gatti (right) fights Thomas Damgaard in 2006. (Photograph by Ray Bailey.)

COVER BACKGROUND: Pictured is the Convention Hall interior in 1995. (Photograph by John DiSanto.)

BACK COVER: Mike Tyson is pictured in 1995. (Photograph by Pete Goldfield.)

BOXING IN ATLANTIC CITY

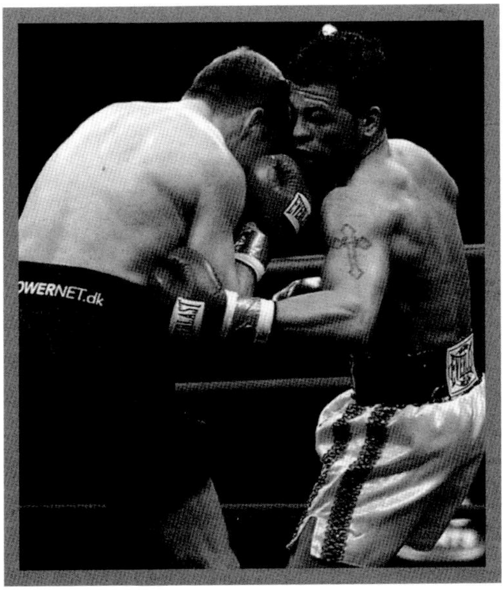

John DiSanto and Matthew H. Ward

ARCADIA
PUBLISHING

This book is dedicated to Jennifer DiSanto, my one and only. —John

This book is dedicated to my Ward girls. —Matt

ISBN 978-1-4671-0707-5

Published by Arcadia Publishing
Charleston, South Carolina

Printed in the United States of America

Library of Congress Control Number: 2021933269

For all general information, please contact Arcadia Publishing:
Telephone 843-853-2070
Fax 843-853-0044
E-mail sales@arcadiapublishing.com
For customer service and orders:
Toll-Free 1-888-313-2665

Visit us on the Internet at www.arcadiapublishing.com

CONTENTS

ACKNOWLEDGMENTS

With an image-driven book such as this, we clearly could not have completed the project without help from a number of excellent photographers. Atlantic City Boxing Hall of Famer Ray Bailey was especially helpful, contributing nearly 50 images. The late Pete Goldfield's photographs proved to be the backbone of this book. Unfortunately, he is not here to enjoy his work as it appears in this publication. However, we hope that our use of his photographs serves as a tribute to his talent and also nudges the AC Boxing Hall of Fame to remember Pete with an induction sometime in the near future. Other photographers who helped us along the way were Darryl Cobb Jr., Bill Baron, Jano Cohen, and Bill Camarota. Additional images were contributed by a number of friends and associates, including Detroit collector Bob Ryder, the Veteran Boxers Association—Ring One of Philadelphia, George (Wilson) Silvano, the son of famed cut man Jimmy Wilson, the New Jersey Boxing Hall of Fame, the Atlantic City Boxing Hall of Fame, and former boxer Guy Gargan. Renowned Atlantic City historian Vicki Gold Levi not only provided images, she also helped guide us through part of our research. Hall of fame boxing promoter J Russell Peltz was quick to help, providing images, serving as a sounding board, and offering excellent feedback. Henry Hascup was our primary fact-checker and saved us much embarrassment with the errors he found while we compiled this book. The Corciones (Erica and Sean), Steve Smoger, George Nelson, Buzz Keough of the *Press of Atlantic City*, Lt. Will Santiago of the Atlantic City Police Athletic League, Frank Bartolini, Luis Cortes, Stephen Ward, Chuck Hasson, and Ray McCline all helped us with details, information, and support. Arcadia Publishing was great to work with, especially Angel Prohaska, J. Banks Smither, and Katie Parry. Matt would like to acknowledge his grandmother, Mildred Caracciolo, who first showed him the "wonders" of Atlantic City. Finally, we would also like to acknowledge all the participants of the Atlantic City boxing scene, both inside the ring and out, for their inspiration. Without all of those mentioned here, this book would not be possible.

INTRODUCTION

The sport of boxing has been a major draw in Atlantic City (AC) since the late 19th century. For over 100 years, pugilists, from club fighters to boxing royalty, fought at AC's numerous venues located in casinos, arenas, and on piers. The gradual increase in boxing activity peaked in the 1980s, when the casino era greatly stimulated the number of fight cards held along the Boardwalk. This culminated with the rise of champion Mike Tyson, who controlled the heavyweight division for three exhilarating years. Four of his memorable title bouts occurred in the city. A decade later, Arturo Gatti ushered in another rise in AC's boxing prominence with his many thrilling appearances at the shore. Despite the number of star boxers and important fights afterward, AC slowly declined as a boxing capital. However, in 2017, the Atlantic City Boxing Hall of Fame began holding induction weekend activities, which brought new interest to the city and reminded fans of AC's important place in boxing's storied history.

Tackling this project was as challenging as it was exciting. Space limitations prevented the inclusion of every deserving subject and forced some difficult content cuts. Further, much of the research for this book was carried out during the COVID-19 pandemic. This hindered the use of many resources, including libraries and historical societies. One fear is that this limitation resulted in the inability to uncover a photograph of the Waltz Dream Arena, a legendary fight club that was at the heart of AC boxing for more than two decades beginning in the 1920s. To date, more boxing shows took place at the Waltz than at any other AC venue. Unfortunately, after months of searching, it appears that no photograph of this locale exists.

In this book, you will see abbreviations used for the world championship titles at stake in many of the bouts detailed. These include WBC (World Boxing Council), WBA (World Boxing Association), IBF (International Boxing Federation), and WBO (World Boxing Organization). Also referenced are the USBA (US Boxing Association) and NABF (North American Boxing Federation), two widely recognized regional titles. In most cases, many other fringe sanctioning bodies are not mentioned in this book. Also used are common abbreviations for boxing terms such as knockout (KO) and technical knockout (TKO). The names of some AC venues changed over the years. However, in this book, the most common name for a venue is used. For example, Convention Hall was originally named the Atlantic City Auditorium and today is known as Boardwalk Hall. However, the venue is best known as Convention Hall. The same is true for many casinos, some of which also experienced name changes for marketing or other reasons. To simplify the narrative, this book uses a single name for each site.

The story of AC boxing is an entertaining ride that involves both the giants of the sport and the working-class fighters who boxed on the thousands of fight cards that occurred on and off the Boardwalk. Most of the events highlighted were the critical matches that took place. However, also included are many smaller fights that deserve recognition as well as some surprising upsets, an eight-second knockout, and even battles between world champion–caliber fighters and unnamed kangaroos.

AC boxing's supporting cast is also spotlighted, including key promoters, referees, trainers, cut men, writers, announcers, training camps, restaurants, bars, and important occurrences like the legalization of gambling in AC.

This book is a collection of the most important, interesting, and exciting milestones of AC boxing history, ranging from 1865 to 2020. We truly hope you enjoy reading it as much as we did putting it together.

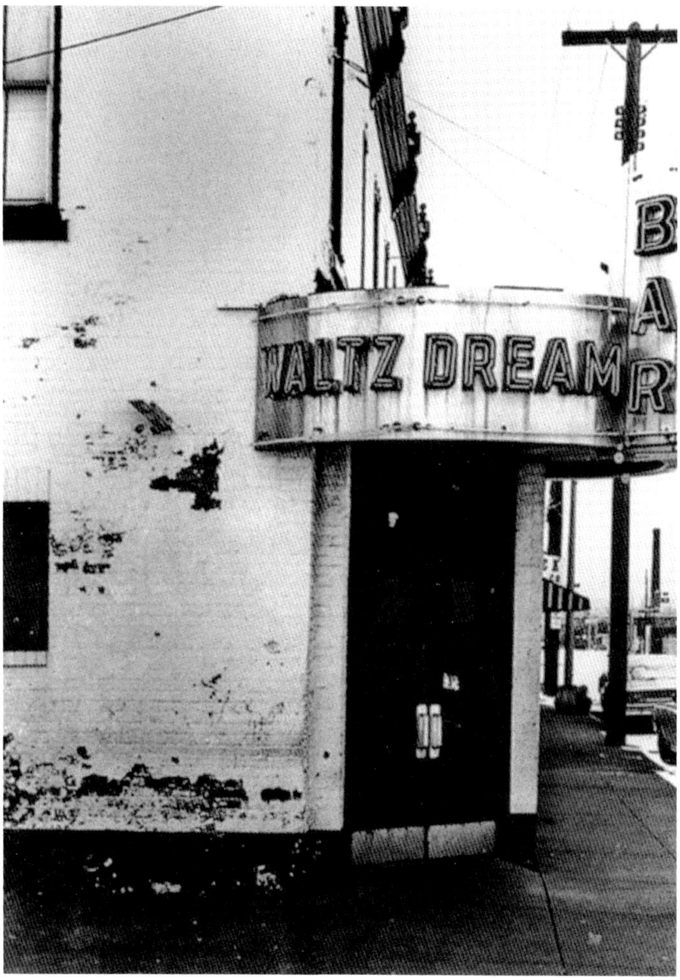

WALTZ DREAM BAR. In Atlantic City's Northside section of town, the Waltz Dream Arena was such a popular and important part of the culture, both as a jazz club and a boxing venue, that a neighborhood bar opened around the corner after the original Waltz burned down. The new place was named the Waltz Dream Bar in homage to the original locale. This photograph dates back to the 1970s. (Photograph by Bill Camarota.)

1

Beginning

1865–1963

Atlantic City boxing began in the late 19th century with a handful of shows at outdoor fairgrounds and venues like Herculaneum Park and the Atlantic City Ballpark. The expansion of train services during this time was an early selling point for the city and helped AC's popularity grow as a vacation and sports destination. Hometown pugilist Horace Leeds was the local boxing star of the day, with at-home fights against Young Griffo, Owen Ziegler, Willie Clark, and Bull McCarthy. By the 1900s, nearby cities, especially Philadelphia, furnished many of the fighters who competed in AC's early boxing matches.

In the 1920s, the Waltz Dream Arena debuted as a fight venue, and by 1925, after promoter Joe Miller took over, it became the center of boxing in AC for decades. Located in the Northside section of town, the indoor arena offered regular shows featuring both club fighters and big names. However, its biggest distinction was being a venue open to Black boxers who often headlined shows there, a rarity for the times. The Waltz also welcomed then-controversial "mixed-race" matches.

By 1930, AC's massive Convention Hall opened and became an important alternate location. With its five-figure seating capacity, AC finally had a site to host big matches year-round. Although the Waltz was still the busier venue, Convention Hall began staging the more significant events.

During this time period, AC also became an important training locale. Ring stars from all over the world came to AC to prepare for their bouts. In the 1940s, Laoma Byrd opened her famous training camp in nearby Pleasantville. The camp flourished in the 1950s and hosted many top names of the sport.

In 1963, Joey Giardello defeated Dick Tiger to win the middleweight title at Convention Hall in front of 12,000 fans. The success of AC's first world championship fight appeared to set the stage for big things to come. Sadly, this was not the case. The AC boxing scene went completely dark for the next 10 years.

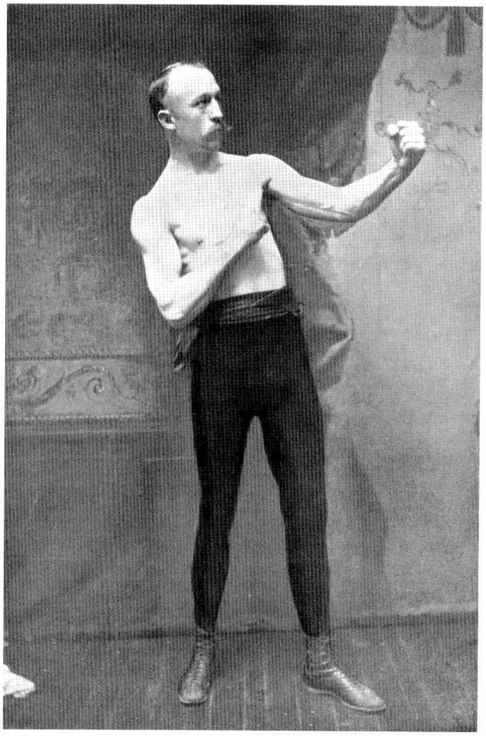

"THE FIGHTING QUAKER." Horace M. Leeds was born in AC on November 1, 1865, to a prominent family in the area. Known as "The Fighting Quaker" during his bare-knuckle boxing career, Leeds fought and trained with notable fighters of his day, including Willie Clark, Al O'Brien, Billy Leedom, Prof. John H. Clark, Dominick McCaffrey, and James J. Corbett. Leeds's excellent footwork, speed, and crafty defense helped him avoid punishment in matches. (Author's collection.)

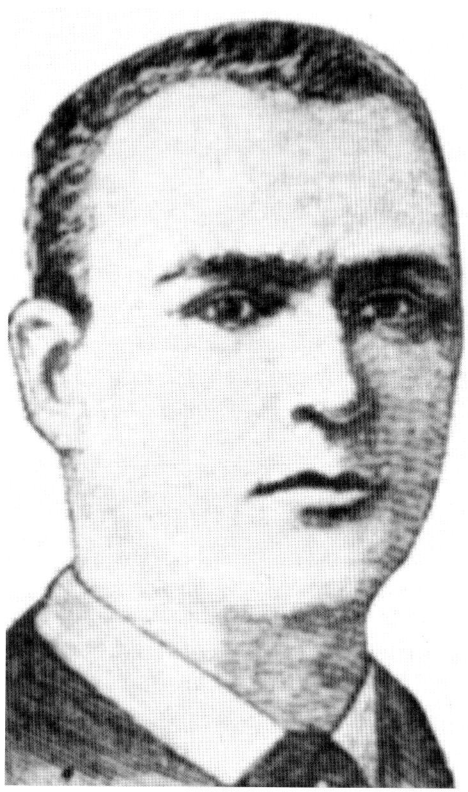

DOMINICK MCCAFFREY. Dominick McCaffrey was a bare-knuckle boxing pioneer from Pittsburgh who stepped in the ring with noteworthy fighters such as John L. Sullivan and James J. Corbett. He managed bare-knuckle fighter Horace Leeds of AC during his July 4, 1893, victory over Philadelphia's Al O'Brien at the Polo Grounds. Later that summer, McCaffrey traveled to AC, where he easily defeated a local amateur boxing star named John F. McCormick on August 15. (Author's collection.)

Newspaper Decision. Owen Ziegler, former American amateur champion, faced hometown hero Horace Leeds in the main attraction of an athletic carnival held at Inlet Amusement Park on August 20, 1894. The fight, witnessed by about 4,000 fans, was quite close. Since no knockout occurred, the bout was officially declared a no-decision, which was standard for the day. Gamblers often relied on "newspaper decisions" to settle their bets, going along with a pre-selected publication's opinion on who won the fight. Ziegler, a Philadelphian, fought more than 100 professional fights, but this was his only appearance in Atlantic City. (Author's collection.)

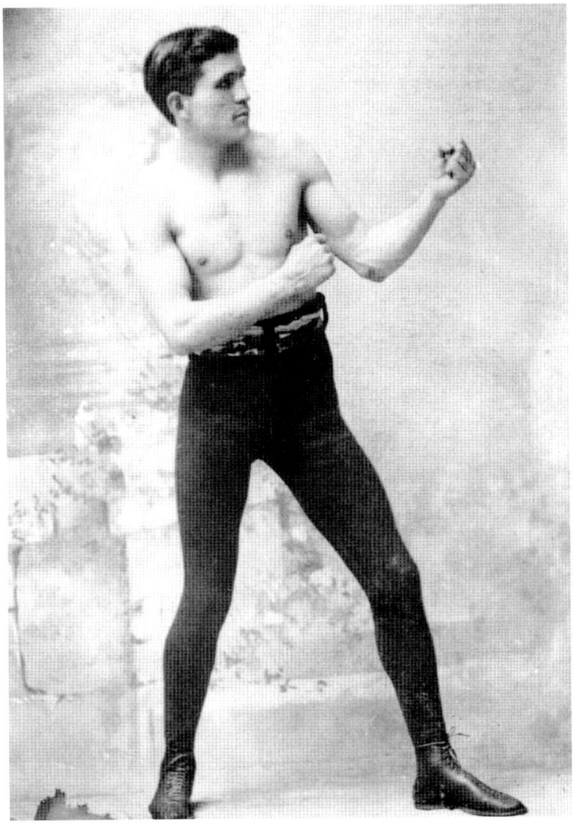

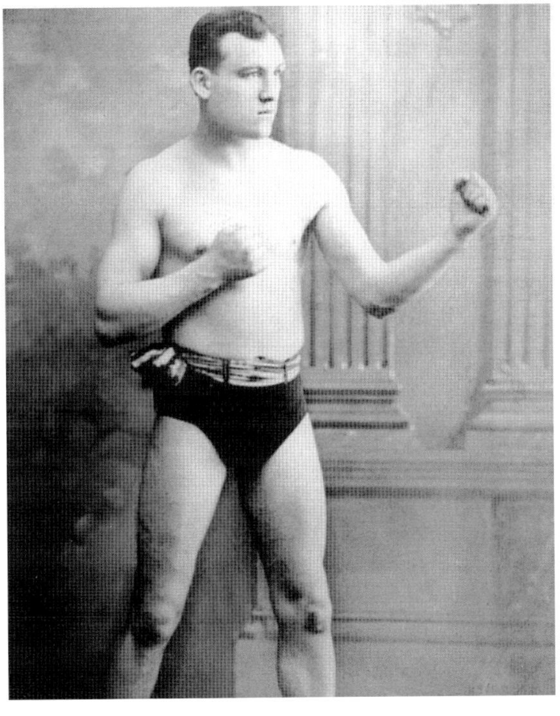

Dirty Fighter. "Mysterious" Billy Smith was a bare-knuckle boxer from the Pacific Northwest who fought professionally between 1890 and 1915. Over the course of his career, he was disqualified at least 11 times. Smith gained a reputation as the "dirtiest fighter who ever lived" by incorporating illegal moves such as elbows, knees, butts, and biting into his boxing style. Smith fought Jimmy Mann in Atlantic City on April 1, 1895. (Author's collection.)

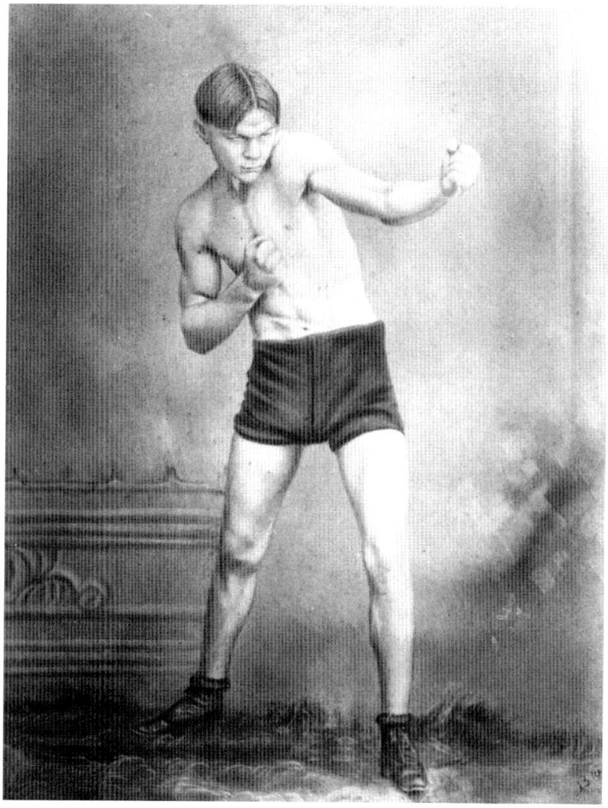

RARE VISIT. Jimmy Simister was an experienced featherweight who rarely fought outside his hometown of Philadelphia. During his 162-bout career, Simister fought less than 20 times in other cities. One of those trips was a stop in Atlantic City, where he beat Billy Abramowitz by a six-round decision on December 15, 1903. Simister's career spanned from 1896 to 1909. (Author's collection.)

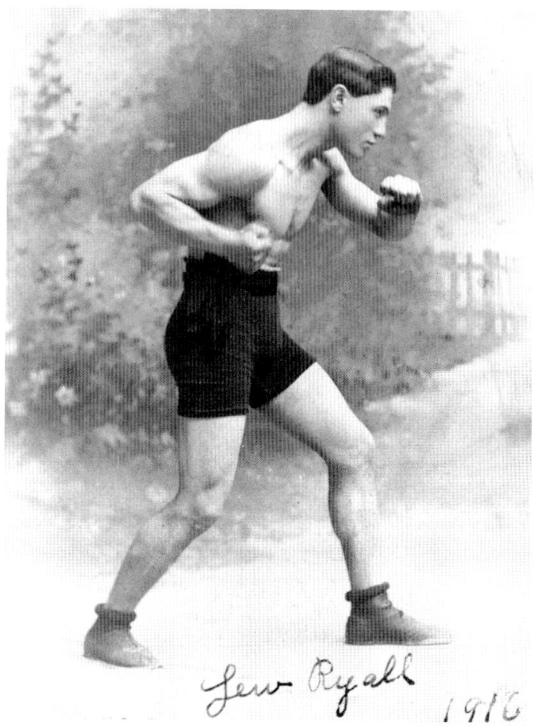

LEW RYALL. Slugger Lew Ryall faced many fine fighters in his 154 pro bouts, including Joe Grim, Kentucky Rosebud, Ellwood McCloskey, Eddie Lenny, Jimmy Simister, Kid Beebe, Sammy Smith, and Pat Bradley. In 1900, Ryall fought in Atlantic City three times, including a no-decision with Jack Ashton at the Quay House and two 15-round bouts against Billy Maharg at the Regular Football Club. After a draw in the first bout, Ryall won the second fight with Maharg by decision. (Author's collection.)

LITERARY INSPIRATION. Jack Britton, born William J. Breslin, was a veteran of over 300 professional boxing matches between 1904 and 1930. One of these was a victory against "KO" Willie Loughlin at the Atlantic City Sports Club on July 11, 1918. The two-time world welterweight champion lost his title to Mickey Walker in 1922. Some literary historians and scholars believe this fight was the inspiration for Ernest Hemingway's 1927 short story *Fifty Grand*, which tells the tale of fictional fighter Jack Brennan's preparation for his match against challenger Jimmy Walcott. (Author's collection.)

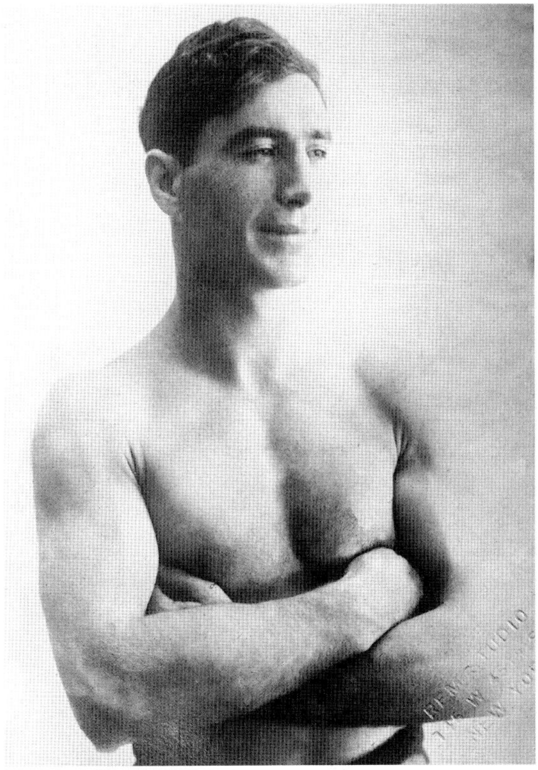

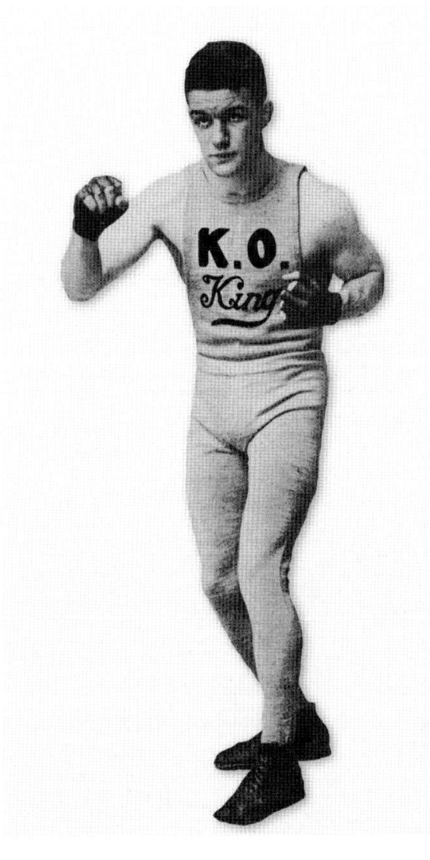

KO ARTIST. George "KO" Chaney was a left-handed knockout artist from Baltimore who scored 78 KOs in his 178 career bouts. He fought twice in Atlantic City, winning both bouts by fifth-round knockout. On August 12, 1918, Chaney stopped Mickey Donley of Newark, New Jersey. Eighteen days later, Chaney put Philadelphian Eddie O'Keefe down for the count with a left hand to the body. (Author's collection.)

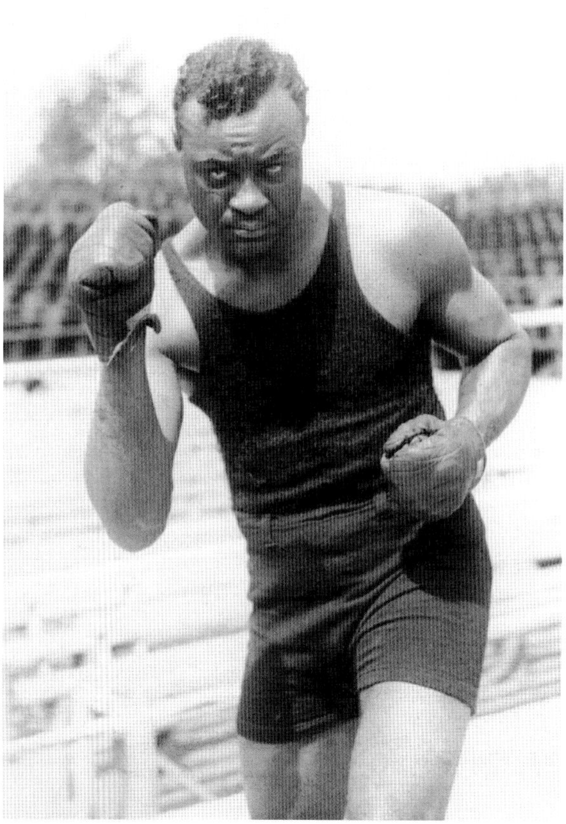

DENIED HIS CHANCE. Harry Wills fought professionally from 1911 to 1932 and held the "Colored Heavyweight Championship" on three occasions. Despite being one of the top fighters of his time, Wills was never given the opportunity to challenge the White heavyweight greats of the day, such as Jack Dempsey. Records show that Wills fought in AC on two occasions in 1918, including a successful title defense against Jeff Clark. (Author's collection.)

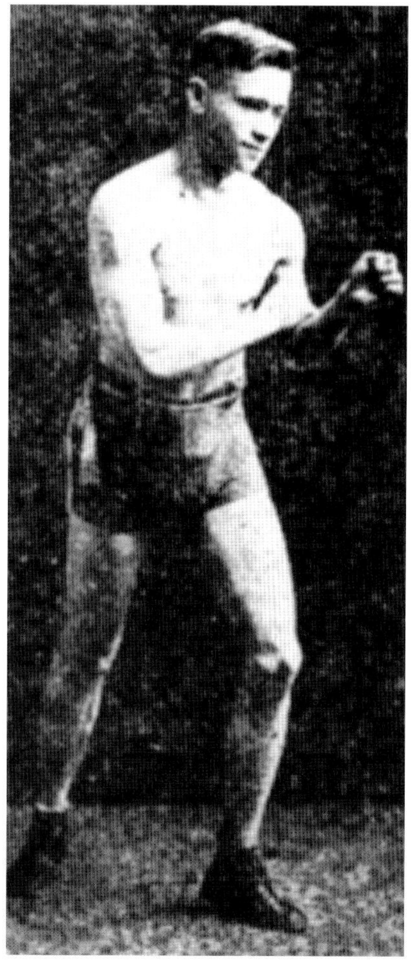

NAVY BOXER. Atlantic City featherweight Johnny Ray interrupted his boxing career to enlist in the Naval Reserves during World War I. He was stationed in Cape May, Philadelphia, and New York, where he served both as a recruiter and a boxing instructor. After his ring career resumed in 1920, he fought in his hometown 10 times between 1920 and 1927, mostly at the Waltz Dream Arena. (Author's collection.)

"THE OXNARD CYCLONE." Near the end of his great career, heavyweight Sam McVea, "The Oxnard Cyclone," appeared in Atlantic City on July 7, 1921, where he beat Jeff Clark. McVea, denied a title shot due to the color of his skin, was famous for rivalries with Jack Johnson, Sam Langford, Joe Jennette, and Harry Wills. McVea fought once more, another 10-round bout with Clark, before dying from pneumonia on December 23, 1921. He was 37. (Author's collection.)

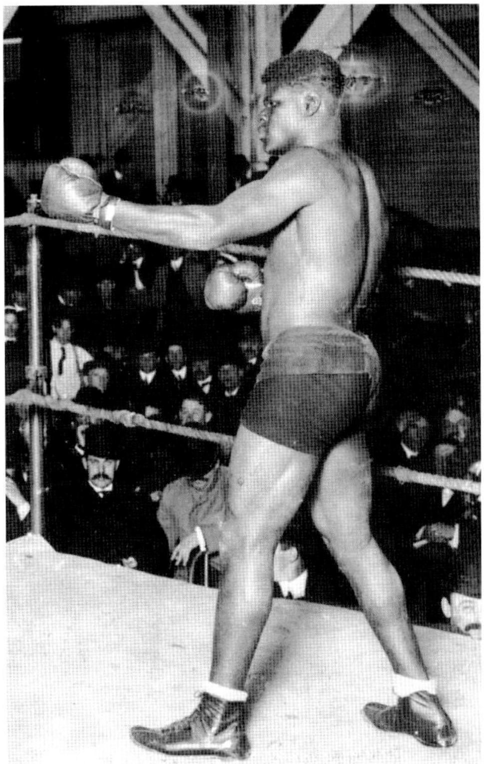

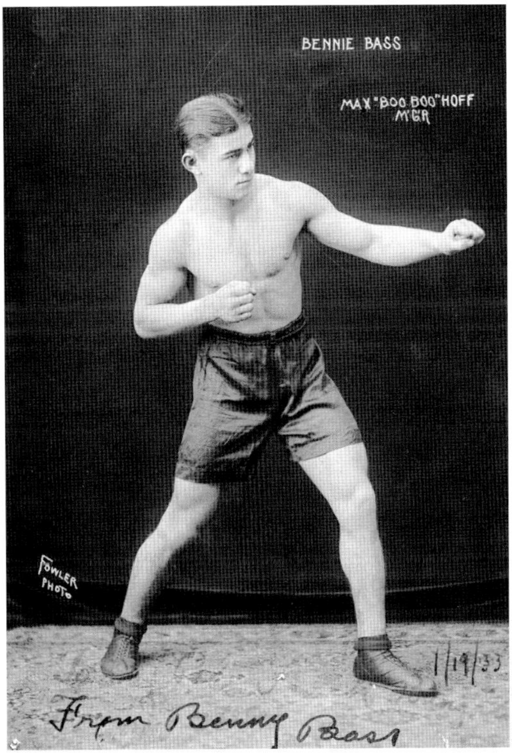

"THE LITTLE FISH." Two-division world champion Benny Bass fought an array of top ring talent between 1919 and 1940. Born in the Ukraine, "The Little Fish" came to Philadelphia at the age of three and started fighting professionally at 15. His 243 bouts included 23 Atlantic City fights, all wins, at the Waltz Dream Arena, Bacharach Ball Park, Bader Field, the AC Airport, and a 10-round decision over Young Patsy Wallace before 6,000 fans at Convention Hall. (Author's collection.)

BOXING

Northside A. C.

3 Six-Round Bouts

2 Eight-Round Bouts

WALTZ DREAM—OHIO AVE., NEAR ARCTIC

MONDAY, APRIL 27th, 1925

MIKE CAMAROTA (Promoter) **JOE WENKE (Matchmaker)**

Frankie VINCENT vs. Clarence Kid BOOYE
Kid HENRY vs. Al EDWARDS
Mike FERINA vs. Carl NAGLE
Young Peter JACKSON vs. Silent PURYEAR
Pedro CAMPO vs. Tommy FARLEY

Prices, $1.00, $1.50, $2.00 (War tax extra)

PHONE MARINE 1727-M **FIRST BOUT 8.30 P. M.**

WALTZ DREAM ARENA. Between 1921 and 1948, the Waltz Dream Arena was AC's primary fight venue. Originally a jazz club, the Waltz offered weekly boxing cards under the auspices of the Northside Athletic Club. Located on Ohio Avenue between Arctic and Baltic Avenues, the single-story building had a seating capacity of 3,000 and was the site of more than 750 boxing shows, more than any other Atlantic City venue to date. (Vicki Gold Levi.)

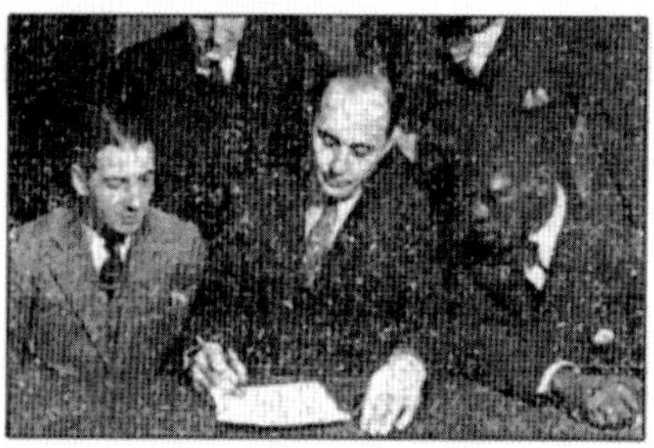

CLUB PHONE 5-9504

NORTHSIDE A. C.

NORTH OHIO AVENUE

ATLANTIC CITY, N. J.

BOXING EVERY FRIDAY NIGHT — 52 SHOWS A YEAR

JOE MILLER, *Promoter*
Home Phone
4-5107

JOE WENKE, *Matchmaker*
10 N. 13th Street, Phila., Pa.
Phone: LOCust 9444

THE PROMOTER. Joe Miller (center) purchased the Waltz Dream Arena in 1925 and turned it into the most consistent and important AC boxing venue of the pre-casino era. Miller offered high-quality shows featuring rising prospects, club fighters, and visiting stars. Miller also welcomed African American fighters and allowed "mixed-race" matches between Black and White boxers. He sold the Waltz around 1941 and opened a newsstand and sandwich shop on the Boardwalk. (George Wilson Silvano and Chuck Hasson.)

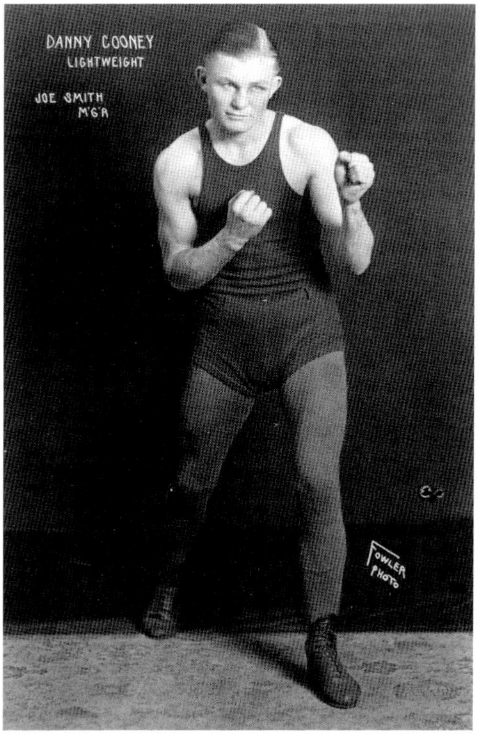

WALTZ DREAM REGULAR. Danny Cooney was from the Trenton suburb of Roebling, New Jersey. During his 11-year boxing career, he fought nine times at the Waltz Dream Arena during the 1920s, including bouts with Atlantic City's Tommy Cooney, Pleasantville's Gene Morretti, Philadelphia's Ray Mitchell, Cleveland's Alex Hart, and Camden's Roxie Allen. He only lost once at the shore: a third-round knockout at the hands of Philadelphian Jack Gallagher in 1929. (Author's collection.)

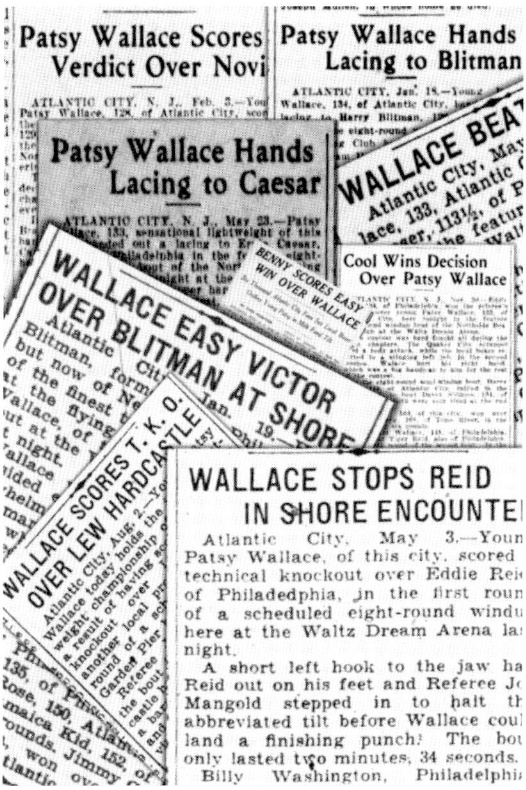

YOUNG PATSY WALLACE. For every champion-caliber fighter who trained and fought in AC, there were countless others like Young Patsy Wallace. Wallace fought 64 times as a professional and ended his career with an even record. Between 1924 and 1935, the man who fought a majority of his fights as a lightweight fought an impressive 44 times in his hometown. Most of these fights were featured at the Waltz Dream Arena. (Author's collection.)

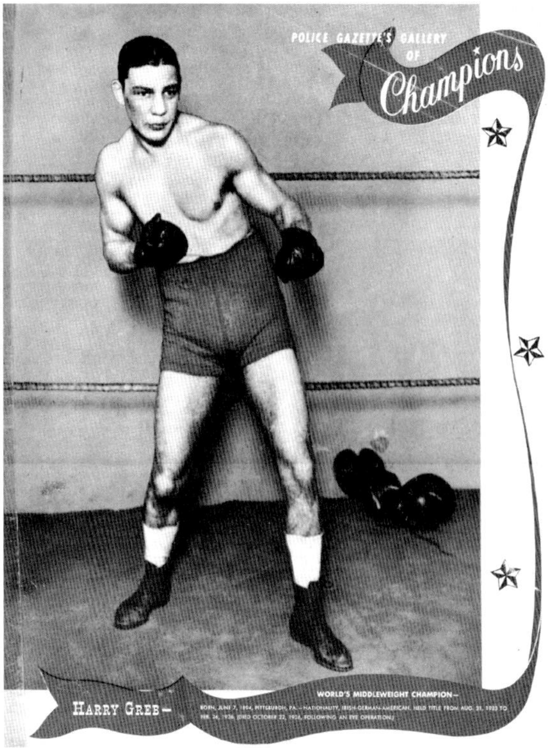

"THE PITTSBURGH WINDMILL." Harry Greb was an all-time great with 299 career bouts against the best of his era. World middleweight champion between 1923 and 1926, "The Pittsburgh Windmill" had a swarming style and fought any opponent regardless of his size. His only stop in Atlantic City came on August 12, 1925, against Cincinnati's Pat Walsh at the Atlantic City Airport. Greb scored four knockdowns, won by second-round knockout, and donated his purse to charity. (Author's collection.)

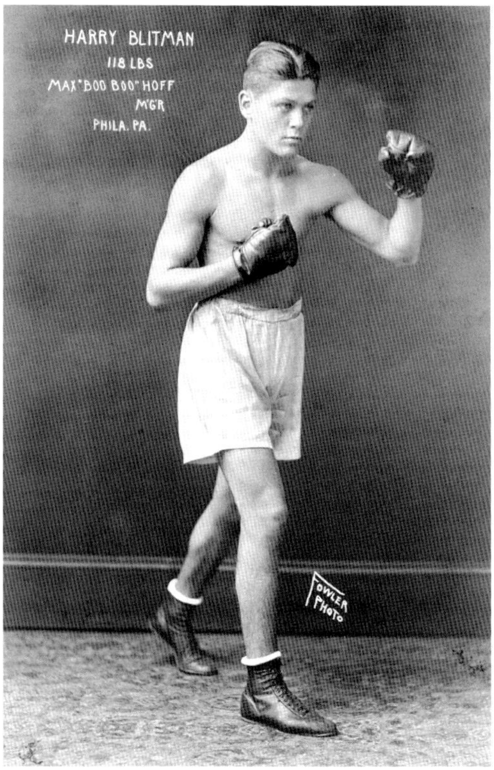

"HANDSOME HARRY." Southpaw Harry Blitman frequently appeared in Atlantic City, including his 1926 pro debut at Bacharach Hall. "Handsome Harry" never earned a title shot, despite beating champion Tony Canzoneri in a non-title bout. During his eight-year career, Blitman only lost 11 of his 78 fights, with 29 of his bouts taking place in Atlantic City. His only loss at the resort came against AC's Young Patsy Wallace in 1932. (Author's collection.)

EDDIE REED. Lightweight Eddie Reed was a speedy Philadelphia boxer who made 23 trips to Atlantic City in the 1920s and 1930s against excellent opposition, including Camden's Roxie Allen, New Yorker Babe Herman, Philadelphians Harry Blitman, Harry "Kid" Brown, and Al Gordon, and Atlantic City fighters Tommy Cooney, Young Patsy Wallace, and Young Harry Wills. Nineteen of these bouts took place at Waltz Dream Arena. (Author's collection.)

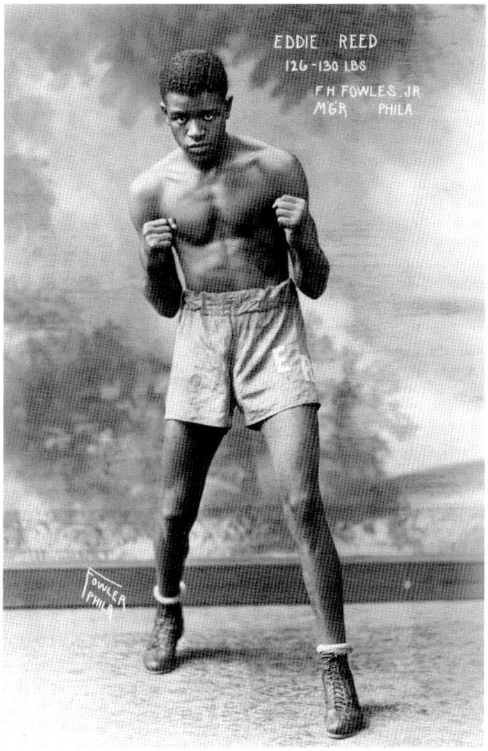

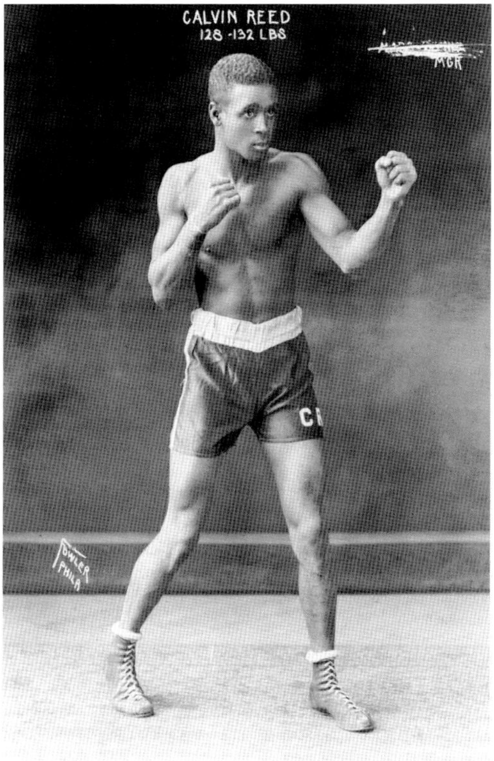

CALVIN REED. Lightweight Calvin Reed made his pro debut in Atlantic City on August 17, 1928, with a draw against local Eddie Palmer. Reed fought 18 more times in the city, including bouts with Benny Bass, Harry Blitman, Ernie Caesar, and Mickey Blair. All of his AC bouts took place at the Waltz Dream Arena, except for his eight-round fight with Bass at Bacharach Ball Park on July 26, 1929. (Author's collection.)

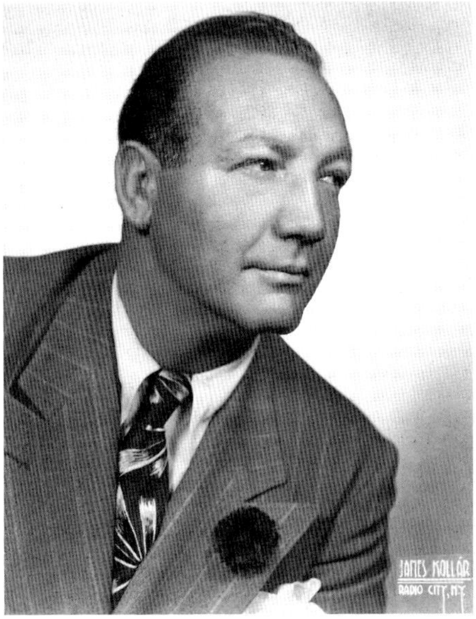

CHAMPION OF BOXING AND HOLLYWOOD. Prior to capturing the world light heavyweight title in 1932, "Slapsie" Maxie Rosenbloom's career took him to AC, where he defeated Jamaica Kid on July 23, 1926. Rosenbloom was not just known for his ring accolades. He also had a successful career as a character actor in Hollywood. Rosenbloom is credited with 79 film and television appearances, including *Nothing Sacred* and *Each Dawn I Die*. He often played a loveable, punch-drunk character. (Author's collection.)

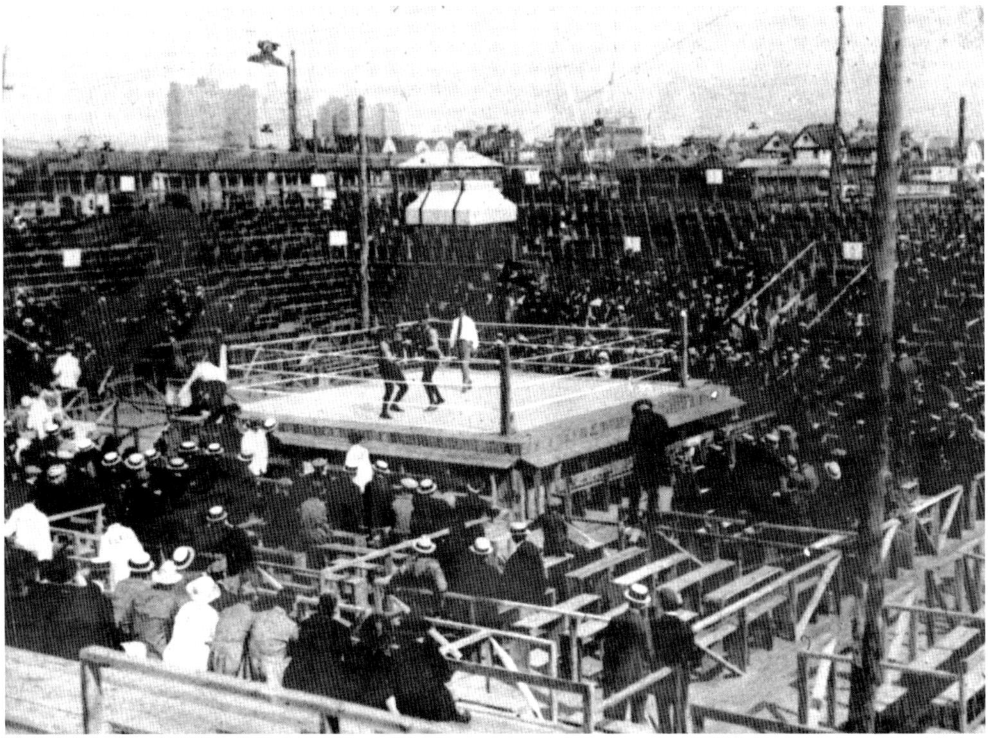

DEMPSEY IN TRAINING. Heavyweight champion Jack Dempsey prepared for his 1921 title defense against Georges Carpentier outdoors at the Atlantic City Airport (pictured) with daily crowds of up to 1,000 fans watching. Dempsey knocked out Carpentier in boxing's first million-dollar gate on July 2, 1921, in Jersey City. In 1926, Dempsey returned to train for Gene Tunney in private workouts at AC's Greyhound Park. Dempsey lost the title to Tunney on September 23, 1926, in Philadelphia. (Author's collection.)

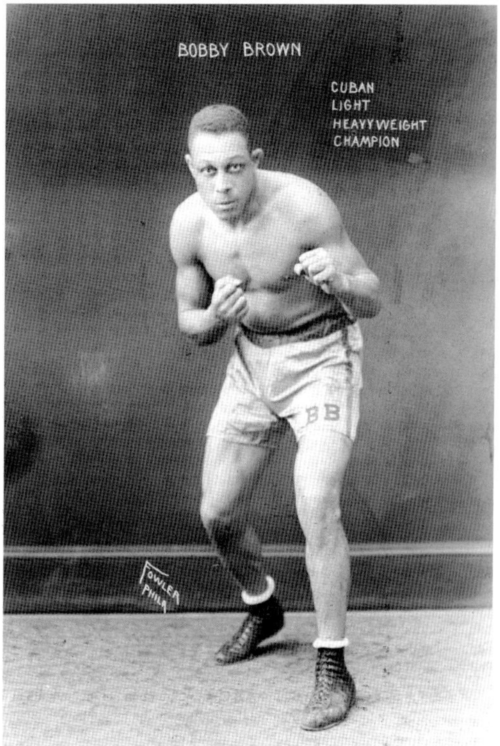

"THE CUBAN WONDER." Bobby Brown was nicknamed "The Cuban Wonder," despite being born in Pennsylvania and fighting mostly out of Chester and Philadelphia. The hard-punching light heavyweight went undefeated in Atlantic City, scoring 11 victories, nine by knockout, between 1927 and 1928. His best win at the shore was an eight-round newspaper decision over Battling Levinsky on August 15, 1927, at the dog track. Brown's career was cut short by his 1929 death from pneumonia. (Author's collection.)

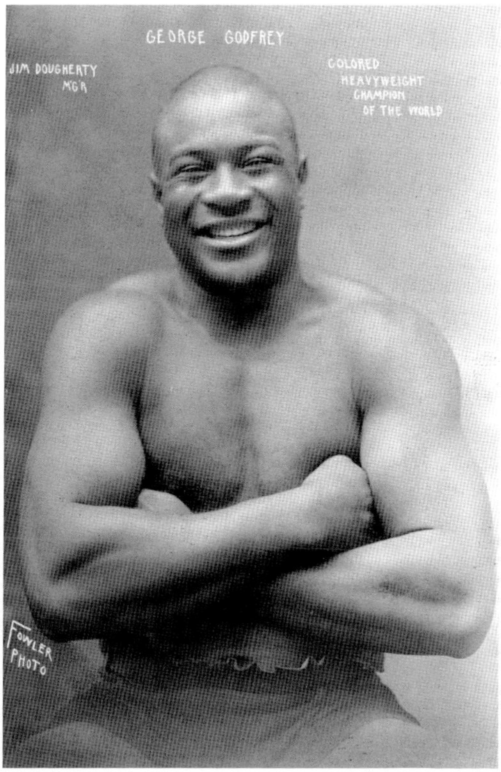

"COLORED HEAVYWEIGHT CHAMPION." George Godfrey was a heavyweight contender during the 1920s. The tall and talented boxer might have become world champion had he not been African American. Barred from a legitimate title shot, Godfrey was relegated to winning the "Colored Heavyweight Championship." He defended this title by a first-round knockout against Clem Johnson at Waltz Dream Arena on November 21, 1927. The win made Godfrey the leading contender for champion Gene Tunney but to no avail. (Author's collection.)

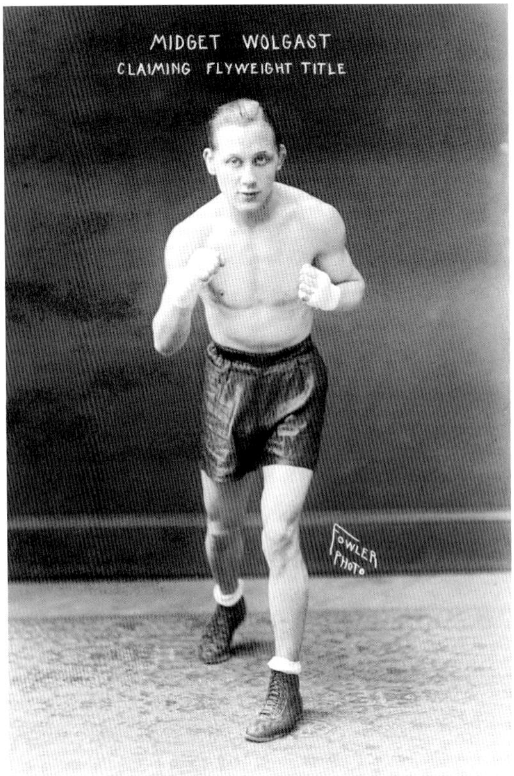

FAST INSIDE THE RING AND OUT. Midget Wolgast won the flyweight championship in 1930 at the age of 19. He fought 25 of his 212 career bouts in Atlantic City, including wins over Cpl. Izzy Schwartz, Marty Gold, and Willie Davis. Considered one of the quickest fighters ever, Wolgast was fast outside the ring too. His partying lifestyle dulled his skills and made him outgrow the 112-pound limit. Gossip claims he romanced legendary star Mae West. (Author's collection.)

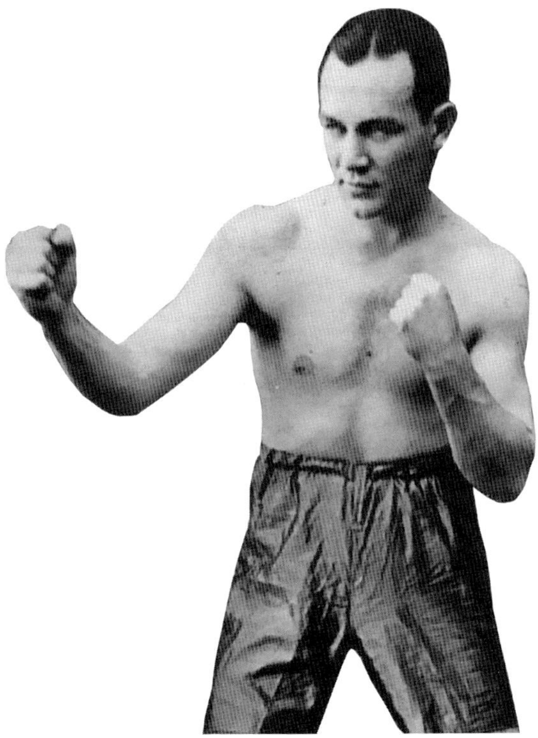

HISTORIC DECISION. Atlantic City lightweight Tommy Farley fought 90 professional bouts between 1922 and 1931, including 33 at the Waltz and 3 at Bacharach Ball Park. Under new state rules, Farley's 10-round decision over Pleasantville's Gene Moretti on March 19, 1928, at the Waltz was the first official points decision rendered in AC. Previously, bouts not ending in a knockout were ruled a no-contest. Famed referee Harry Ertle was also the only judge. (Veterans Boxers Association Ring One.)

NOT TOO COOL FOR AC. Philadelphian Eddie Cool, "The Pride of Tacony," fought 142 professional bouts, including 23 in AC at the Waltz, Garden Pier, and Convention Hall. He defeated lightweight champion Lou Ambers in a 1936 non-title fight at home but never received a rematch for the belt. Cool's career and life were cut short due to years of alcohol abuse. He died from liver disease in 1947 at the age of 35. (Author's collection.)

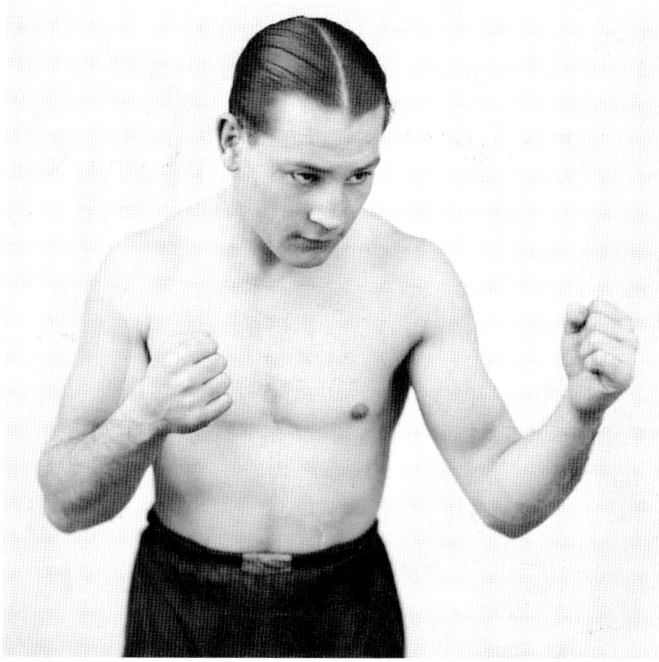

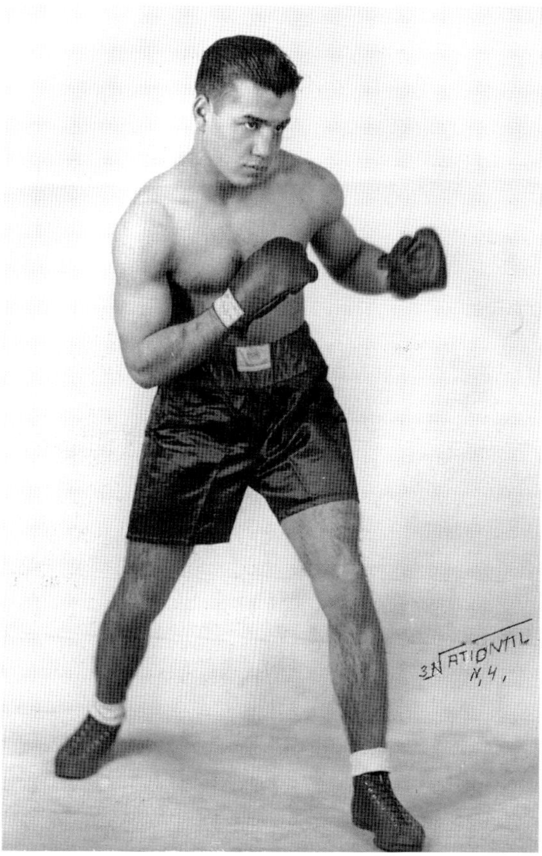

CAREER LAUNCH. Tony Falco launched his lengthy professional career at Waltz Dream Arena in 1929, a venue he would return to often during his nine-year career. Once the number-five contender, Falco's 93-39-7 record included 33 stops in Atlantic City with bouts against Eddie Cool, Mickey Blair, Lew Raymond, Ernie Caesar, and George Gibbs. (Author's collection.)

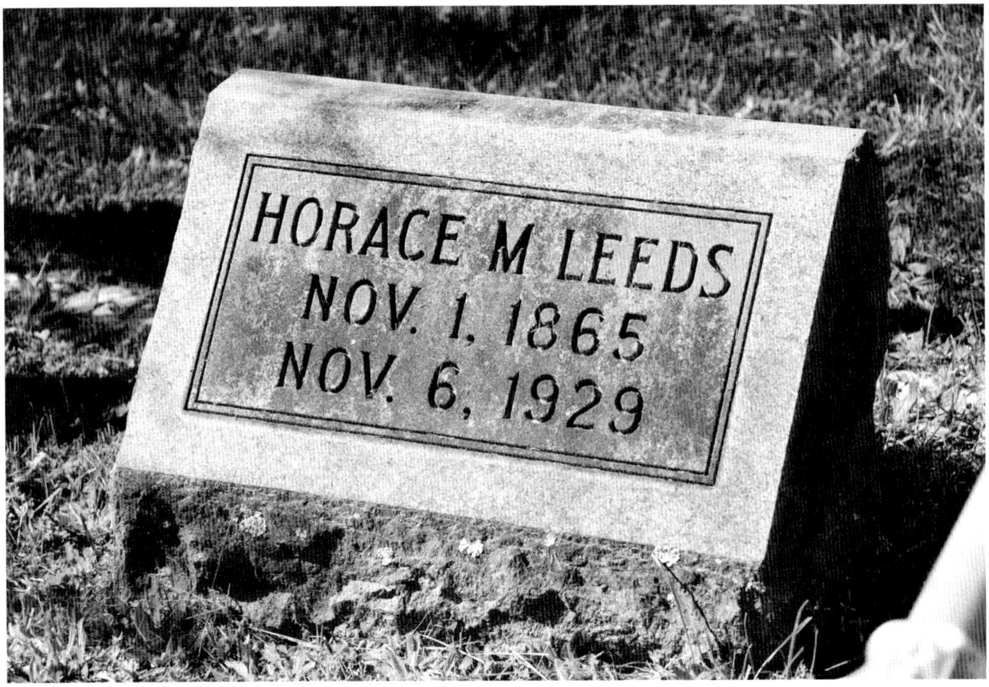

Final Resting Place. Horace Leeds, AC's bare-knuckle boxer, was a lifelong resident of the city. Credited with fighting one of the first main events in the history of AC, a February 1887 contest with Willie Clark, Leeds trained for his numerous amateur and professional fights on the city's beaches. Leeds died at the age of 64 in 1929 and is interred at the Atlantic City Cemetery in nearby Pleasantville. (Photograph by John DiSanto.)

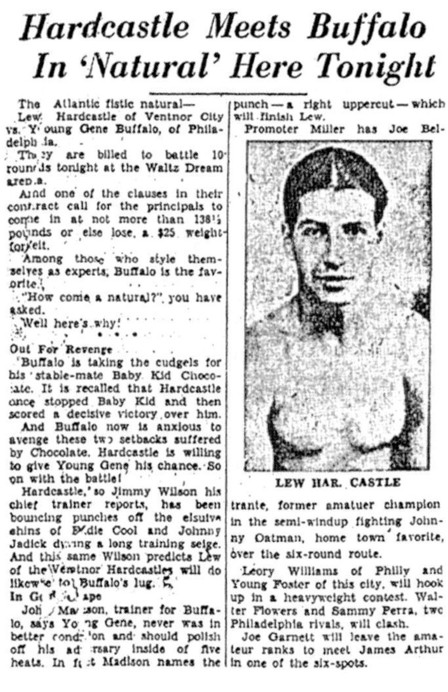

Hardcastle Meets Buffalo In 'Natural' Here Tonight

The Atlantic fistic natural—
Lew Hardcastle of Ventnor City vs. Young Gene Buffalo, of Philadelphia.

They are billed to battle 10 rounds tonight at the Waltz Dream arena.

And one of the clauses in their contract call for the principals to come in at not more than 138½ pounds or else lose a $25 weight forfeit.

Among those who style themselves as experts, Buffalo is the favorite.

"How come a natural?" you have asked.

Well here's why!

• • •

Out For Revenge

Buffalo is taking the cudgels for his stable-mate Baby Kid Chocolate. It is recalled that Hardcastle once stopped Baby Kid and then scored a decisive victory over him.

And Buffalo now is anxious to avenge these two setbacks suffered by Chocolate. Hardcastle is willing to give Young Gene his chance. So on with the battle!

Hardcastle, so Jimmy Wilson his chief trainer reports, has been bouncing punches off the elsuive chins of Eddie Cool and Johnny Jadick during a long training seige. And this same Wilson predicts Lew of the Ventnor Hardcastles will do likewise to Buffalo's lug.

In G[illegible]ape

John Madison, trainer for Buffalo, says Young Gene, never was in better condition and should polish off his adversary inside of five heats. In fact Madison names the punch—a right uppercut—which will finish Lew.

Promoter Miller has Joe Beltrante, former amatuer champion in the semi-windup fighting Johnny Oatman, home town favorite, over the six-round route.

LEW HAR. CASTLE

Leory Williams of Philly and Young Foster of this city, will hook up in a heavyweight contest. Walter Flowers and Sammy Perra, two Philadelphia rivals, will clash.

Joe Garnett will leave the amateur ranks to meet James Arthur in one of the six-spots.

"Prospects of the Month." Lew Hardcastle fought 28 times in AC, with most of his fights held at the Waltz Dream Arena. In 1931, the featherweight fought 12 times, dropping one fight to Lew Franklin at the Waltz. *The Ring* magazine honored him as the "Prospect of the Month" in the September 1931 issue. Other AC-area "Prospects of the Month" included welterweight Gene Moretti in January 1930 and heavyweight Austin Johnson in June 1945. (Chuck Hasson.)

Atlantic City's Boxing Mecca. Opened in 1929 and located at 2301 Boardwalk, Convention Hall is a massive venue that has hosted a variety of sporting events, concerts, political conventions, and the Miss America Pageant. Originally called the Atlantic City Auditorium, and later Boardwalk Hall, it began holding fight cards in 1930. By the 1980s, it was the site for the city's biggest boxing bouts, with more than 200 fight cards to date. (Author's collection.)

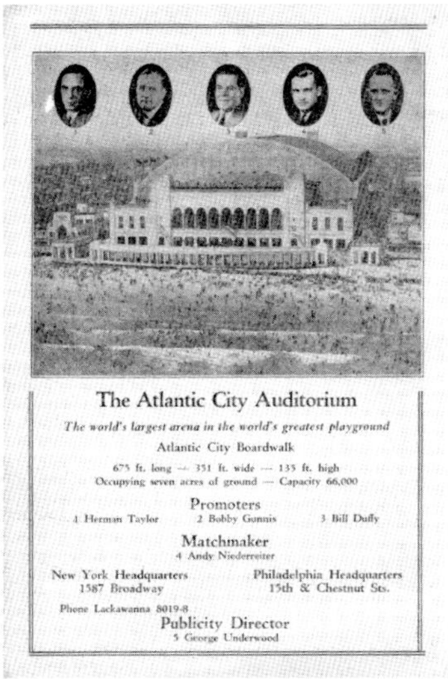

The Atlantic City Auditorium

The world's largest arena in the world's greatest playground

Atlantic City Boardwalk

675 ft. long — 351 ft. wide — 135 ft. high
Occupying seven acres of ground — Capacity 66,000

Promoters

1 Herman Taylor 2 Bobby Gunnis 3 Bill Duffy

Matchmaker

4 Andy Niederreiter

New York Headquarters
1587 Broadway

Philadelphia Headquarters
15th & Chestnut Sts.

Phone Lackawanna 8019-8

Publicity Director

5 George Underwood

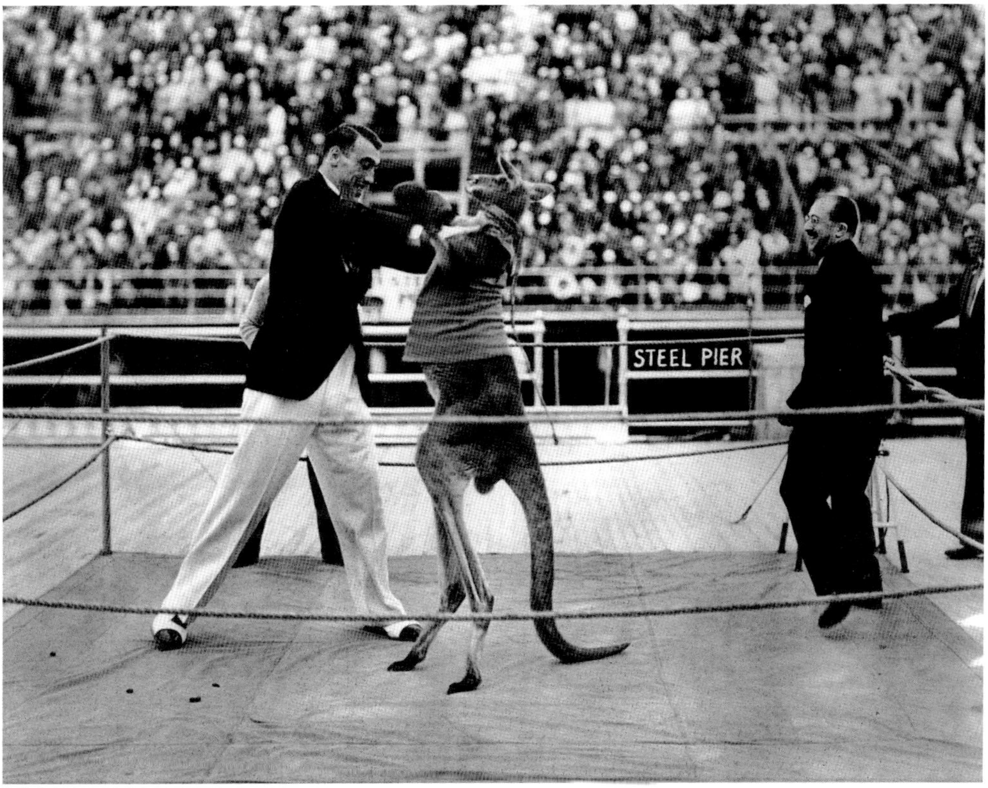

Future Champ Draws Large Crowd. The barnstorming tour of future heavyweight champion Primo Carnera stopped in Atlantic City on August 30, 1930. The "Ambling Alp" faced fellow Italian Riccardo Bertazzolo in a scheduled 15-round fight at Convention Hall before a crowd of 10,500. Carnera scored a third-round TKO, improved his record to 37-2, and continued his march toward the title. Primo returned to AC to battle this kangaroo on Steel Pier in 1933. (California State University Archives/Everett Collection.)

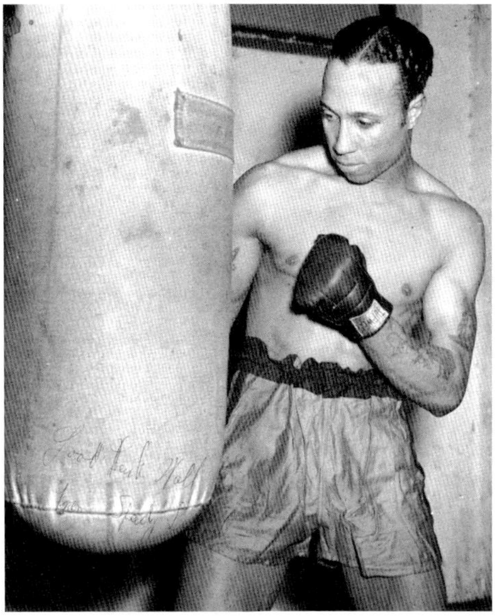

SPEEDY MIDDLEWEIGHT. Walter "Speedy" Duvall fought in Atlantic City 10 times during the 1930s and 1940s at venues like Waltz Dream Arena, Million Dollar Pier, and Convention Hall. His first start in AC was April 13, 1934, against local Leroy Jones, a fight he won on points. Duvall was also the 17th knockout victim of Billy Fox during his legendary 44-bout knockout streak. Duvall fell in round seven at the Waltz. (Author's collection.)

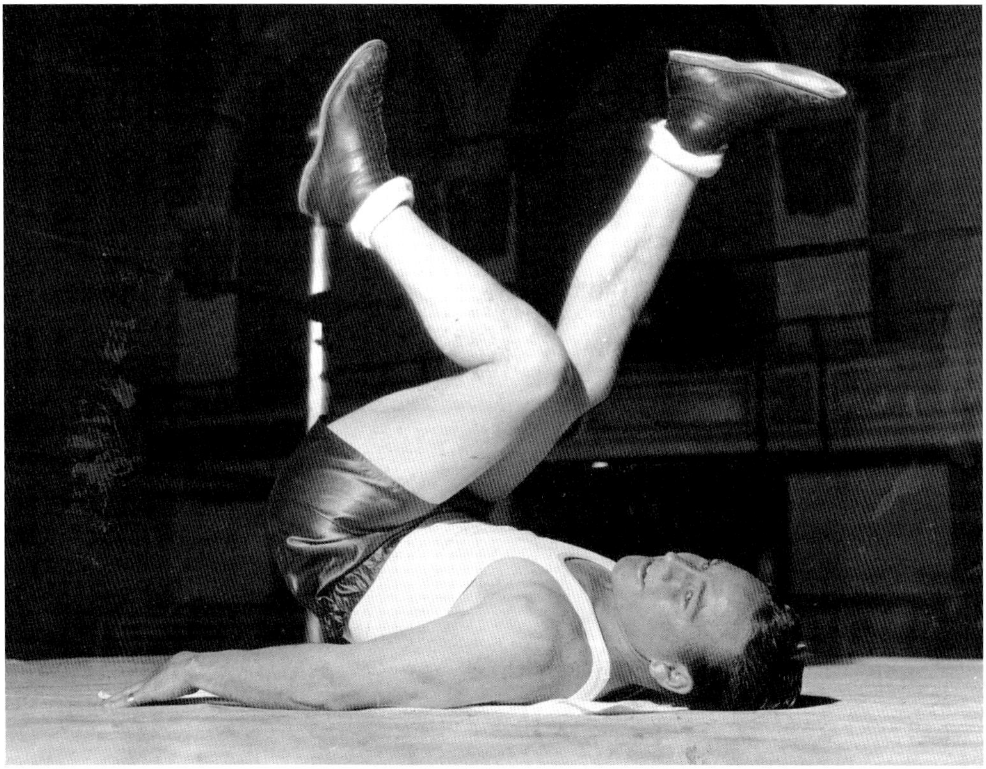

"THE BABY-FACED ASSASSIN." Irish-born boxer Jimmy McLarnin came to AC in 1934 to train for his May 28 fight against Barney Ross in the first of three world welterweight title fights over a one-year span. After capturing the title in 1933, McLarnin came up short by a split decision against Ross in their first bout. McLarnin regained and then lost the title in the final two bouts of their series. (Author's collection.)

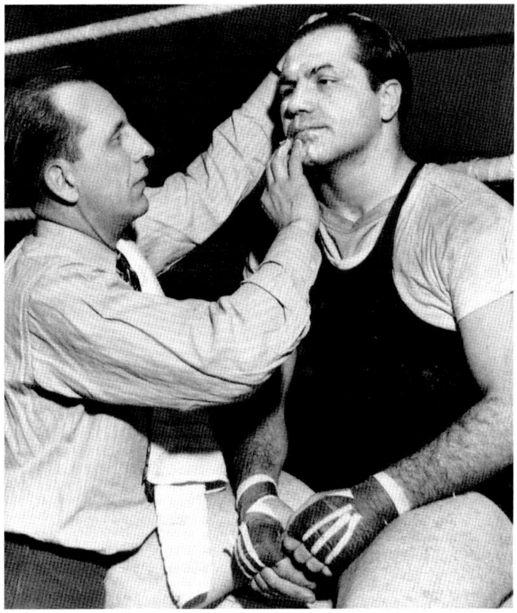

WINNING COMBINATION. Heavyweight contender of the 1930s and 1940s, Gus Dorazio once challenged champion Joe Louis. He made six winning appearances in AC, including his 1935 debut at the Waltz and a main event victory over local Bobby Jones at Convention Hall in 1940. Boxing legend Jimmy Wilson fought at the Waltz but made his name as a trainer and cut man, working countless corners until his death in 1958. (George Wilson Silvano.)

Young Johnny Buff Wins From Jaramillo

ATLANTIC CITY, N. J., May 13.—Young Johnny Buff, 128, of Atlantic City, was awarded the referee's decision over Cristobol Jaramillo, 123, of New York, in the feature eight-round windup bout of the North Side Boxing Club held here tonight at the Waltz Dream Arena.

"YOUNG JOHNNY BUFF." AC's "Young Johnny Buff," born John Jablonski, selected his ring moniker as a tribute to a fellow Polish American Jersey man and former world bantamweight champion. Young Johnny Buff, a featherweight, fought professionally from 1929 to 1941 but did not have the same level of success as his namesake. He fought 14 times in AC and retired with a losing record. (Author's collection.)

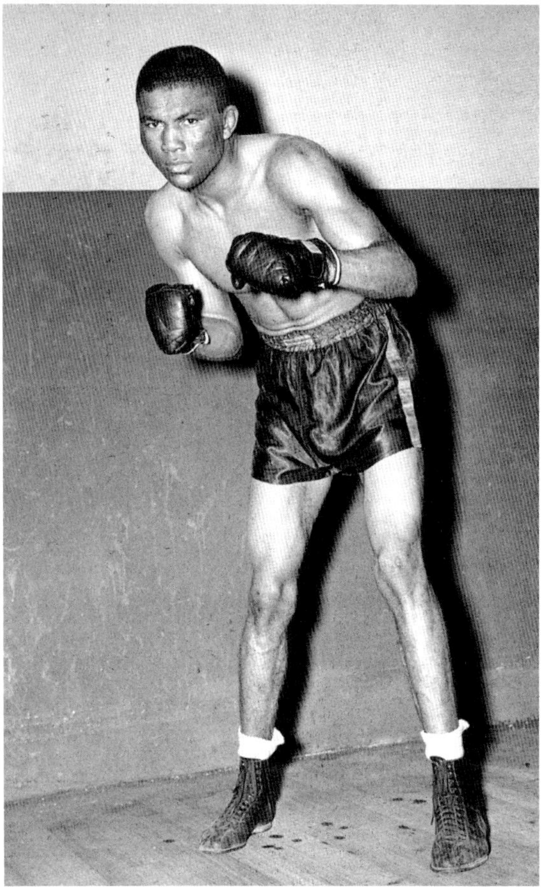

THE "BOBCAT." Early in his career, two-time lightweight champion "Bobcat" Bob Montgomery fought in Atlantic City 18 times during the 1930s and 1940s, including 15 appearances at Waltz Dream Arena. One bout at the Waltz was a second-round knockout of AC's Young Johnny Buff on October 13, 1938, in Montgomery's debut. He also fought at Garden Pier and Convention Hall. Montgomery won them all except a 1940 draw against Norment Quarles. (Author's collection.)

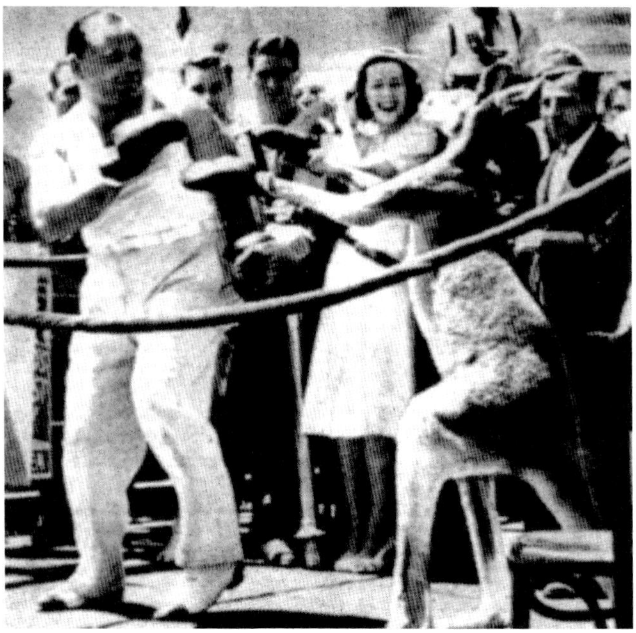

"TWO TON" VERSUS A KANGAROO. After his valiant but losing effort against Joe Louis, "Two Ton" Tony Galento cashed in on the fame that came from knocking down the heavyweight champion. In one money-making stunt, Galento battled two kangaroos on Million Dollar Pier on July 23, 1939. "I'll just clip him a couple in the pouch and flatten him," Galento said before the spectacle. Galento earned $1,000 but had to settle for a draw. (Author's collection.)

Popular Shore Attraction. Young Gene Buffalo was a popular and exciting welterweight battler who fought 46 of 161 bouts (1934–1950) at the shore, including 35 at the Waltz. Buffalo beat future champion Fritzie Zivic and former champion Johnny Jadick, both by 10-round decision. He also went 3-1 against archrival Wicky Harkins, one of them a 15-round victory. Buffalo also defeated Camden's Frankie Blair by a 15-round decision and faced locals including Lew Hardcastle, Bobby Jones, and Ted Bowman. (Author's collection.)

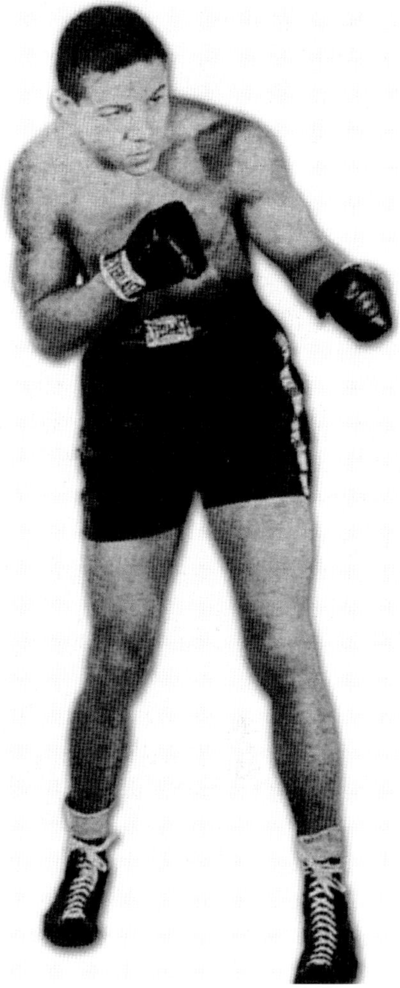

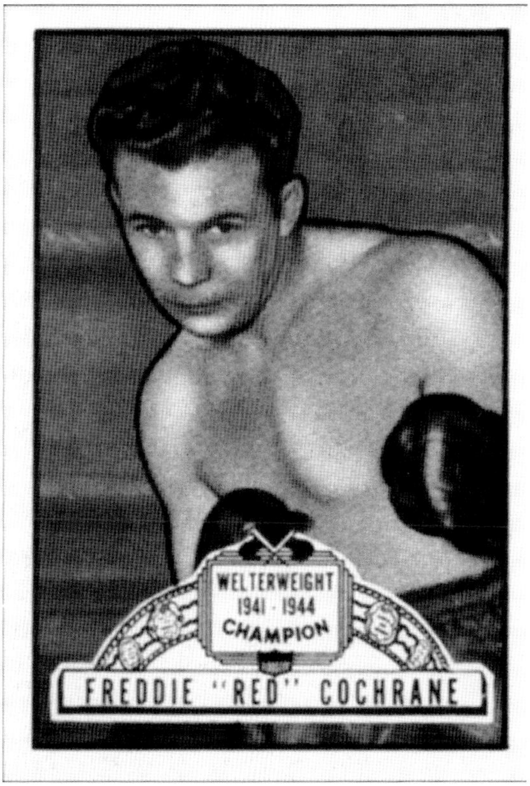

Title Bout Warm-Up. With negotiations underway for a shot at welterweight king Fritzie Zivic, Freddie "Red" Cochrane of Elizabeth, New Jersey, kept sharp with two 1941 bouts in Atlantic City. In February, he stopped Newark's Ray Powell on cuts. Then in March, he flattened Oscar Poindexter, also of Newark, with a left hook in round two. After two more warm-up bouts, Cochrane received his title shot and won the crown by a 15-round decision. (Author's collection.)

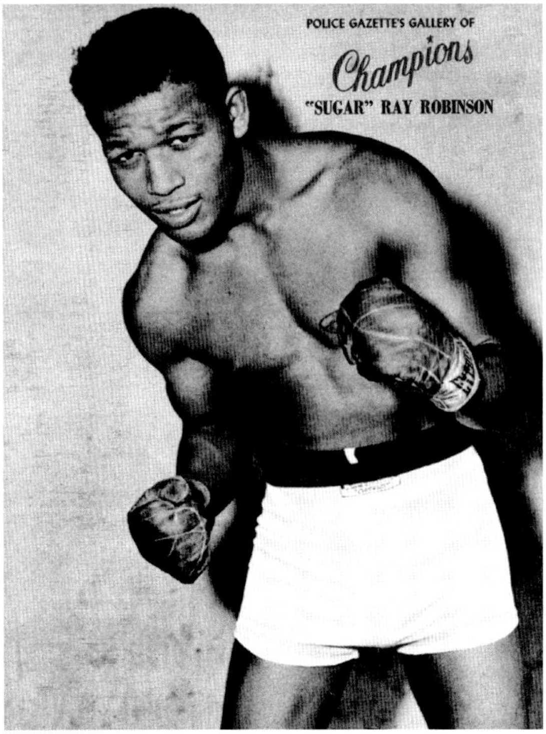

POUND-FOR-POUND. During his first year as a pro, "Sugar" Ray Robinson briefly appeared twice in Atlantic City. Robinson won his 15th fight with a first-round knockout of 89-bout veteran Charley Burns at Waltz Dream Arena on April 24, 1941. Robinson then stopped Maurice Arnault for win number 23 in another one-round knockout at Convention Hall on August 29, 1941. Robinson eventually won world welterweight and middleweight titles and is considered the greatest pound-for-pound fighter in boxing history. (Author's collection.)

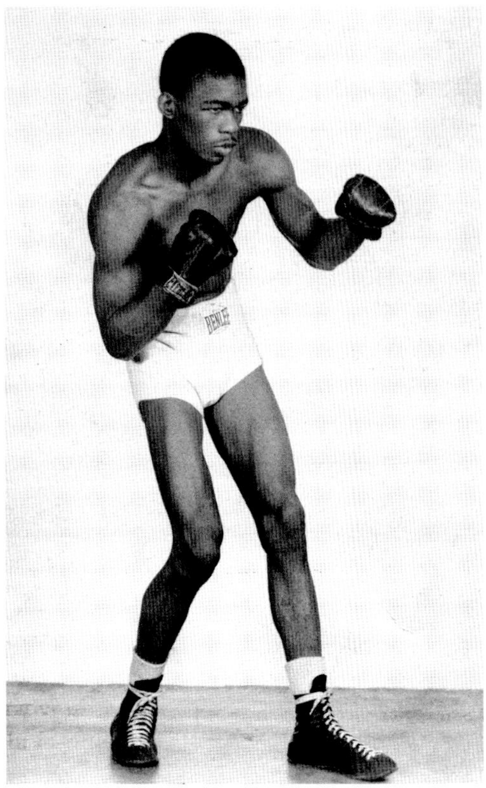

IKE'S EARLY VICTORIES. Trenton lightweight Ike Williams turned pro in 1940. Two years later, he made four successful trips to Waltz Dream Arena to post wins over Pedro Firpo, Angelo Pantellas, Abie Kaufman, and Ruby Garcia. Three years later, Williams won a portion of the lightweight title and then unified the crown with a revenge knockout of Bob Montgomery in 1947. Williams retired in 1955 with a record of 128-24-5, with 60 knockouts. (Author's collection.)

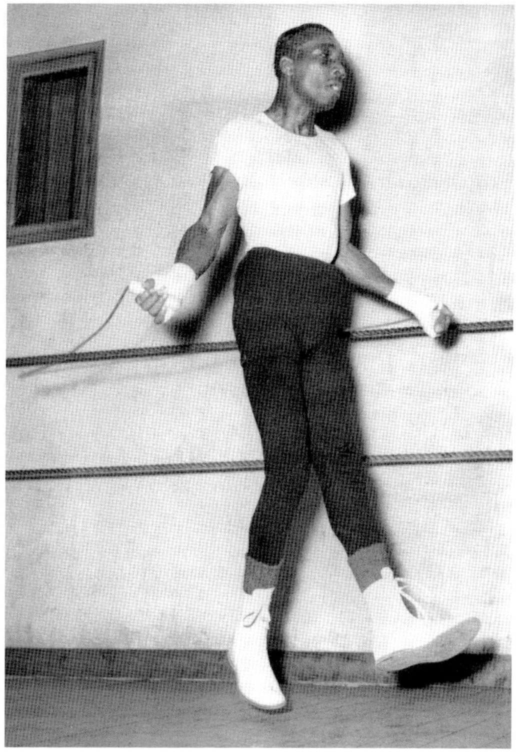

SADDLER CUTS HIS TEETH. In the early days of his 163-bout, three-title career, Sandy Saddler made four stops in Atlantic City, including 1946 wins over Johnny Wolgast at Convention Hall and Pedro Firpo and Joe Rodriguez at Million Dollar Pier. He returned in 1947 to stop Leslie Harris at Bader Field. Saddler won his first featherweight title in the initial installment of his four-bout series with Willie Pep in 1948. (Author's collection.)

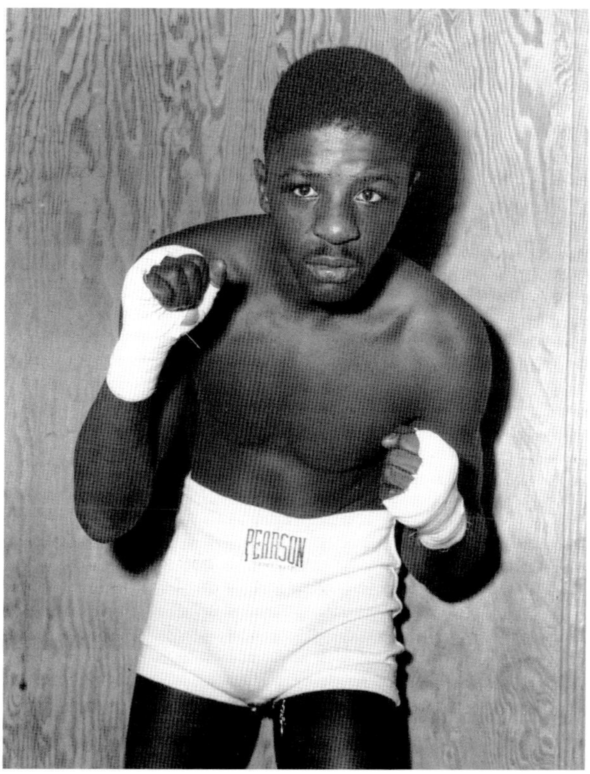

WOULD NOT GIVE AN INCH. Beginning in 1947, featherweight Percy Bassett fought 16 of his first 18 bouts in AC at Bader Field and Waltz Dream Arena. Although he eventually became the number-one contender, Bassett's unwillingness to do business with the mob prevented him from challenging world champion Sandy Saddler. Still, Bassett won the interim world title in 1953 while Saddler served in the Army. In 1955, a detached retina forced Bassett's retirement at the age of 25. (Author's collection.)

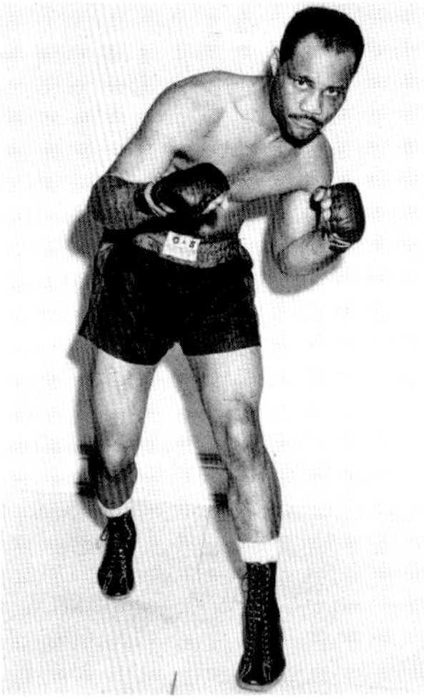

RISING CONTENDER. DC-born heavyweight Gene Jones was based in Camden through most of his career and made frequent appearances in Atlantic City during the 1940s and 1950s. Twelve of his 61 bouts came at Convention Hall, Million Dollar Pier, and Waltz Dream Arena. The biggest of these was a close 10-round decision over Billy Gilliam on January 8, 1948, in the main event of a benefit show at Convention Hall that drew 4,000 fans. (Author's collection.)

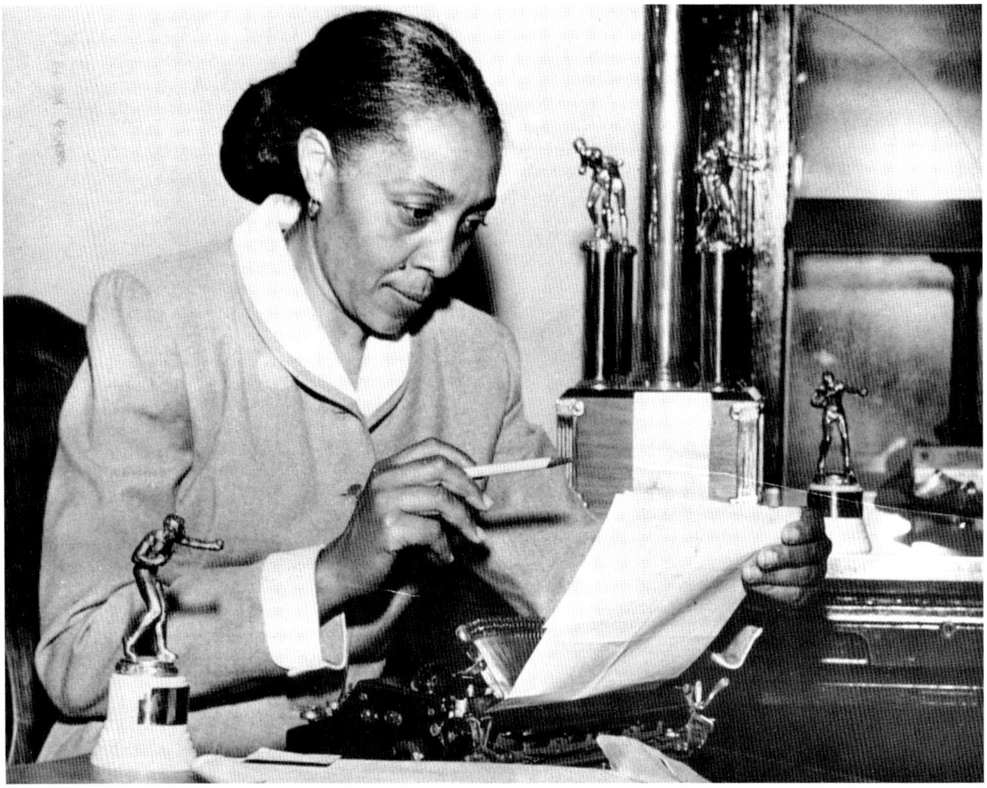

LADY AND THE CHAMPS. In 1944, Laoma Byrd established the South Jersey Athletic Club, a boxing gym and training camp on Wright Street in Pleasantville. The facility was housed in a three-story building that included an indoor ring, two outdoor rings, a kitchen, a dining room, and bedrooms for boxers. Top fighters like Ezzard Charles, Bob Montgomery, Jersey Joe Walcott, Sonny Liston, Sugar Hart, Ike Williams, Gil Turner, and Wesley Mouzon trained there under the watchful eye of Byrd. The camp was active into the 1960s. Byrd died in 2002 at the age of 98. (Author's collection.)

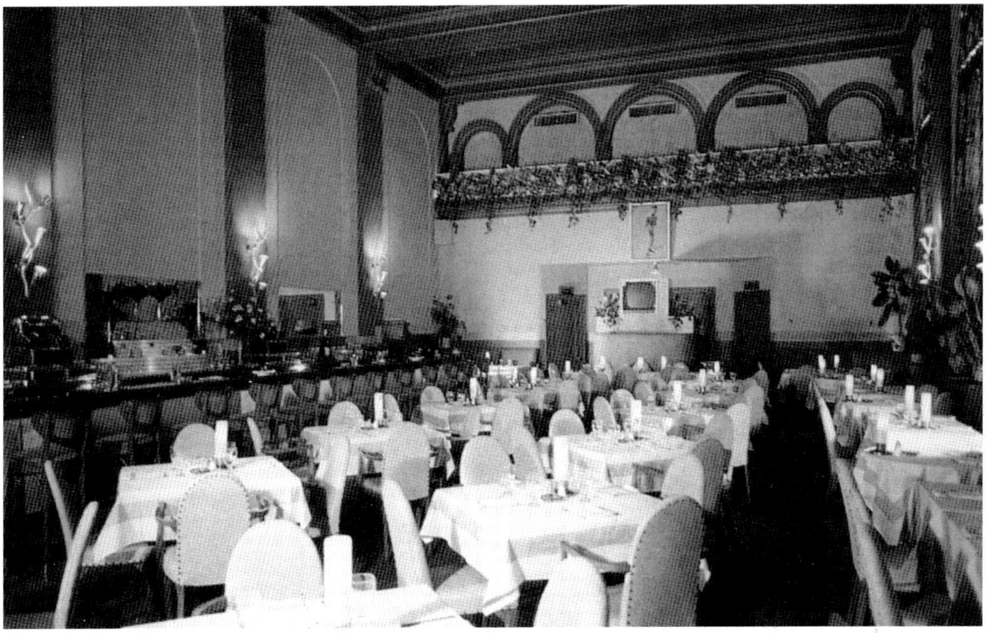

LEW TENDLER'S STEAKHOUSE. Lew Tendler, a top contender during his boxing career, is regarded by many experts to be one of the best boxers who never held a world title. He fought four times in AC, including a 1926 bout against Joe Reno at the Waltz. Following his retirement in 1928, Tendler opened restaurants in Philadelphia, Miami Beach, and Atlantic City. Lew Tendler's Steakhouse in AC was located on the corner of Texas and Atlantic Avenues. (Author's collection.)

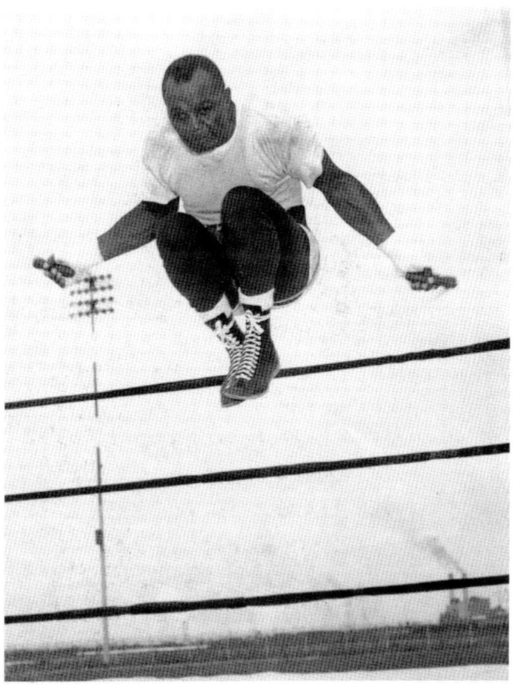

JUMPIN' JOE. Camden's Jersey Joe Walcott was crowned world heavyweight champion when he defeated Ezzard Charles for the title on July 18, 1951, at age 37. Walcott trained in Atlantic City for his September 23, 1952, title defense against Rocky Marciano, who took the title and also won their 1953 rematch. Walcott retired after the rematch. In 1975, Walcott became the New Jersey State boxing commissioner, and he served in that capacity until 1984. (Author's collection.)

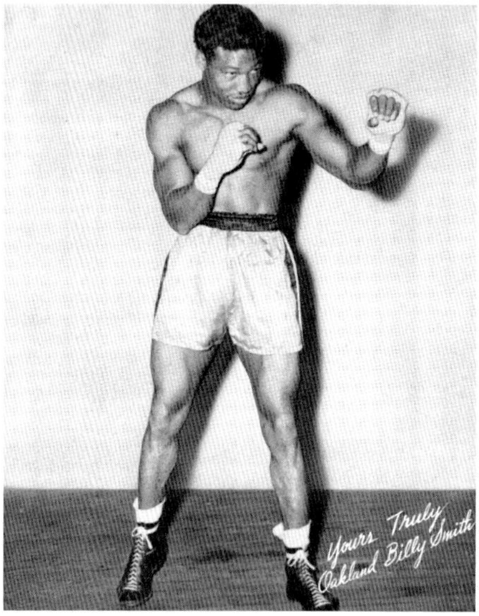

"BOARDWALK" BILLY. "Oakland" Billy Smith was a well-traveled light heavyweight who started boxing in his hometown of Oakland, California. He eventually relocated to Atlantic City and changed his nickname to "Boardwalk" Billy Smith. He fought standouts including Ezzard Charles, Charley Burley, Jimmy Bivins, Bob Satterfield, and Harold Johnson, whom he knocked out in his best win. Smith only fought once in AC but served as deputy sheriff of Atlantic County after his 1955 ring retirement. (Author's collection.)

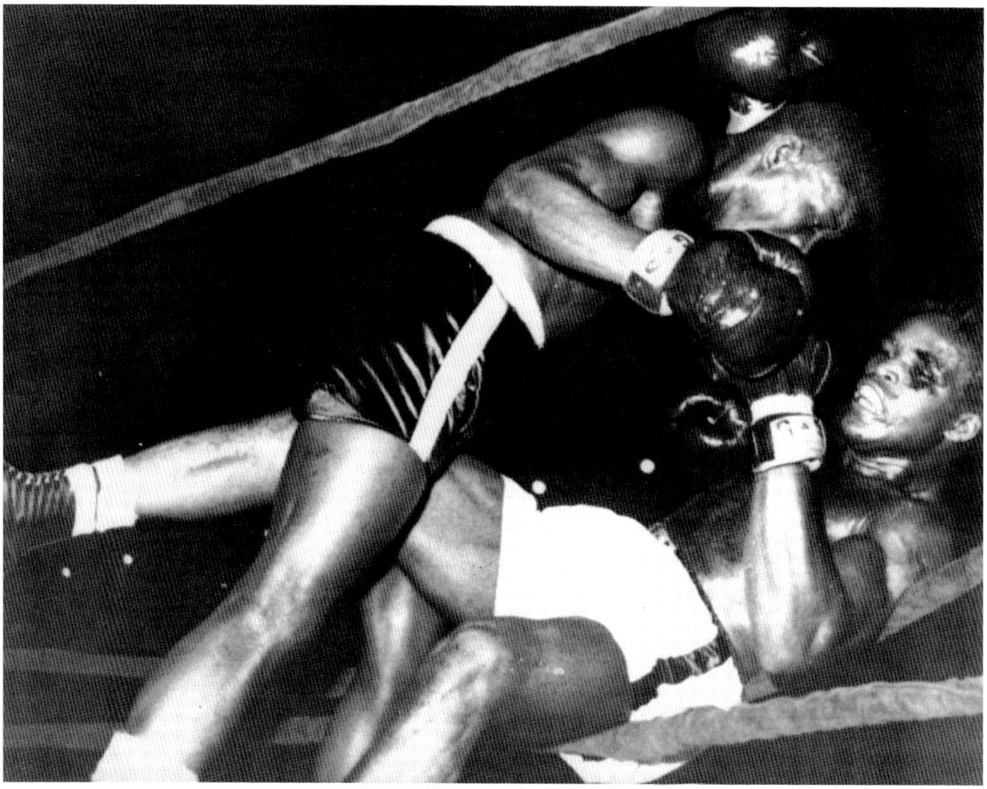

POPULAR TV FIGHTER. Gil Turner's all-action style made him one of the most popular and exciting television fighters of the 1950s. After winning 31 straight fights, Turner lost a welterweight title bid to Kid Gavilan in 1952. While battling his way back up the ranks, Turner (white trunks) beat Virgil Akins over 10 rounds in an important battle of contenders on September 18, 1957, at Convention Hall. Turner's only other AC fight came in 1951. (Author's collection.)

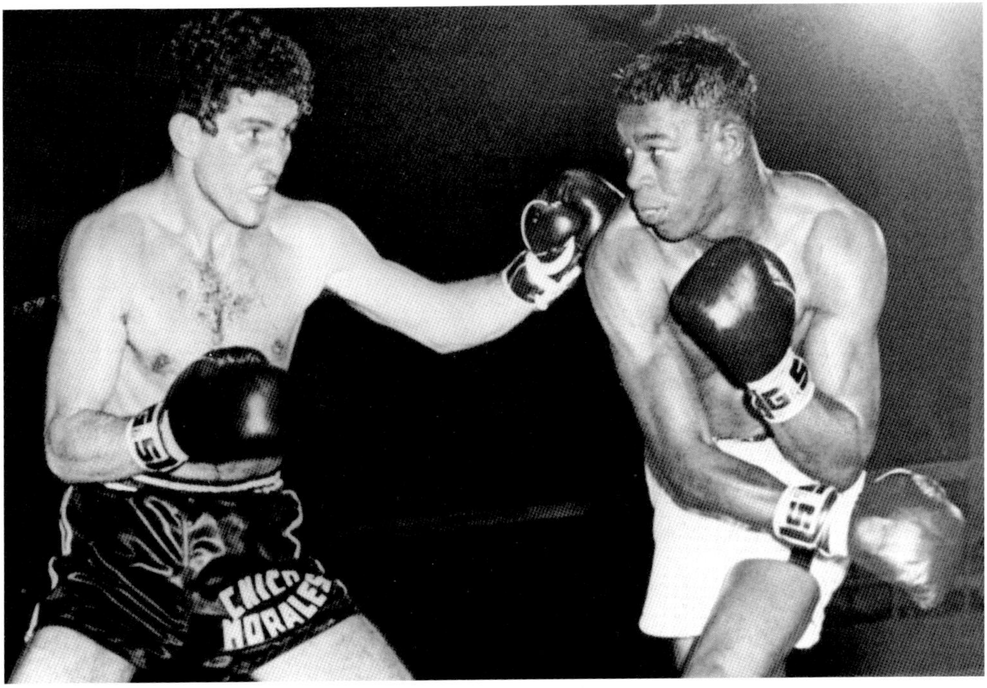

TOP CONTENDER. In his day, Philadelphia's Len Matthews was a hot lightweight prospect. His rise in the ratings included three bouts at Atlantic City's Convention Hall. On July 3, 1959, he defeated Johnny Gonsalves by a 10-round decision. Two fights later, he beat Chico Morales by a decision on September 4, 1959 (pictured). Finally, Matthews stopped Jorge Quintero in the 10th round on August 5, 1960. Within a few months, Matthews became the number-one contender. (Author's collection.)

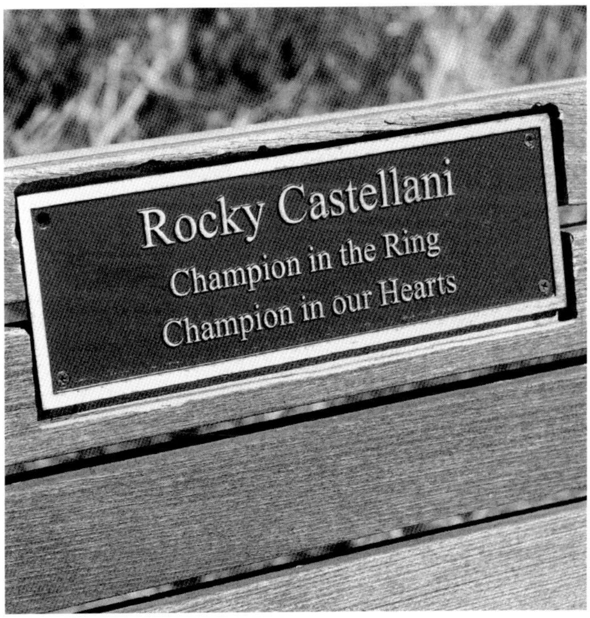

ADOPTED SON. Northeast Pennsylvania native Rocky Castellani, a World War II veteran, was a top middleweight contender who fought boxing greats such as Bobo Olson (for the middleweight title in 1954), "Sugar" Ray Robinson, and Gene Fullmer. Following his boxing career, Castellani retired with his family to AC, where he trained fighters and owned taverns in AC and Galloway Township. A bench is dedicated to Castellani and his wife, Mary, on the Boardwalk in Ventnor City, New Jersey. (Photograph by John DiSanto.)

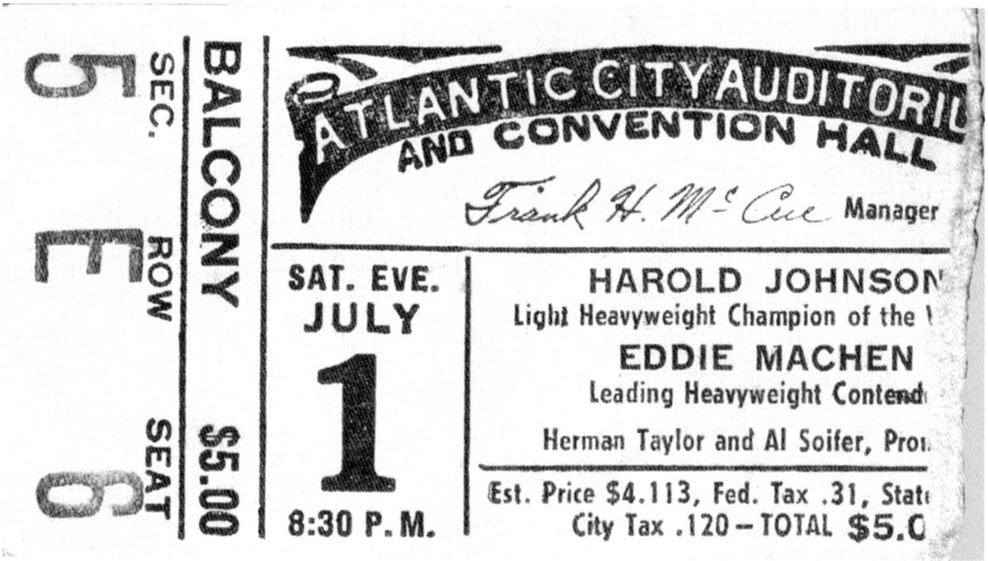

Testing the Waters. Light heavyweight champion Harold Johnson tested the heavyweight waters on July 1, 1961, at Convention Hall against number-two contender Eddie Machen. Johnson won a 10-round decision. The victory put Johnson on the heavyweight division's radar and bolstered his hopes of facing champion Floyd Patterson. That fight never materialized, but his light heavyweight title reign spanned another two years. This was his fourth and final AC appearance. (Author's collection.)

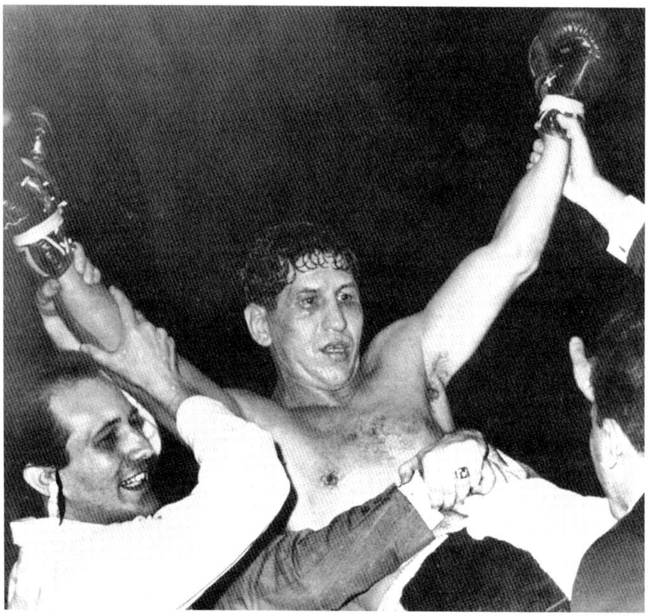

A Champion at Last. After 123 fights, Philadelphia-based New Yorker Joey Giardello finally won the world middleweight championship. He defeated Dick Tiger by a 15-round decision on December 7, 1963, at Convention Hall before a crowd of 12,000. The fight was Atlantic City's first world title bout and its last until the casino era. During his 133-bout career, Giardello only had two other bouts in AC, his first and third pro fights in 1948. (Author's collection.)

2

REBIRTH

1964–1979

After the 1963 title fight between Joey Giardello and Dick Tiger, there were no boxing matches in AC until 1973. That year, promoter Frank Gelb began running shows at Convention Hall's 3,200-seat ballroom. These events featured neighboring fighters like Bridgeton's Richie Kates, Philadelphia middleweight contender Bennie Briscoe, future champion Mike Rossman, Ocean City's Guy Gargan, and Pleasantville's Ernest Bing. These shows were small but would prove significant in Gelb's future standing in the city's boxing scene.

Through most of the 1970s, boxing was sporadic in AC, with only four shows between 1974 and 1976. However, in 1976, Mayor Joseph Lazarow helped drive a referendum to legalize casino gambling in the city. This referendum made it to the general election ballot and was approved by New Jersey voters on November 2, 1976. Given boxing's long-standing liaison with gambling in other gaming meccas, the legalization of gambling and the promise of casinos brought hope to local fight fans that AC might become a new boxing capital.

Instead of authorizing any and all promoters a license to stage fights during AC's rebirth, the commission opted to grant the one existing promoter in AC at that time, Frank Gelb, the sole license to stage boxing cards. This exclusive license lasted until 1981.

On November 4, 1978, the city's first casino, Resorts, hosted the official launch of the new boxing era. In the main event, 1976 gold medalist Howard Davis Jr. beat Luis Davila over 10 rounds. It was the start of everything.

The following summer, Gelb ran a weekly series at Steel Pier. Like his previous Convention Hall shows, Gelb filled these bouts with local talent and relied heavily on Philadelphia fighters as headliners. J Russell Peltz, promoter at the Spectrum in Philadelphia, served as Gelb's matchmaker for the series.

In 1979, Resorts hosted the WBC light heavyweight title fight between Matthew Saad Muhammad and former champion John Conteh in AC's first championship contest in more than 15 years. However, unlike in 1963, AC now had the infrastructure and incentive to make boxing a big part of its future. Big-time boxing was finally coming to AC.

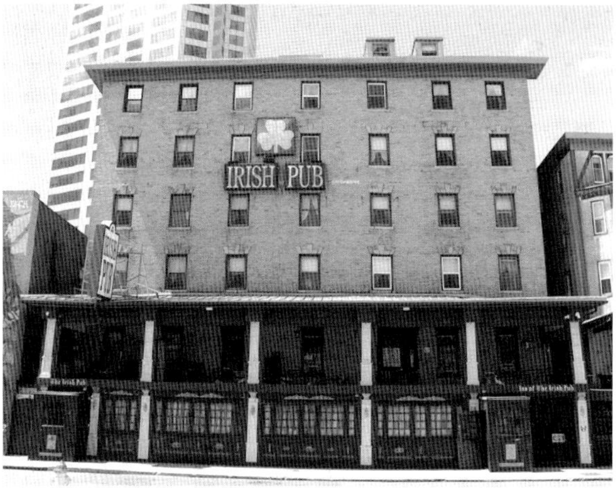

ICONIC WATERING HOLE. Founded in 1972 by Richard and Cathy Burke, the Irish Pub is an iconic tavern and inn housed inside a 19th-century building. The pub's walls are covered in memorabilia from the 1880s to the 1930s, a number of which are associated with the sport of boxing. Located just off the Boardwalk at 164 St. James Place, the Irish Pub is a gathering spot for fight fans and boxing insiders. (Photograph by John DiSanto.)

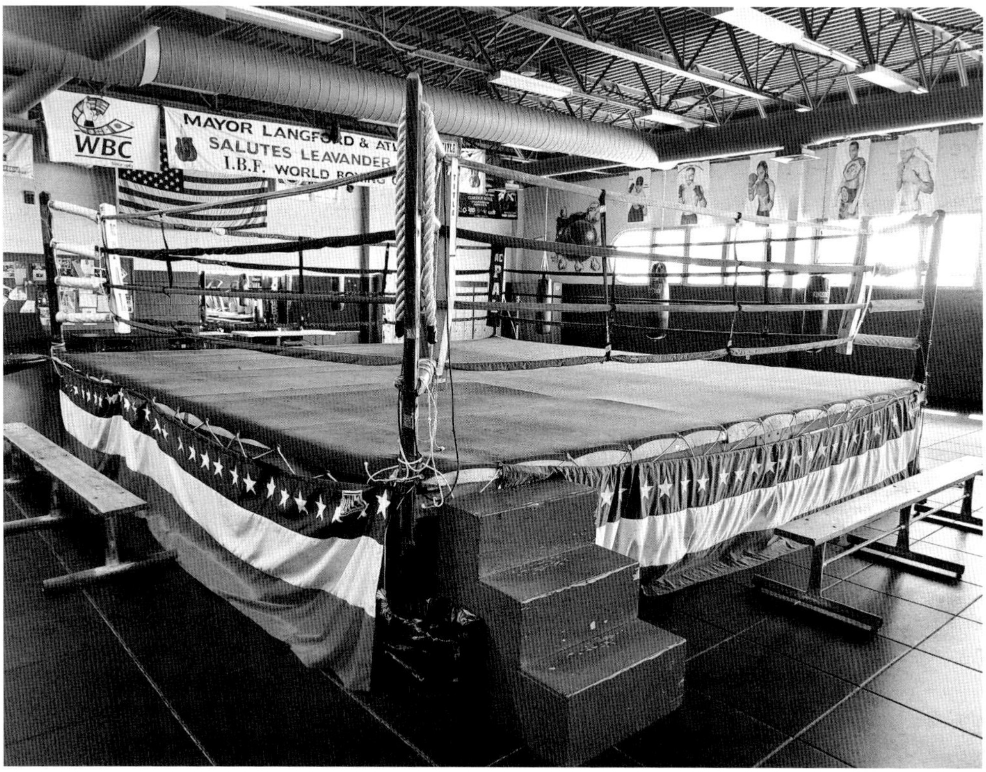

ATLANTIC CITY POLICE ATHLETIC LEAGUE (PAL). Founded by Sgt. Lloyd "Mr. Scope" Ward in 1972, the AC PAL housed one of the East Coast's finest boxing programs and produced amateur and professional champions like Leavander Johnson. It was a temporary training facility for visitors like Evander Holyfield, Mickey Ward, and Mike Tyson and also provided many community and cultural programs. In 1994, the current PAL building, on New York Avenue, was dedicated and named for its founder. (Photograph by Matthew H. Ward.)

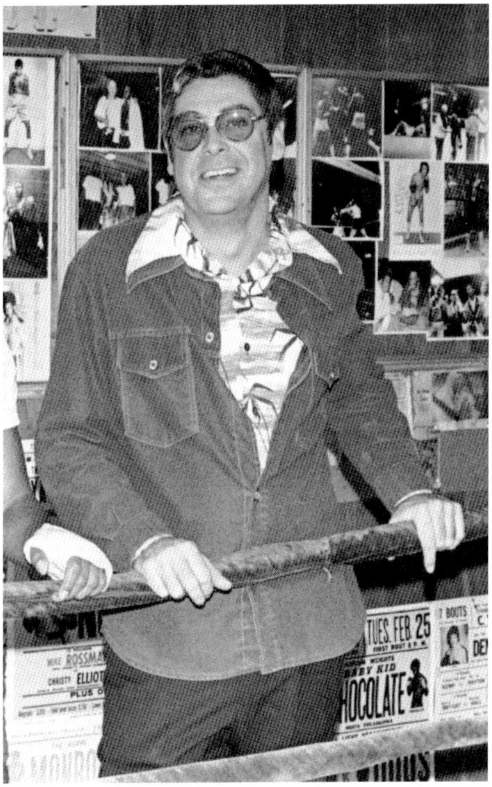

THE GATEKEEPER. When Atlantic City legalized gambling, Frank Gelb was the only licensed boxing promoter in town, and the commission decided that Gelb would be the lone fight promoter for the looming boxing boom. For the next few years, all AC boxing cards went through him, including bouts like Saad Muhammad versus Conteh, which Gelb copromoted with Top Rank. Gelb promoted the first casino fight, a series at Steel Pier, and helped bring championship boxing back in 1979. Each milestone contributed to the sport's rise in AC. (Peltz Boxing Promotions.)

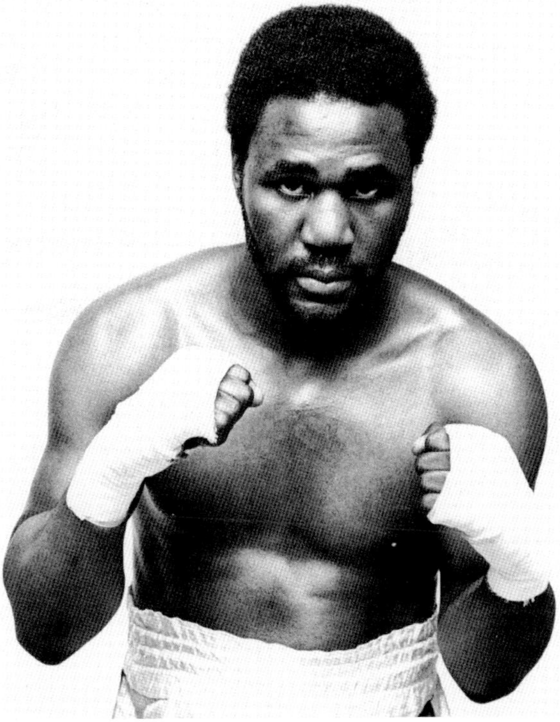

UNDEFEATED IN AC. Two-time world title challenger Richie Kates of Bridgeton, New Jersey, fought the best light heavyweights in one of the division's toughest eras and was undefeated in 10 AC bouts. In the first main event after a 10-year boxing drought in the city, Kates knocked out Ron Oliver in 1973. He was also the cofeature attraction on the first casino fight card in 1978 and headlined a show on Steel Pier in 1979. Kates defeated Roger Russell, Jerry Martin, Richie Bennett, and Jeff Lampkin in AC. (Peltz Boxing Promotions.)

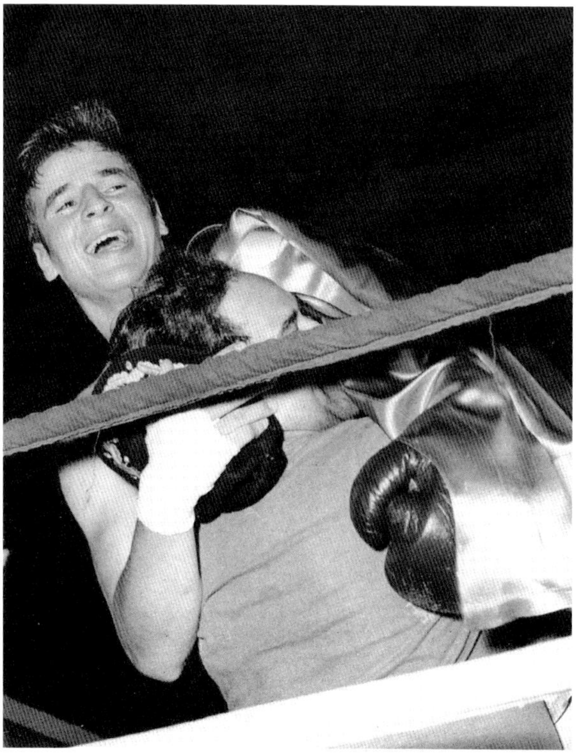

OCEAN CITY FIGHTER. Ocean City middleweight Guy Gargan debuted on June 2, 1973, with a four-round decision victory over Tyrone Taylor in Frank Gelb's second AC promotion in Convention Hall's ballroom (pictured). He returned for three more shows at Convention Hall, two draws with Jasper Brisbane and Skipper Jones and a loss to Archie Andrews in 1976. Gargan retired in 1979 and went on to write for the *Press of Atlantic City*. (Guy Gargan.)

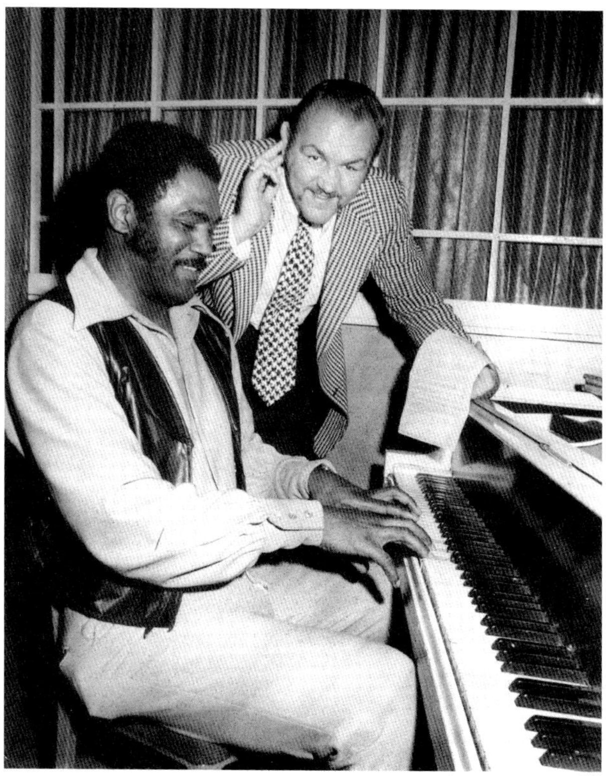

DUBIOUS DECISION. Chuck Wepner and Ernie Terrell (left) met at Convention Hall on June 23, 1973, in a 12-round fight for the vacant National Americas heavyweight title. Although Terrell appeared to have the upper hand throughout the fight, Wepner won the decision rendered by referee Harold Valan, also the lone judge. The surprise verdict kept "The Bayonne Bleeder" on track for his eventual title fight with Muhammad Ali in 1975. (Author's collection.)

"THE JEWISH BOMBER." Mike Rossman became the WBA light heavyweight champion in 1978 with a 13th-round technical knockout of Victor Galindez. His overall pro record was 44-7-3, with 27 knockouts and 11 bouts in Atlantic City. "The Jewish Bomber" fought both his first and last pro fights in AC, as well as bouts with Steven Smith, Matt Ross, Al Bolden, and in his only Atlantic City loss, Dwight Muhammad Qawi. (Author's collection.)

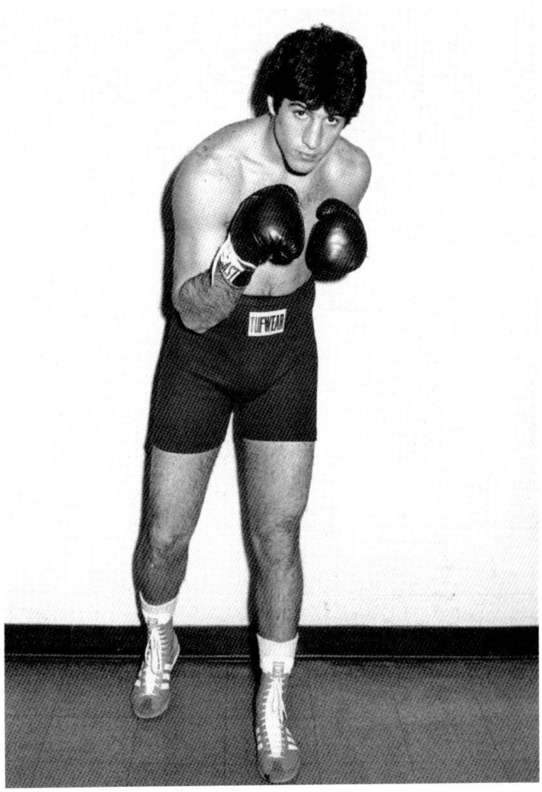

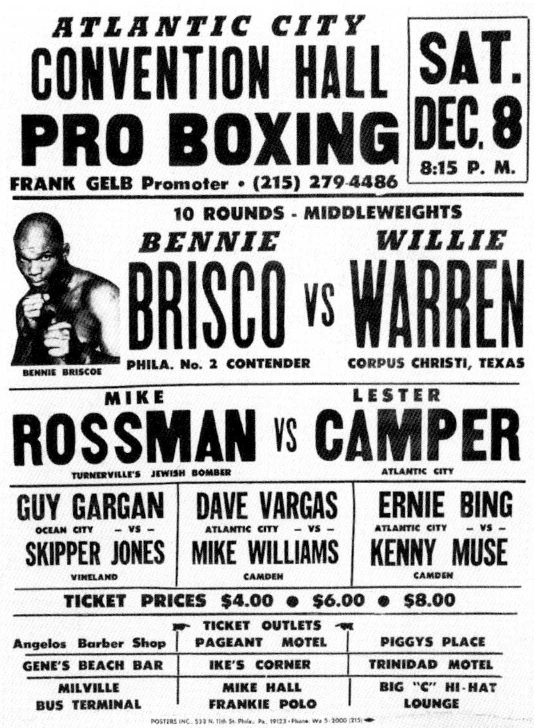

BRISCOE RISKS RANKING. Frank Gelb staged his fourth AC boxing card on December 8, 1973, with number-two middleweight contender Bennie Briscoe headlining against Willie Warren. Briscoe kept his world rating intact by chopping down the sturdy Texan in seven rounds. The event drew a crowd of 2,100 and kept the careers of both Briscoe and Gelb moving forward. "Bad Bennie" returned to the shore two more times before his boxing days ended. (Author's collection.)

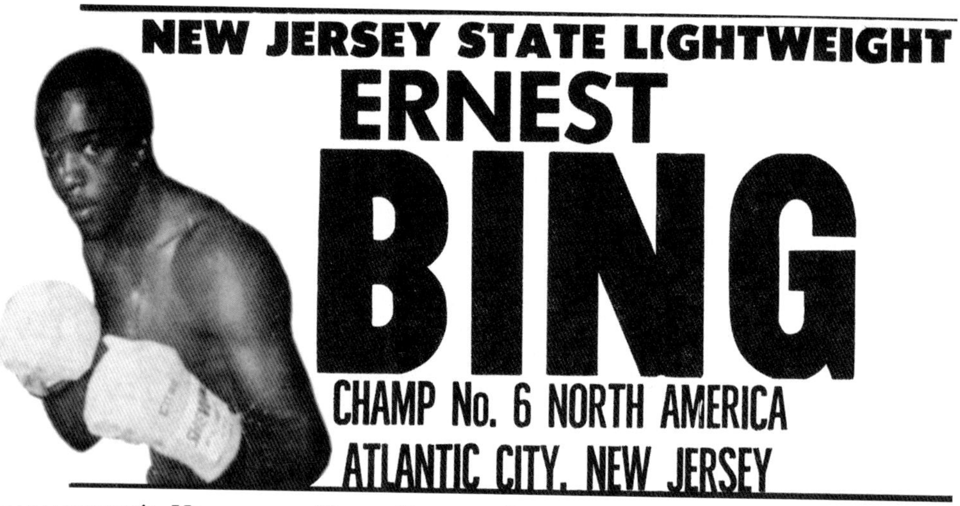

PLEASANTVILLE'S HOMETOWN HERO. Pleasantville's Ernest Bing made his pro debut on December 8, 1973, at Convention Hall. This was the first of 13 total appearances in AC. He went on to fight at numerous other venues, including the West Side Complex, Atlantic City Armory, Steel Pier, Resorts, the Sands, and Claridge. On April 26, 1980, he captured the New Jersey lightweight title in AC with a victory over Newark's Danny Daniels. (Author's collection.)

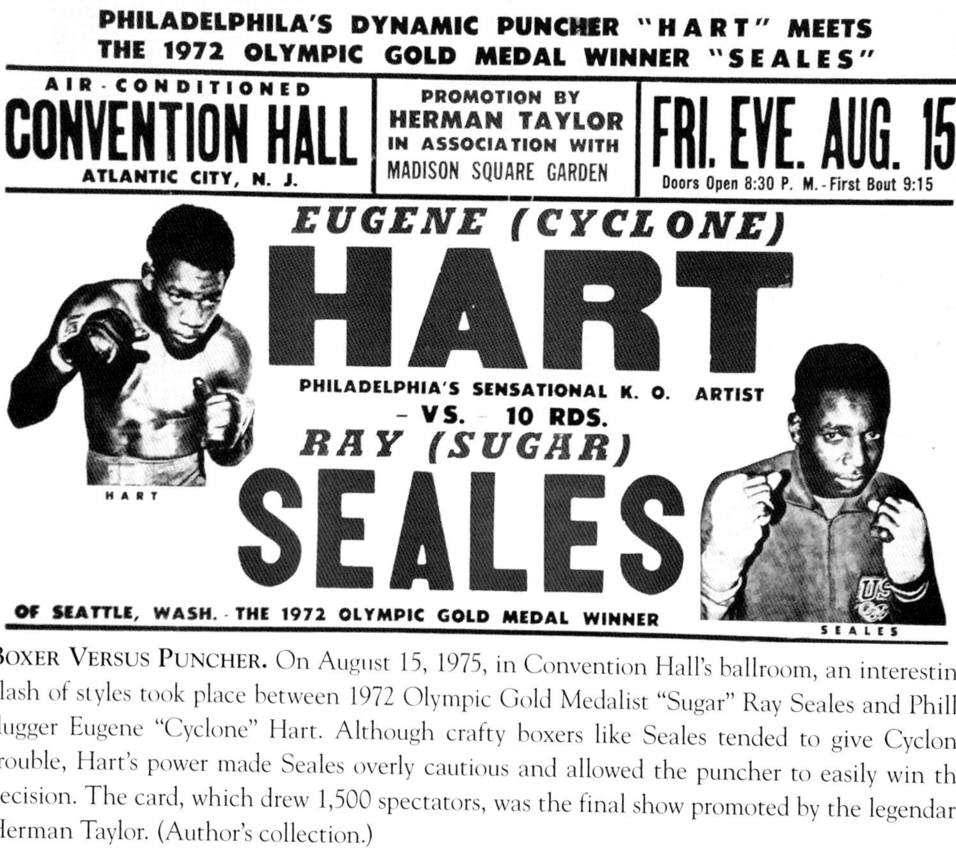

BOXER VERSUS PUNCHER. On August 15, 1975, in Convention Hall's ballroom, an interesting clash of styles took place between 1972 Olympic Gold Medalist "Sugar" Ray Seales and Philly slugger Eugene "Cyclone" Hart. Although crafty boxers like Seales tended to give Cyclone trouble, Hart's power made Seales overly cautious and allowed the puncher to easily win the decision. The card, which drew 1,500 spectators, was the final show promoted by the legendary Herman Taylor. (Author's collection.)

A New Age in Atlantic City. Born in AC on December 17, 1923, Joseph Lazarow served as mayor of the seaside resort town between 1976 and 1982, a period that saw the introduction of the gambling industry to the city. The historic referendum that legalized gambling in the struggling city was passed in November 1976, with Resorts opening as the first casino on May 26, 1978. (Author's collection.)

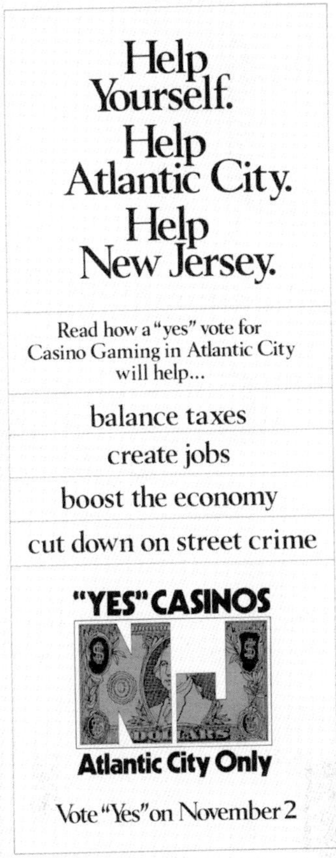

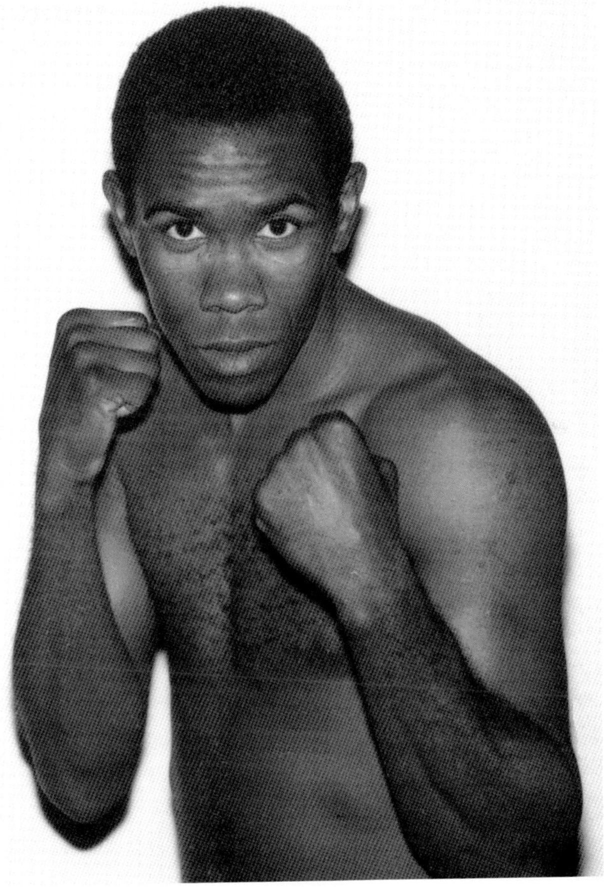

Casino Boxing Is Born. Atlantic City's very first casino fight card occurred on November 4, 1978, in the Superstar Theatre at Resorts International. Howard Davis Jr., a 1976 Olympic gold medalist, was tapped to headline the show in his ninth professional bout. He defeated Luis Davila by a 10-round decision. This was the first of 13 AC appearances for Davis. The five-bout card was promoted by Frank Gelb. (Photograph by Pete Goldfield.)

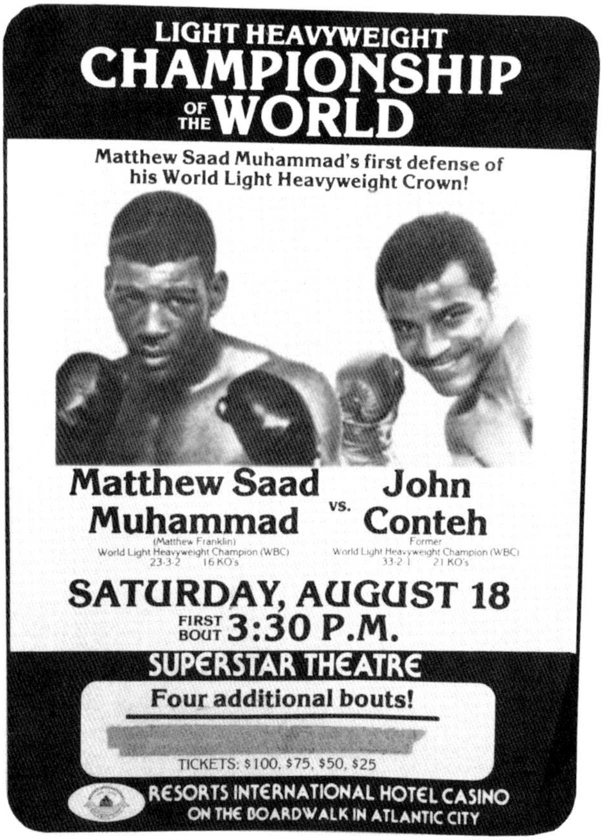

EPIC DEFENSE. On August 18, 1979, Matthew Saad Muhammad defended his WBC light heavyweight title for the first time with a 15-round decision over former champion John Conteh at Resorts. A bloody Saad Muhammad made another one of his famous comebacks, securing the victory with two late-round knockdowns. This was the first world championship bout in AC since 1963. In the rematch at Resorts seven months later, Saad Muhammad won by fourth-round technical knockout. (Author's collection.)

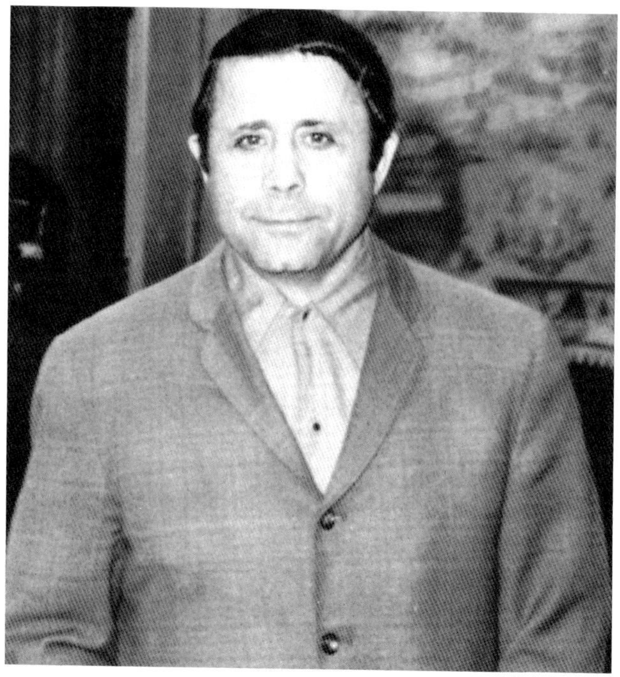

TEA LEAVES. Cut man and trainer Adolph Ritacco worked with fighters like Joey Giardello, Bud Smith, Jimmy Carter, and Kitten Hayward. Ritacco is also remembered for a brief and controversial association with Matthew Saad Muhammad. Known for homemade coagulants that he claimed consisted mainly of tea leaves, Ritacco ran into trouble when he used his concoction in Saad Muhammad's 1979 title defense against John Conteh. Adolph's solution helped the champion retain his belt, but Ritacco was suspended for using a foreign substance. (Author's collection.)

IN THIS CORNER. Ed Derian began his career announcing roller derby contests at the Philadelphia Arena and later became a staple at the Spectrum fights. When the boxing scene shifted from Philly to Atlantic City, Derian migrated with it and became the most prominent man with a microphone during the city's boxing rebirth. Derian worked up and down the Boardwalk, including the weekly Tropicana shows in the 1980s, and announced cards into the 21st century. (Photograph by Pete Goldfield.)

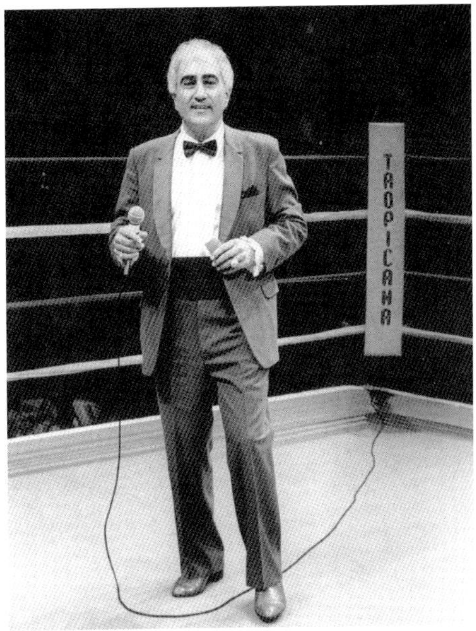

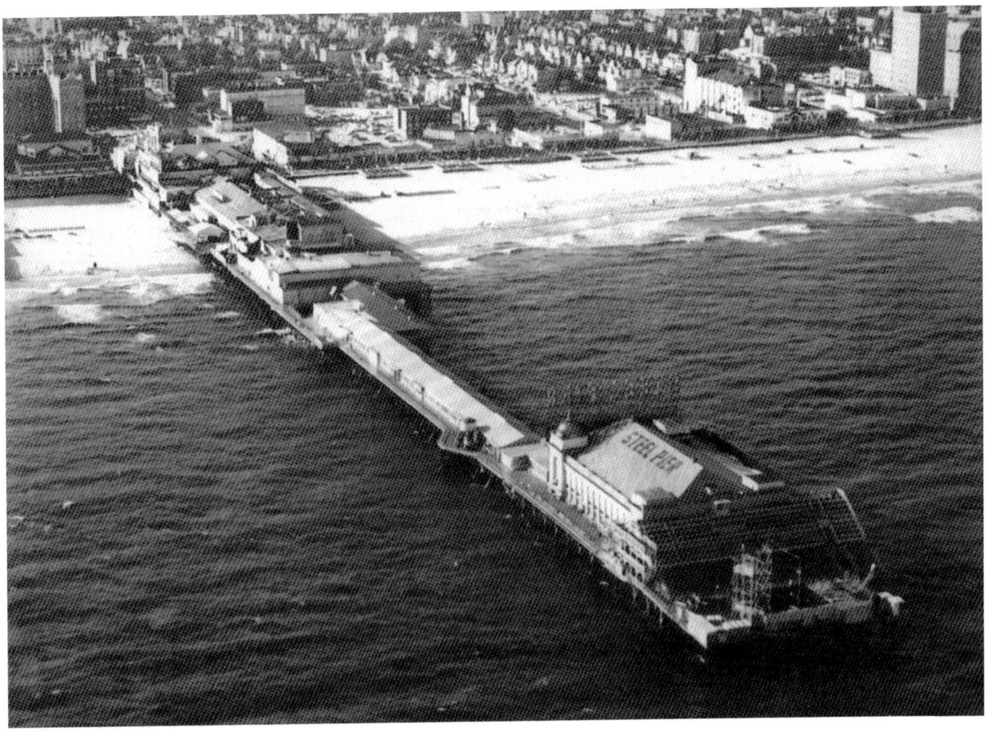

STEEL PIER. Built in 1898, AC's "oldest theme park" was known mainly for concerts, cotton candy, and a famous diving horse. Steel Pier was the site for nine boxing events in 1979, just before casino prizefighting surged. The fights were promoted by Frank Gelb with matches made by J Russell Peltz. Jeff Chandler, Bennie Briscoe, Dwight Muhammad Qawi, Eddie Mustafa Muhammad, Richie Kates, Tex Cobb, Duane Bobick, and Jerry Martin highlighted the series. (Author's collection.)

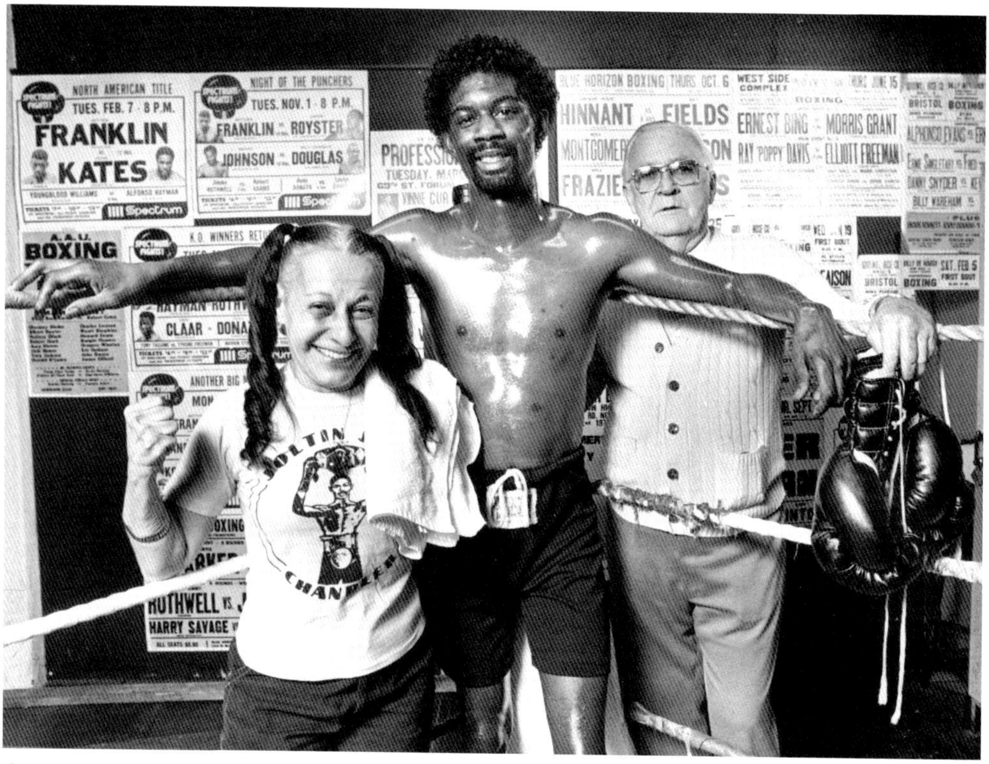

Best of the Bantamweights. "Joltin'" Jeff Chandler won the WBA bantamweight title in 1980 and made nine successful title defenses through 1984. He appeared in AC 13 times at venues like Resorts, the Sands, Convention Hall, and Steel Pier. These appearances included six title fights against Julian Solis, Eijiro Murata, Miguel Iriarte, Gaby Canizales, Oscar Muniz, and Richie Sandoval. Chandler is pictured here with manager "KO" Becky O'Neill and trainer Willie O'Neill. (Author's collection.)

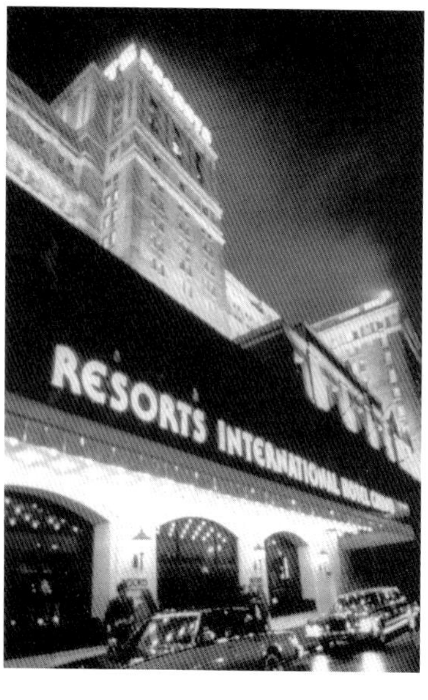

Resorts International. AC's first gambling site, Resorts International Hotel Casino, also became the first hot spot for casino boxing. Fights were held in two different rooms at Resorts, the 400-seat Rutland Room and its primary venue, the 1,300-seat Superstar Theatre. Resorts has hosted more than 200 boxing events, including many world title bouts. More than 175 of the fights at Resorts occurred during the 1980s. (Author's collection.)

3

Boom

1980–1985

The Atlantic City fight scene bloomed in the 1980s. While the entire decade of the 1970s only offered fans about 25 shows, 1980 alone featured 24. Most of these were at Resorts, including one title bout, the rematch between Matthew Saad Muhammad and John Conteh. The number of shows doubled the following year, with more high-profile title fights involving Saad Muhammad, Jeff Chandler, Alexis Arguello, Michael Spinks, and Sean O'Grady.

Other star acts developed during this time. Frank Fletcher never won a world title but was arguably the most entertaining fighter of this AC era. Dwight Muhammad Qawi (then Dwight Braxton) took the light heavyweight title from Saad Muhammad at the end of 1981 and became another important attraction. Joining Resorts as key boxing sites were Bally's, Golden Nugget, Playboy, and the Sands.

In 1982, nearly 140 boxing shows occurred in AC. More than 50 of these were at the Tropicana, where weekly Tuesday night fights became a new haven for boxing fans. The Sands offered more than 40 shows that year, while other casinos like the Claridge and Harrah's also got in on the action. Big visiting attractions, such as "Marvelous" Marvin Hagler, Aaron Pryor, and Wilfredo Gomez, brought more title fights to the city. Spinks, Chandler, Qawi, and Fletcher continued to be key AC regulars.

Near the end of 1982, AC gambled on staging a bigger-scale event on the Boardwalk. The nine casinos at that time collaborated to present a world title fight between Qawi and Eddie Davis at Convention Hall, a fight in which Qawi defended his title in front of 7,201 enthusiastic fans. In terms of attendance, it was the biggest AC boxing event since the 1963 Giardello versus Tiger fight and set the stage for future big boxing cards at the venue.

Over the next few years, boxing output continued to be strong. In 1983, there were nearly 120 shows, and 1984 offered just over that number. In 1985, a record 143 shows took place along the Boardwalk. In terms of quantity, this was AC's all-time peak.

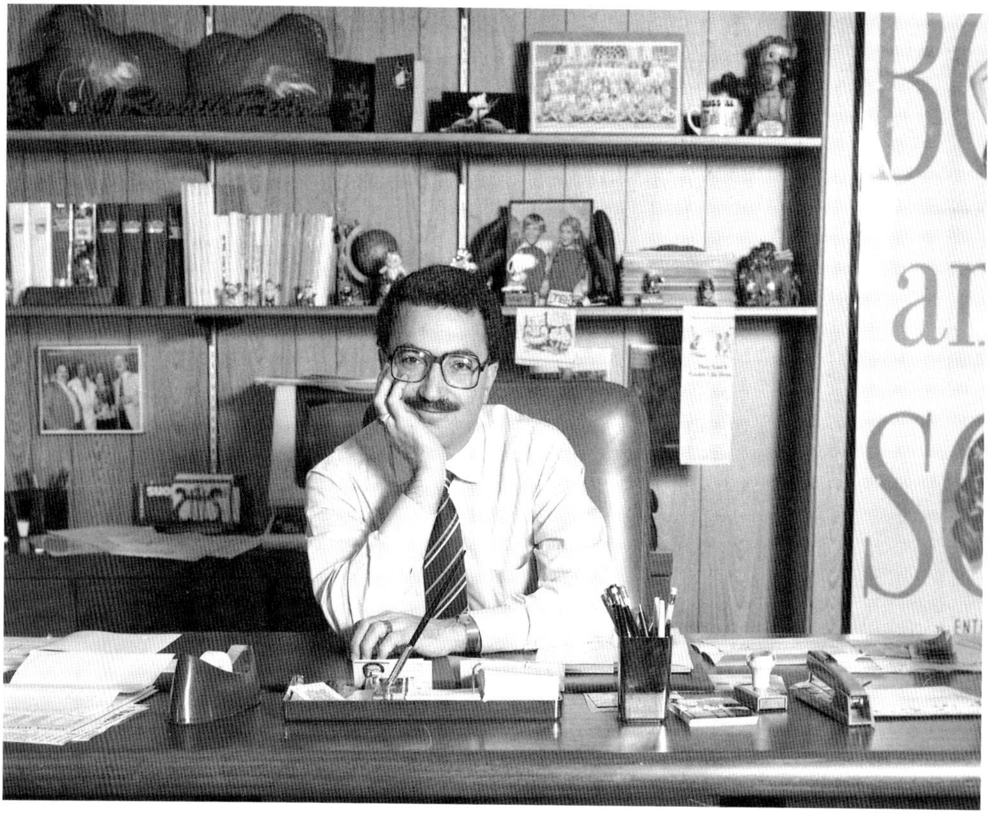

Blue Collar Boxing Promoter. Philadelphia boxing guru J Russell Peltz ventured to AC and contributed to the city's rise as a new boxing capital. Peltz was a matchmaker for early Frank Gelb shows, then promoted his own casino cards beginning in the early 1980s, mainly at the Sands, Resorts, and later Bally's. Using the "fans-first" approach that made his Philadelphia promotions thrive, Peltz was responsible for some of the Boardwalk's best bouts. He promoted fights for 50 years. (Photograph by Pete Goldfield.)

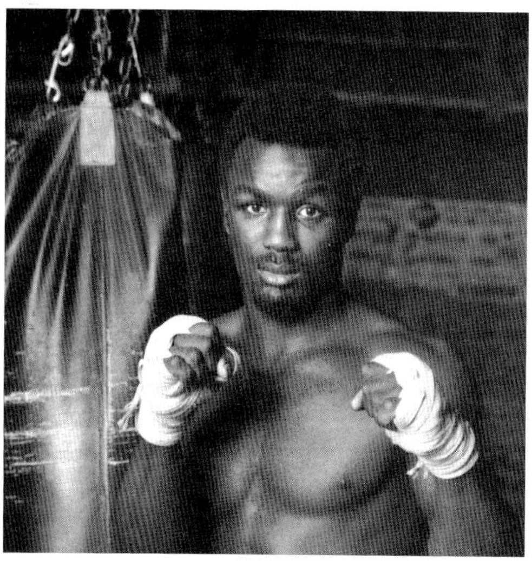

Curtis Parker. Middleweight Curtis Parker made 17 appearances at Bally's, Playboy, Golden Nugget, Claridge, Harrah's Marina, and the Sands. He won the USBA title in 1980 with a TKO of David Love and scored other AC victories over Mike Colbert, Tony Braxton, and Frank Fletcher. However, losses to Mustafa Hamsho and Wilford Scypion kept Parker from a world title fight. Trained by Willie Reddish through most of his career, Parker went 11-6, with 6 KOs, at the shore. (Photograph by Pete Goldfield.)

Top Rank. Promoter Bob Arum's Top Rank made its AC debut in the late-1970s before partnering with the cable network ESPN in 1980 to launch the ESPN Boxing Tournament. This competition gave rising boxers their first national exposure and crowned the winners ESPN champions. The series also helped bolster ESPN's boxing reputation. Top Rank remained a major presence in AC through the late 1990s, promoting nearly 200 shows along the Boardwalk. After several years away, Arum returned to AC to promote occasional events beginning in 2004 featuring major attractions like Floyd Mayweather, Miguel Cotto, Sergio Martinez, Guillermo Rigondeaux, and others. (Author's collection.)

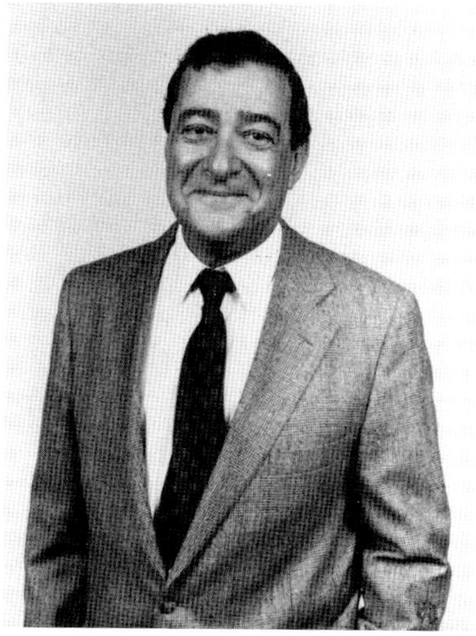

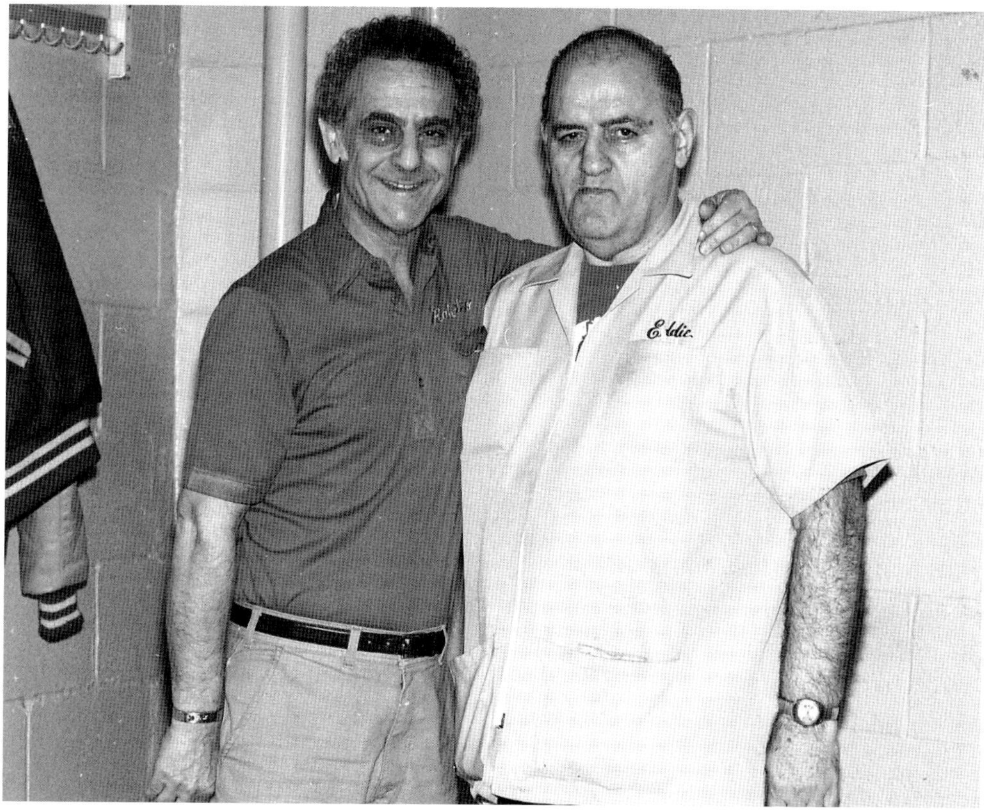

Cut Men. Two of the busiest cut men during the 1980s and 1990s were Ralph Citro (left) and Eddie Aliano. Both worked countless corners in AC during the boom years. Nicknamed "The Clot," Aliano worked with champs like Jeff Chandler and Matthew Saad Muhammad. Citro worked with Riddick Bowe, plus Thomas Hearns, Michael Moorer, and the rest of Emanuel Steward's Kronk team. Citro was also a record-keeper who published the *Computer Boxing Update*. (Photograph by Pete Goldfield.)

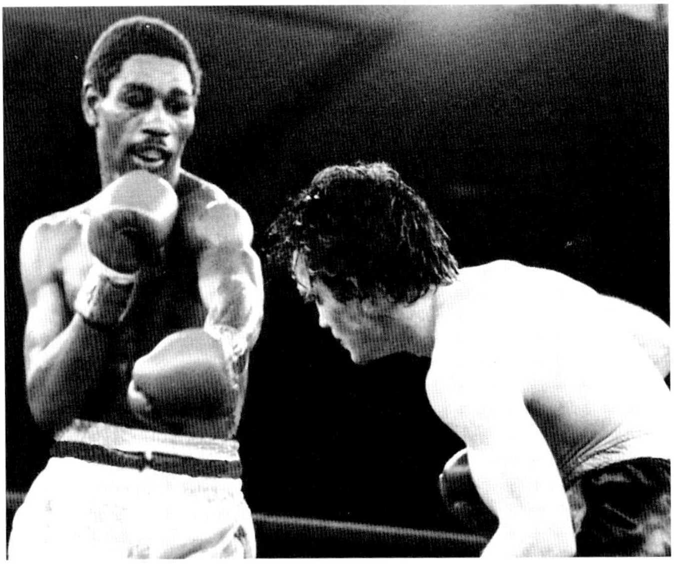

O'GRADY BEATS KENTY. In his second try for the lightweight title, Sean O'Grady took the WBA championship from Hilmer Kenty on April 12, 1981, at Bally's. O'Grady (dark trunks) knocked down the champion in both the second and eighth rounds and won by a unanimous decision. It was Kenty's first career loss and the only time either fighter appeared in Atlantic City. (Bob Ryder.)

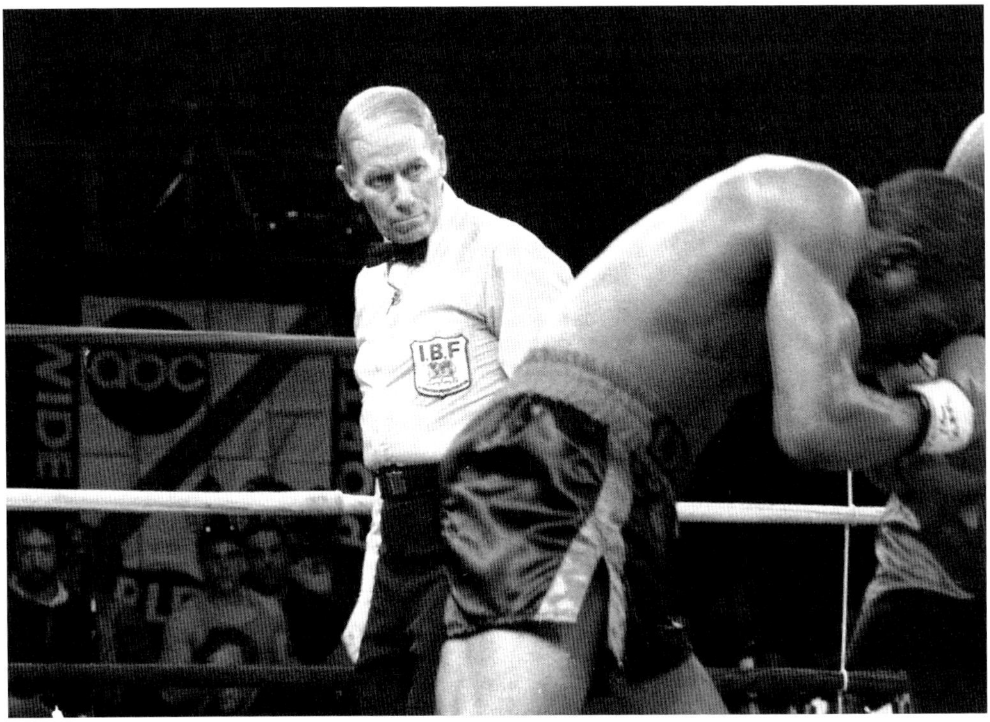

CONTROVERSIAL COUNTER. Paul Venti began refereeing fights in the late 1960s and started working in Atlantic City by 1975. He landed key assignments including bouts featuring Jeff Chandler, Frank Fletcher, and Hector Camacho. His biggest job, the 1981 light heavyweight title fight between Matthew Saad Muhammad and Murray Sutherland, proved controversial when it appeared Sutherland beat Venti's fight-ending 10-count. However, the contentious call remained. (Photograph by Pete Goldfield.)

Saad Muhammad's Last Stand. In 1981, Matthew Saad Muhammad returned to AC for three consecutive WBC light heavyweight title defenses. On February 28, he stopped Vonzell Johnson in 11 rounds at Bally's. Two months later at Resorts, he knocked out Murray Sutherland in the ninth round. Finally, on September 26, he struggled to stop Jerry Martin in 11 rounds at the Golden Nugget. Saad Muhammad's exciting championship run ended in his next bout. (Photograph by Pete Goldfield.)

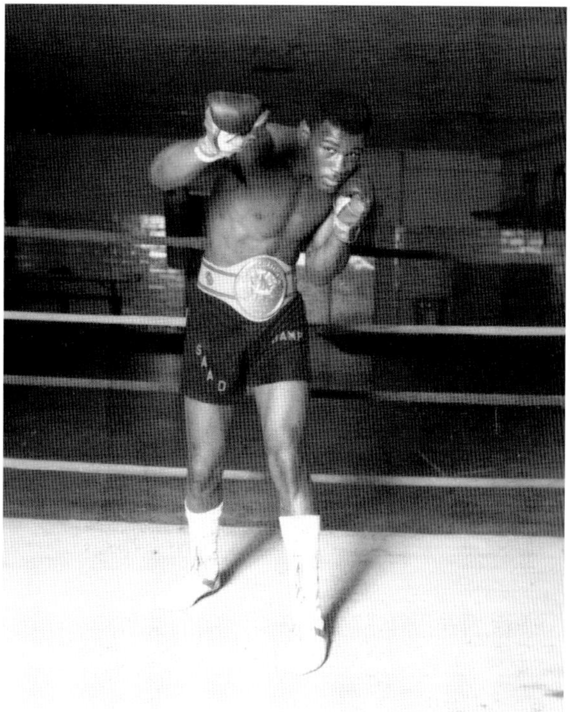

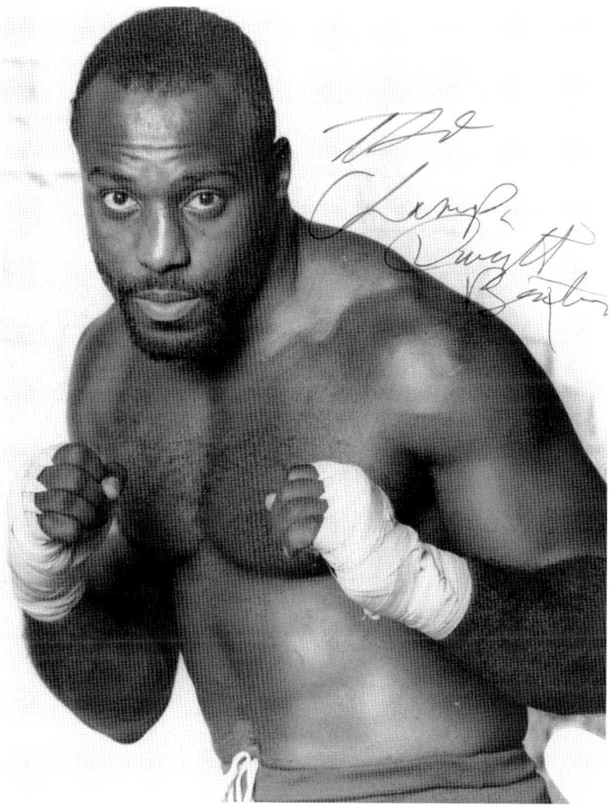

"The Camden Buzzsaw." Dwight Muhammad Qawi (formerly Dwight Braxton) was a fan favorite who made 23 starts in Atlantic City, including many important career milestones. He won the ESPN Tournament in 1980 and knocked out former world champion Mike Rossman in 1981. Qawi also won, defended, and lost the WBC light heavyweight title in Atlantic City. Overall, he went 21-2, with 14 knockouts in AC. (Photograph by Pete Goldfield.)

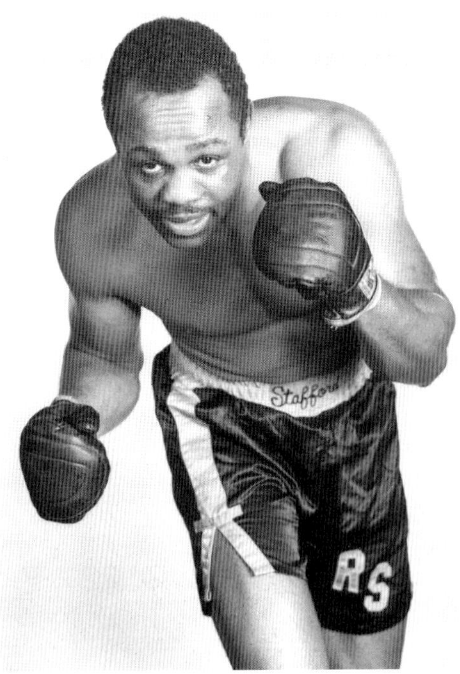

ESPN Champ. Roger Stafford won the ESPN Tournament in 1980, which earned him a fight with former champion Pipino Cuevas. In his biggest career win, Stafford beat Cuevas in Las Vegas. The fight was named the "Upset of the Year" by *The Ring*. Roger fought in Atlantic City 10 times, including wins over Kevin Howard, Johnny Cooper, Tony Suero, Darryl Fuller, and Robert Adams. (Photograph by Pete Goldfield.)

Sands

Copa Room

The Sands famed theatre showcases dazzling headline entertainment, spectacular revues and fast paced sporting events.

The Copa Room. In the 1980s, the Sands' 800-seat Copa Room was AC's version of an old-school boxing club, despite the glitzy casino trappings. Frank Fletcher headlined the first Sands show on June 14, 1981, and eventually, big names like Jeff Chandler, Michael Spinks, Aaron Pryor, Pernell Whitaker, Marvin Johnson, Meldrick Taylor, and Eusebio Pedroza fought there too. Originally known as the Brighton Hotel, the Sands hosted just under 200 cards, with nearly 160 of them during the 1980s. Peltz Boxing staged many of the shows, but others, including Main Events, Top Rank, Butch Lewis, and Sylvester Stallone's Tiger Eye Boxing, were also active there. (Author's collection.)

"THE EXPLOSIVE THIN MAN." Three-division champion Alexis Arguello fought in Atlantic City four times, including a dramatic TKO of Ray Mancini in defense of his WBC lightweight title on October 3, 1981, at Bally's. Arguello stopped Mancini in round 14, preventing the brave challenger from winning the title for his father. However, Mancini accomplished that goal the following year. During the 1980s, Arguello also knocked out Cornelius Boza Edwards, Kevin Rooney, and Claude Noel in AC. (Author's collection.)

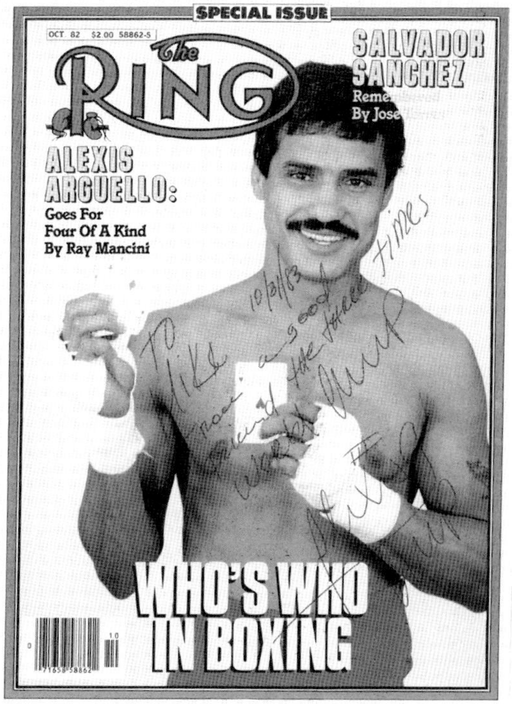

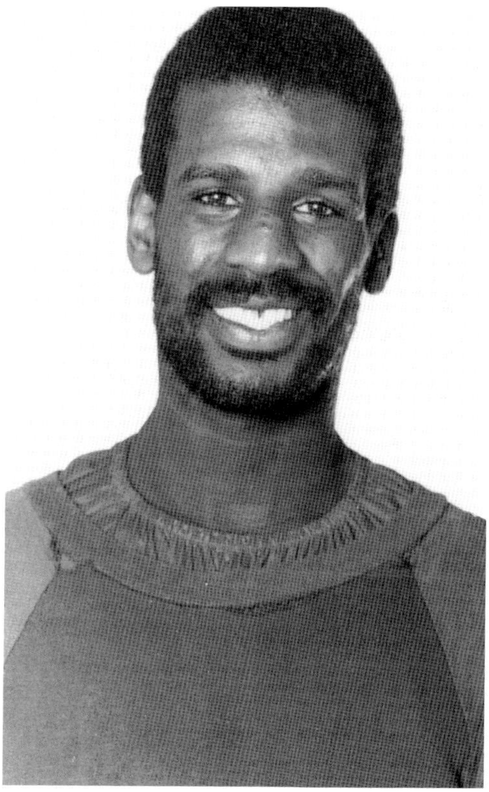

SPINKS JINX. Michael Spinks, an essential casino-era participant, fought 13 times at the shore between 1980 and 1988. These fights included eight light heavyweight title bouts against Vonzell Johnson, Mustafa Wasajja, Murray Sutherland, Jerry Celestine, Johnny Davis, Eddie Davis, David Sears, and Dwight Muhammad Qawi. Trained by legend Eddie Futch, Spinks also knocked out Gerry Cooney at heavyweight, which led to a showdown with Mike Tyson, the only man ever to beat Spinks. (Photograph by Pete Goldfield.)

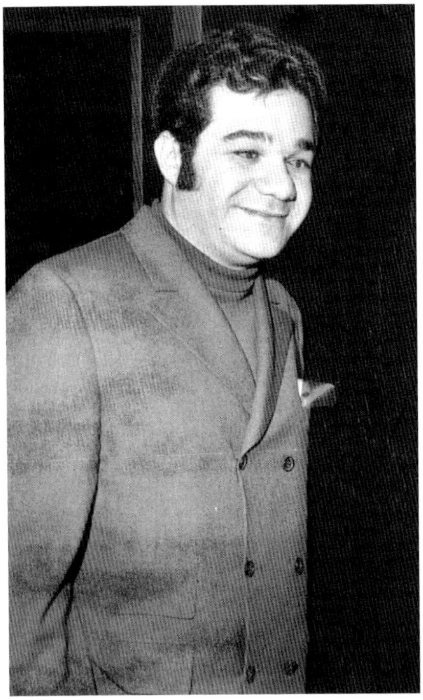

TUESDAY NIGHT FIGHTS. Legendary promoter Don Elbaum was a key figure during Atlantic City's busiest boxing era. His weekly Tuesday night shows with copromoter Teddy Menas at the Tropicana (1981 to 1986) totaled nearly 200 and played a big part in making AC the boxing capital that it became. Elbaum, a boxing jack-of-all-trades, not only promoted events, he was also a boxer, manager, adviser, writer, and publicist in his decades-long career. (Author's collection.)

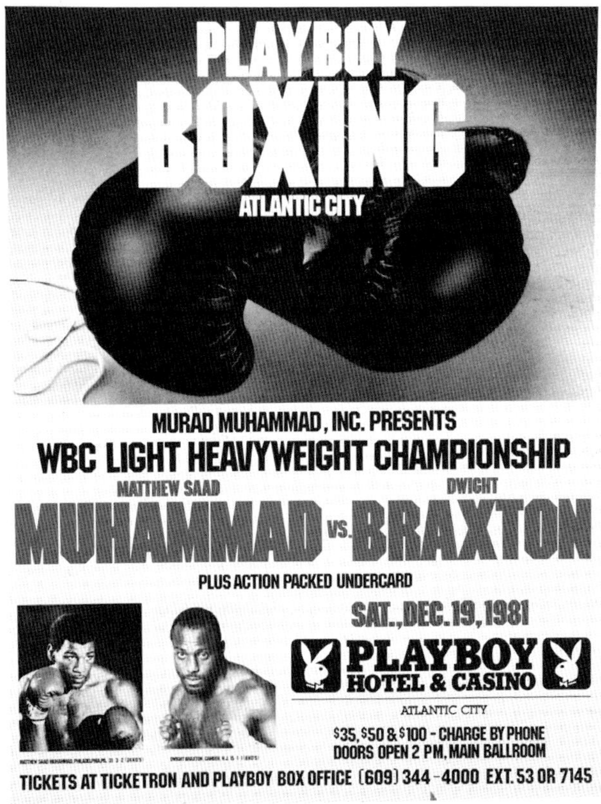

QAWI DETHRONES SAAD. Dwight Muhammad Qawi (then Dwight Braxton) brought the remarkable title reign of Matthew Saad Muhammad to an end on December 19, 1981, at the Playboy Hotel and Casino. Famous for battling back from the brink of defeat, "Miracle Matthew" ran out of miracles against Qawi, who knocked Saad Muhammad down and relentlessly attacked him until referee Arthur Mercante stepped in to stop it in the 10th round. (Author's collection.)

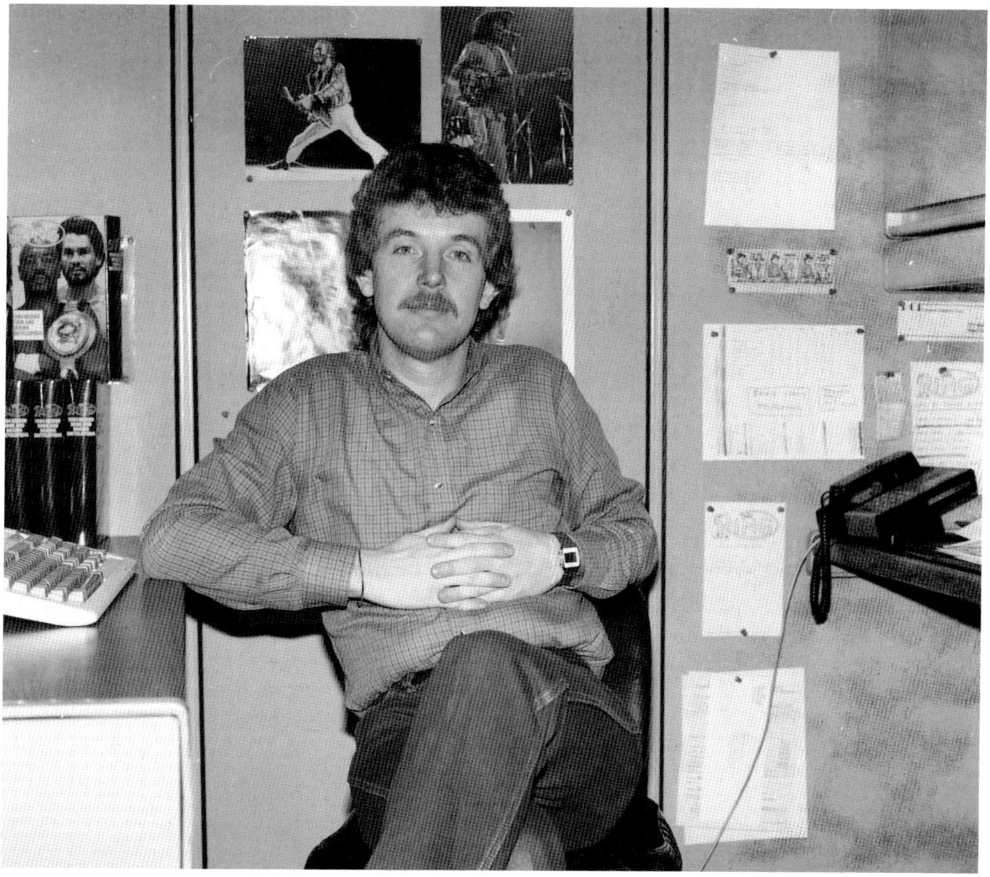

Editor-in-Chief. When casino boxing came to Atlantic City, Nigel Collins was a fixture at ringside, capturing the scene as a correspondent and writer for various publications. Collins became the assistant editor of *The Ring* in 1983 and then editor-in-chief in 1985. He held the position for four years. Collins authored the book *Boxing Babylon* in 1990 before returning to *The Ring* in 1993 to again serve as editor-in-chief until 2011. (Photograph by Pete Goldfield.)

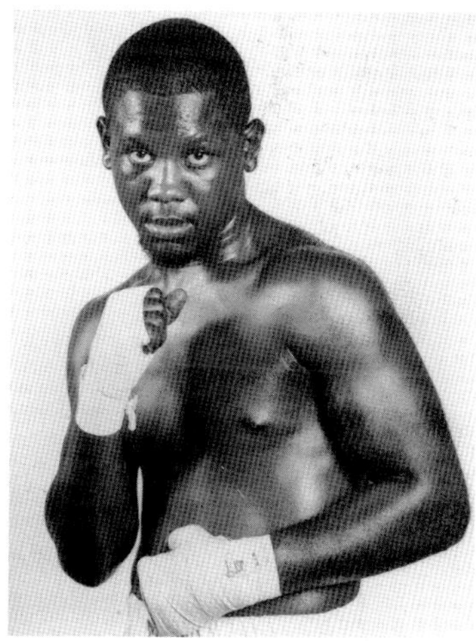

Spoiler Alert. Welterweight Kevin Howard was best known for his 1984 nationally televised knockdown of "Sugar" Ray Leonard in Worcester, Massachusetts. Despite losing to Leonard, Howard was popular in his native Philadelphia and Atlantic City. Known as "The Spoiler" for his ability to make opponents look bad, Howard fought 15 of his 30 professional bouts in AC. In 1982, he defeated Micky Ward's half-brother and future trainer, Dicky Eklund, at the Sands. (Peltz Boxing Promotions.)

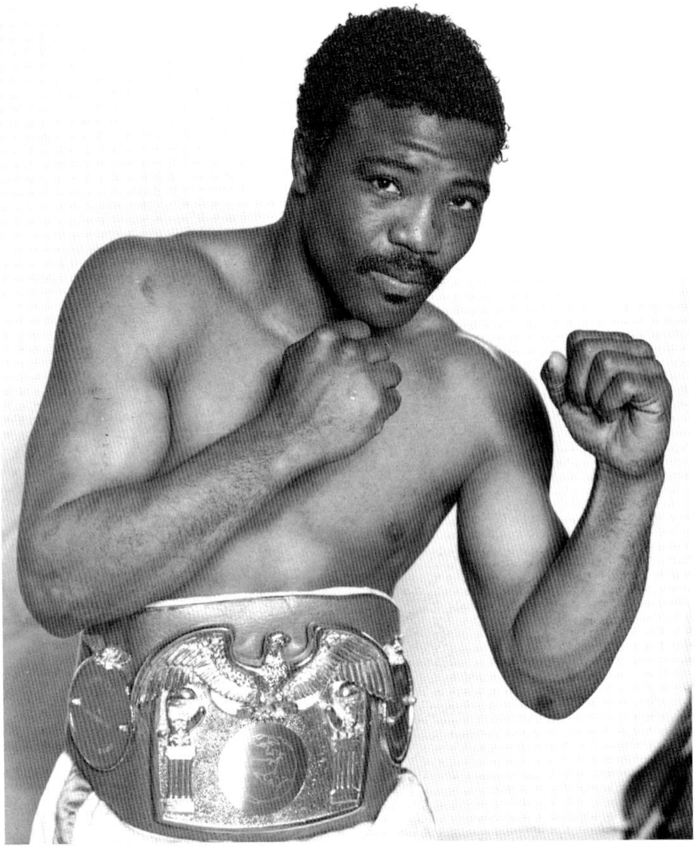

Hawk Time. Thrill-a-minute junior welterweight champion Aaron "Hawk" Pryor brought his entertaining show to the Playboy on March 21, 1982, for the fifth defense of his title against Miguel Montilla. He returned to stop Sang Hyun Kim in three rounds at the Sands on April 2, 1983. Finally, Pryor made his 10th and final defense, a decision victory over Gary Hinton on March 2, 1985, at the Sands. (Photograph by Pete Goldfield.)

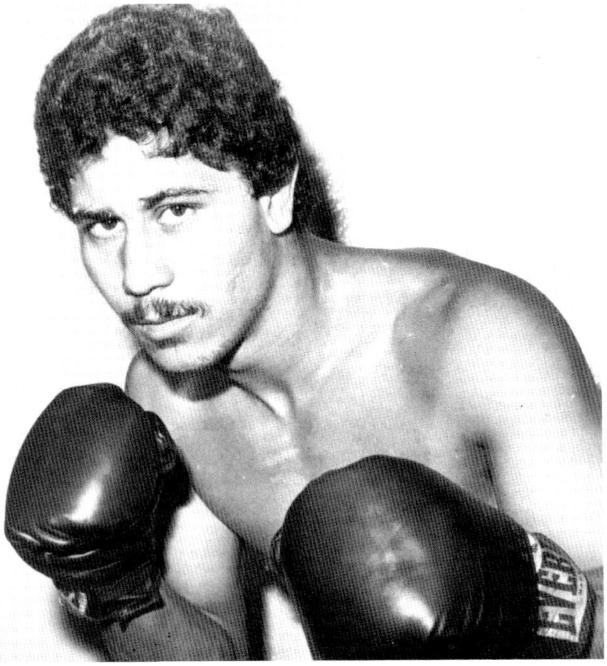

"Bazooka" Gomez. After losing for the first time (to Salvador Sanchez in a featherweight title challenge), Wilfredo "Bazooka" Gomez resumed his long reign as WBC junior featherweight champion, making his 14th title defense with a sixth-round TKO of future champ Juan Meza on March 27, 1982, at the Playboy. This was the only AC appearance by both fighters. Gomez made two more defenses before winning both the featherweight and junior lightweight titles. (Author's collection.)

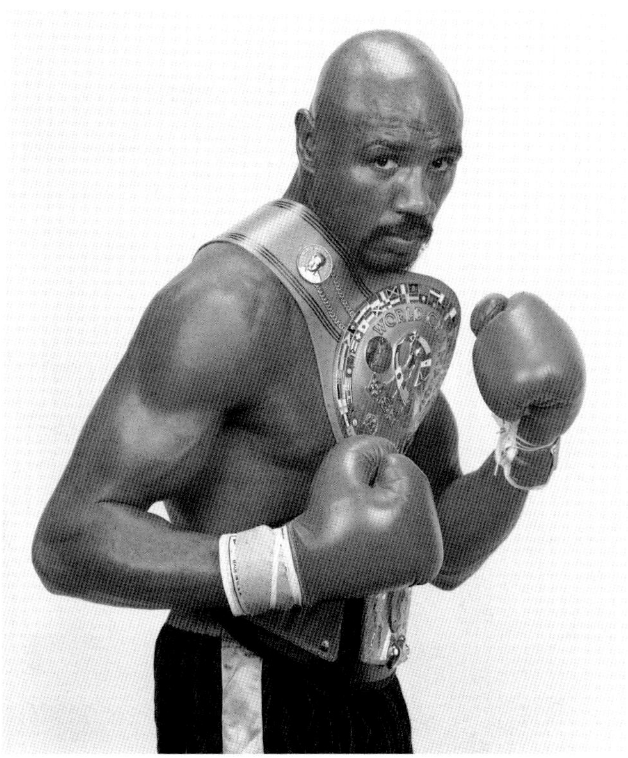

SIMPLY MARVELOUS. Middleweight champion Marvin Hagler's only stop in AC was an impressive one. On March 7, 1982, Hagler defended his title for the fourth time with a 67-second technical knockout of 10th-ranked contender William "Caveman" Lee at Bally's. Annoyed that the television announcers refused to call him by his preferred name, "Marvelous Marvin Hagler," the champ legally changed his name shortly after the fight. (Photograph by Pete Goldfield.)

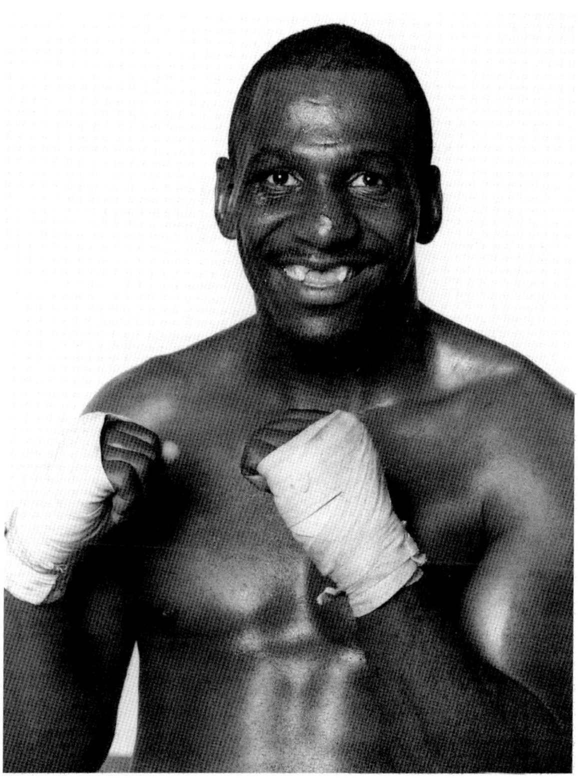

"THE ANIMAL." Frank "The Animal" Fletcher was one of AC's most exciting performers between 1980 and 1985. With his mother, Lucille, wildly cheering from ringside, Fletcher won the ESPN middleweight tournament in 1980 and the USBA title in 1981. His most memorable AC wars included wins over Ernie Singletary, Clint Jackson, Tony Braxton, James "Hard Rock" Green, Curtis Ramsey, Caveman Lee, and Jimmie Sykes. Even his losses to Wilford Scypion and Curtis Parker were thrilling. (Photograph by Pete Goldfield.)

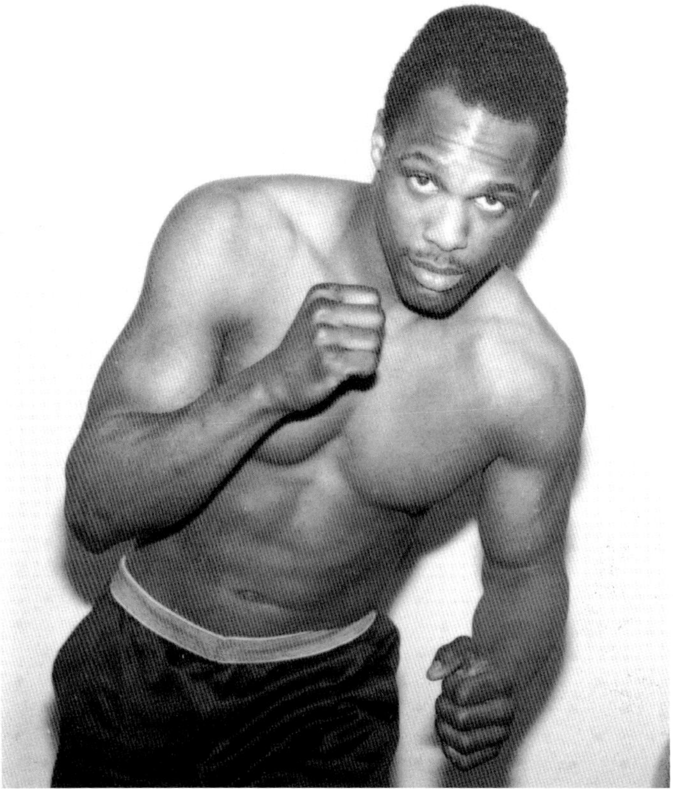

SENSATIONAL. After a distinguished amateur career, junior middleweight "Sensational" Davey Moore won the WBA championship in his ninth professional fight. He fought in AC eight times, including two title defenses. Moore made his second defense with a 10th-round TKO of former champ Ayub Kalule on July 17, 1982. In his next bout on January 29, 1983, Moore knocked out Gary Guiden in round four of his third defense. Both bouts were at Bally's. (Photograph by Pete Goldfield.)

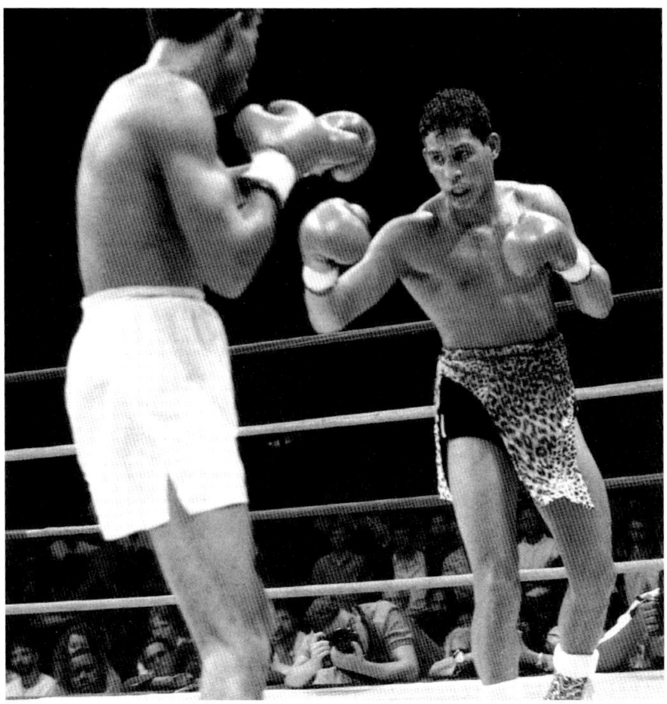

MACHO MAN. Flamboyant Hector "Macho" Camacho was undefeated in his 12 Atlantic City appearances, including big bouts against Roberto Duran, "Sugar" Ray Leonard, Howard Davis Jr., and Vinny Pazienza. He posted an overall record of 79-6-3, with 38 KOs, in a career that spanned 30 years (1980–2010) and six weight divisions. He won WBC titles at junior lightweight and lightweight and WBO belts at junior welterweight twice. (Photograph by Pete Goldfield.)

Boardwalk Blockbuster. On November 20, 1982, all nine Atlantic City casinos, Resorts, Golden Nugget, Harrah's, Tropicana, Bally's, Claridge, Playboy, Caesars, and the Sands, joined forces to bring championship boxing back to Convention Hall. Dwight Muhammad Qawi defended his WBC light heavyweight title by 11th-round TKO over Eddie Davis. Also, Mustafa Hamsho beat Bobby Czyz, and Tony Ayala Jr. stopped Carlos Herrera. Attendance for the show was 7,201, and Convention Hall became the site for future big events. (Author's collection.)

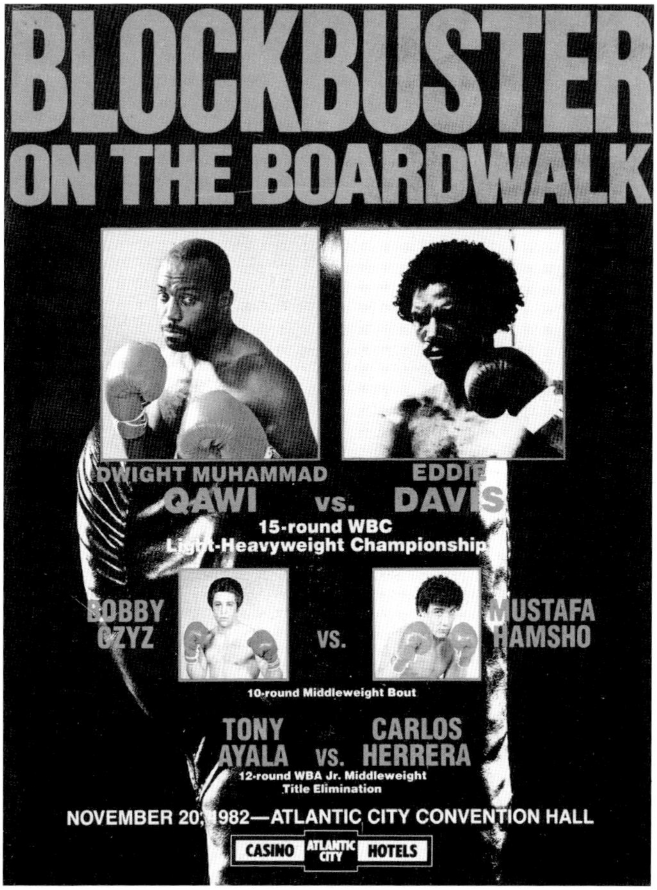

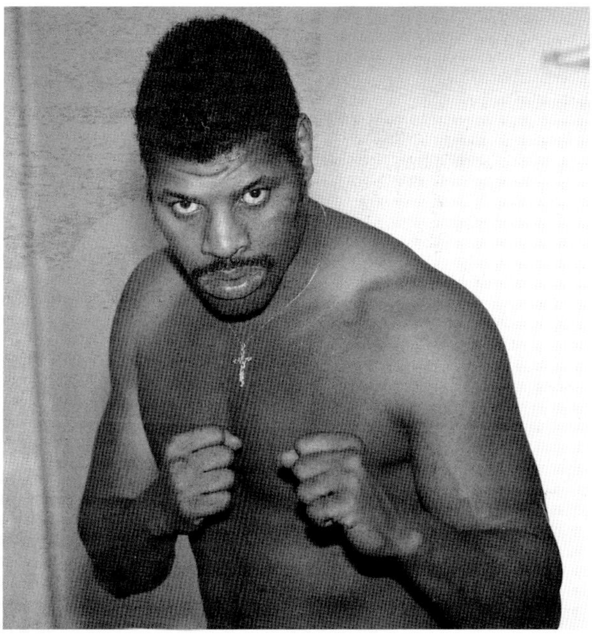

Impaired Vision. Former heavyweight champion Leon Spinks made his 1982 cruiserweight debut against Ivy Brown in AC. On March 6, 1983, at Harrah's Marina, Spinks lost by sixth-round technical knockout to former cruiserweight champion Carlos De Leon, who battered Spinks so badly that Leon, with both eyes practically swollen shut, retired in his corner. De Leon later regained the WBC title three more times and defended it once in AC. (Photograph by Pete Goldfield.)

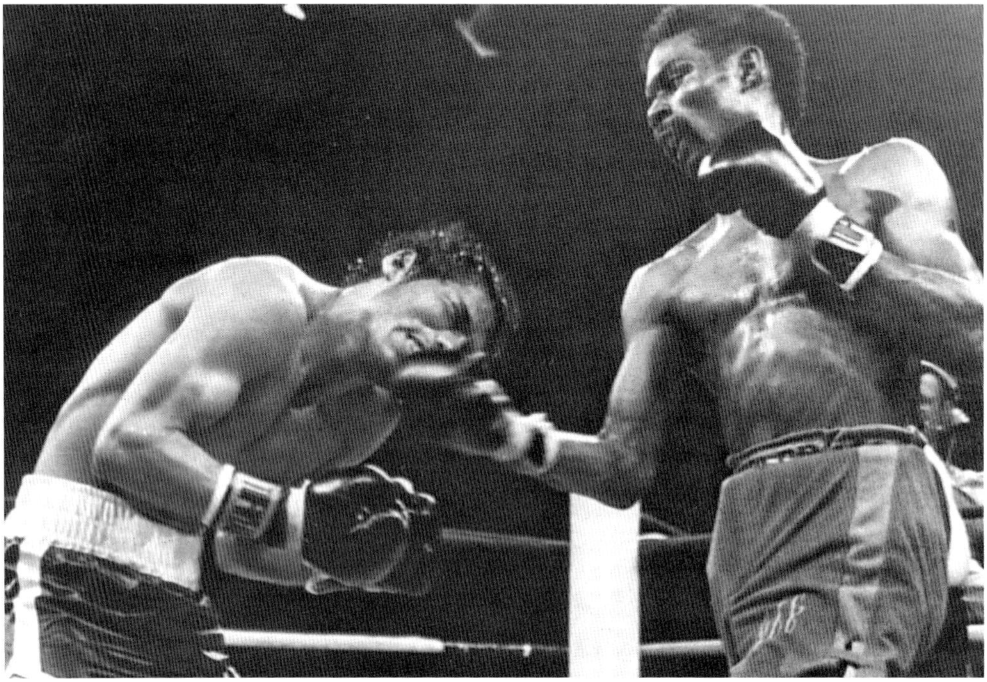

CHANDLER'S PEAK. Bantamweight champion Jeff Chandler defended his WBA title for the seventh time against tough Texan Gaby Canizales on March 13, 1983, at Resorts. Chandler won by unanimous 15-round decision in perhaps the finest performance of his hall-of-fame career. This was Chandler's ninth appearance in Atlantic City and improved his record to 30-0-2, with 16 KOs. Canizales went on to win the bantamweight title three years later. (Photograph by Pete Goldfield.)

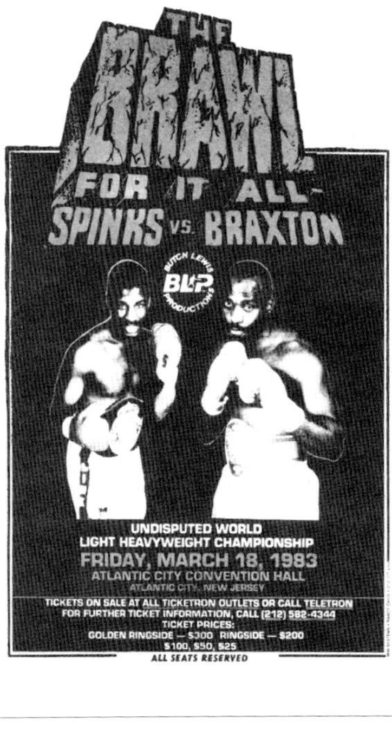

UNDISPUTED CHAMP. In a highly anticipated light heavyweight showdown, WBA champion Michael Spinks out-boxed WBC champion Dwight Muhammad Qawi (then Dwight Braxton) over 15 rounds to unify the world title at Convention Hall on March 18, 1983. Although fans, including the 7,000 in attendance, expected a knockout from these two big punchers, the unanimous decision still produced one clear-cut, unified champion. Spinks held these titles until he moved up and won the IBF heavyweight championship in 1985. (Author's collection.)

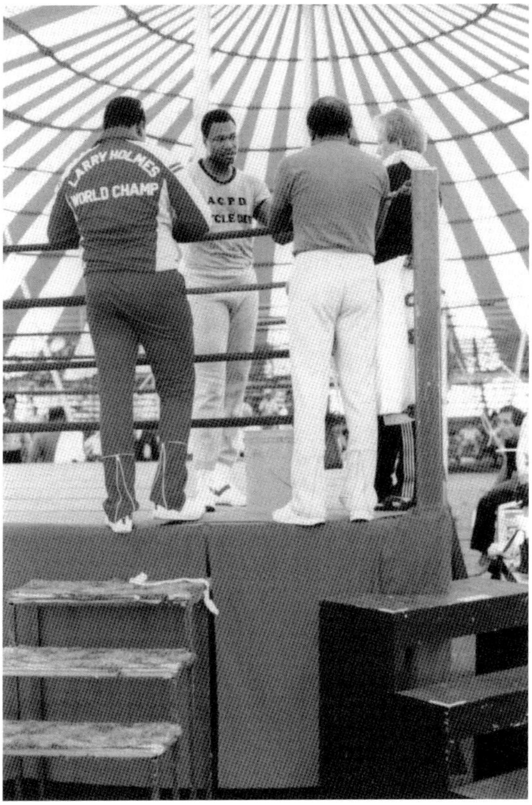

"**THE EASTON ASSASSIN.**" Larry Holmes, "The Easton Assassin," made the 16th defense of his WBC heavyweight championship with a sixth-round TKO of Scott Frank on September 10, 1983, at Harrah's Marina. Holmes, 44-0, relinquished the WBC title after this bout but assumed the IBF belt and remained champion until 1985. This was the first of three AC appearances. Holmes is pictured here training in an outdoor tent one week before the fight. (Photograph by John DiSanto.)

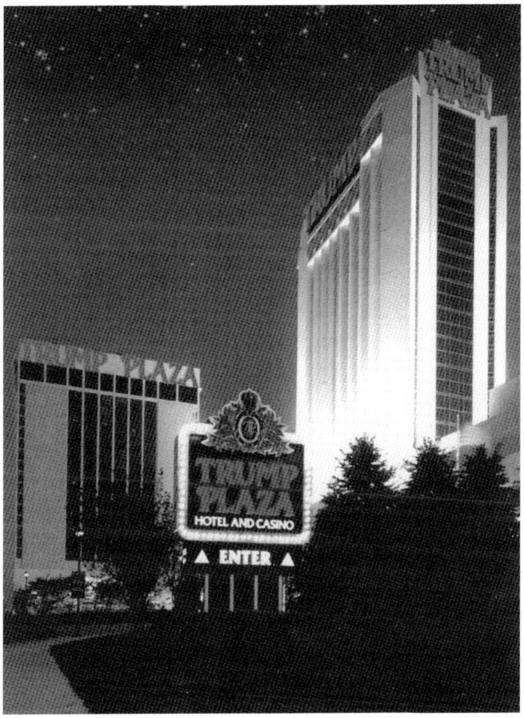

TRUMP PLAZA. Perhaps the best location on the Boardwalk, directly off the Atlantic City Expressway and right next to Convention Hall, Trump Plaza became the centerpiece of AC boxing during its heyday. Although the number of cards hosted within the hotel itself was relatively modest, Donald Trump and his primary property presented numerous other fights next door at Convention Hall, either in the main arena or one of its smaller annexes. (Author's collection.)

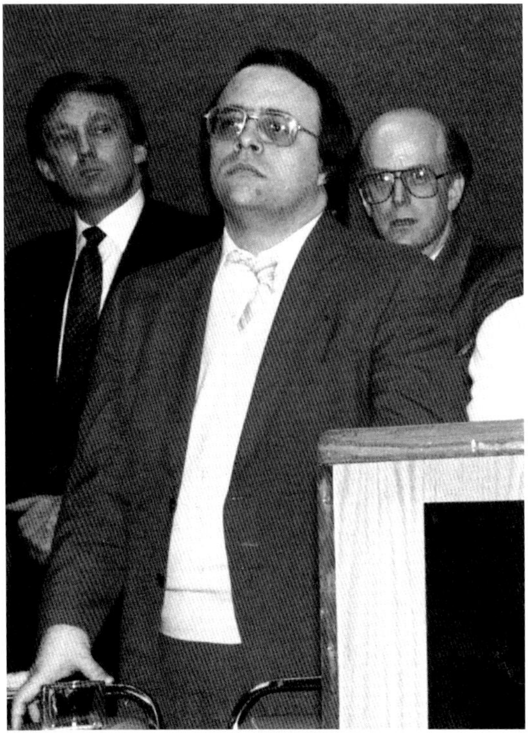

MAIN EVENTS. Dan Duva (shown flanked by Donald Trump and Shelly Finkel) began promoting fights at Ice World in Totowa, New Jersey, before his company, Main Events, entered the big time with the first Leonard versus Hearns fight. His large stable of championship-caliber fighters, including much of the 1984 USA Olympic boxing team, became an important part of the AC scene. When Dan died in 1996, his wife, Kathy Duva, took the reins and directed Main Events into the present day with fighters like Arturo Gatti and Sergey Kovalev. (Photograph by Bill Baron.)

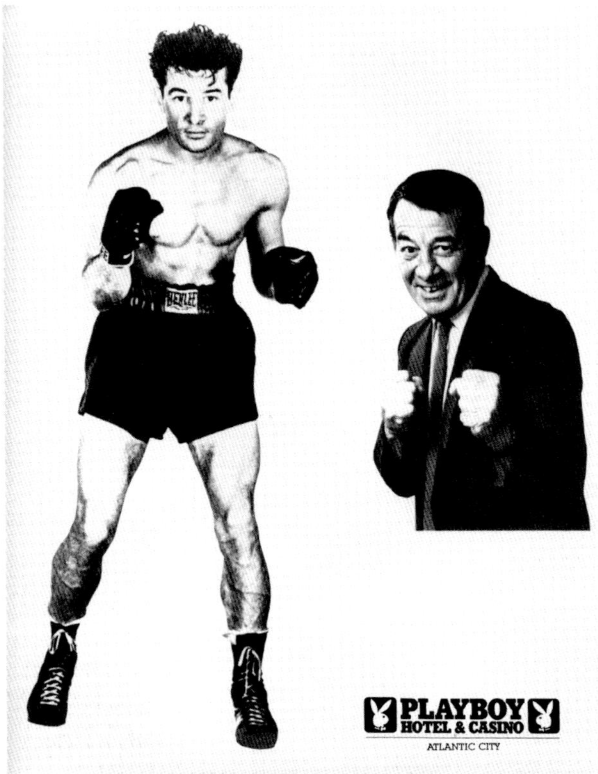

BOXING AMBASSADOR. Although he never fought in Atlantic City during his storied career, former middleweight champion Rocky Graziano was recruited by the Playboy Casino to serve as its boxing ambassador. In this role, Graziano, along with fellow greeter Paddy DeMarco, was a popular staple at ringside and added some championship luster to Playboy's boxing shows. The casino ran nearly 40 boxing cards, including three world title bouts between 1981 and 1984. (Author's collection.)

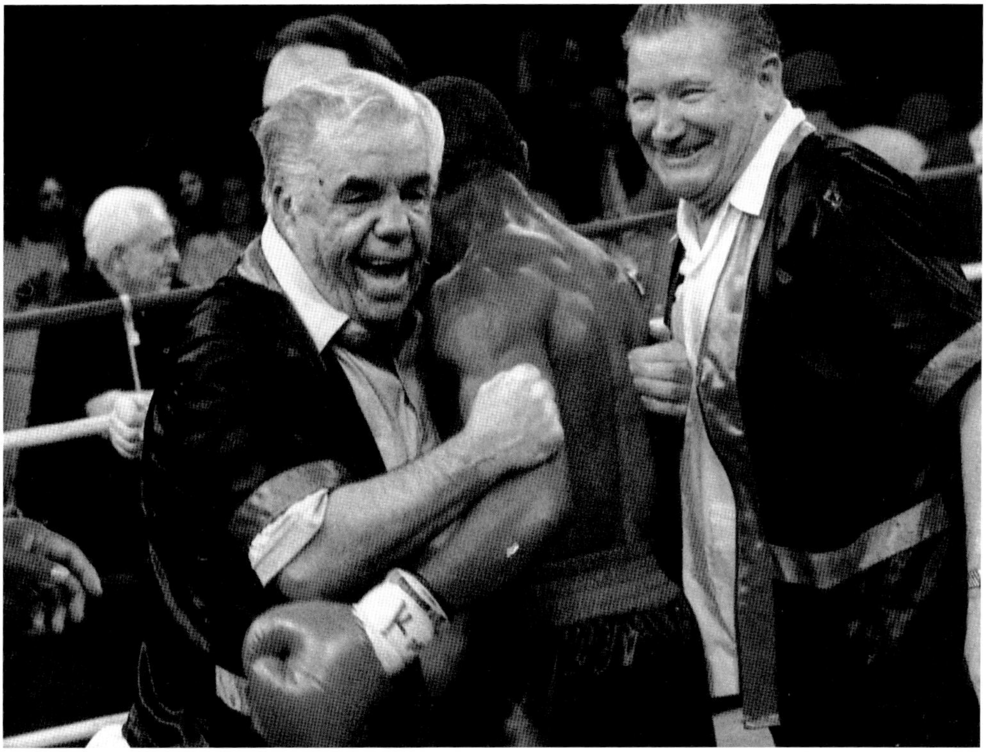

He Loved His Fighters. Lou Duva handled many great boxers, including many of the 1984 Olympic boxing team members, during their professional careers. His stable included Evander Holyfield, Pernell Whitaker, Meldrick Taylor, Tyrell Biggs, Johnny Bumphus, Rocky Lockridge, Tony Ayala Jr., Vinny Pazienza, and Andrew Golota. Duva is also credited with bolstering the training career of George Benton. Already highly respected, Benton reached a new level when he began guiding many of Duva's fighters. Boxing was Duva's life, and as he told *KO* magazine in 1997, "I love my fighters." (Photograph by Pete Goldfield.)

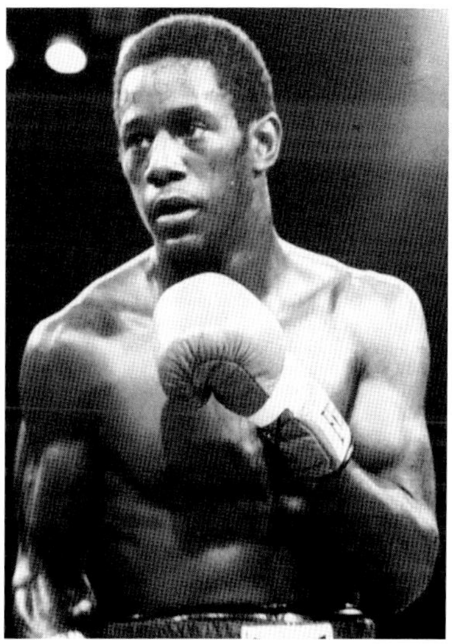

"Bump City." Johnny "Bump City" Bumphus, one of four world champions who started their boxing careers in Tacoma, Washington, was a popular AC attraction with 16 appearances. His biggest bout there came on January 22, 1984, when he fought and defeated Argentina's Lorenzo Garcia at the Sands to capture the WBA junior welterweight title. Bumphus held the title until June 1, 1984, when he lost to Gene Hatcher in his first title defense. (Author's collection.)

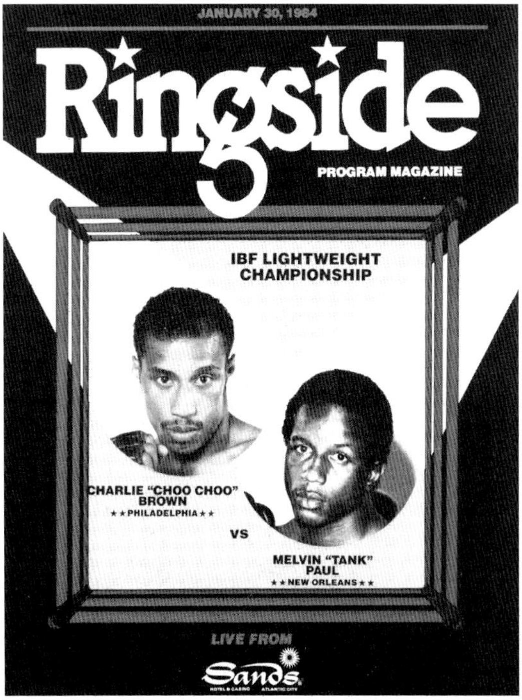

"CHOO CHOO" WINS NEW IBF BELT. Charlie "Choo Choo" Brown came off the floor to win the newly created IBF lightweight championship on January 30, 1984, at the Sands. Brown dropped Melvin Paul twice early in the bout before scoring a narrow 15-round split decision victory. Luckily for Brown, his slim lead on the scorecards was enough to negate his last-round trip to the canvas. This was one of 19 Atlantic City starts for Brown. Paul made seven appearances. (Author's collection.)

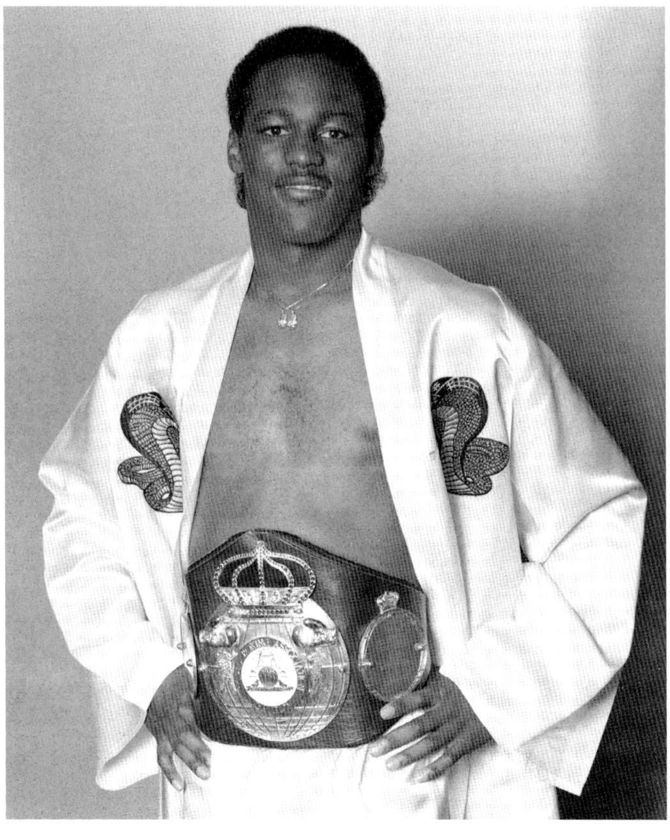

"LONE STAR COBRA." Fort Worth, Texas, welterweight Donald Curry fought five times in AC, including a 12-round decision win against Marlon Starling that earned him NABF and USBA titles. The fight also landed Curry a world title shot, which he won. Curry returned to AC in 1984 for his second title defense, another decision over Marlon Starling. After six more successful defenses, Curry lost his title in a 1986 AC upset. (Photograph by Pete Goldfield.)

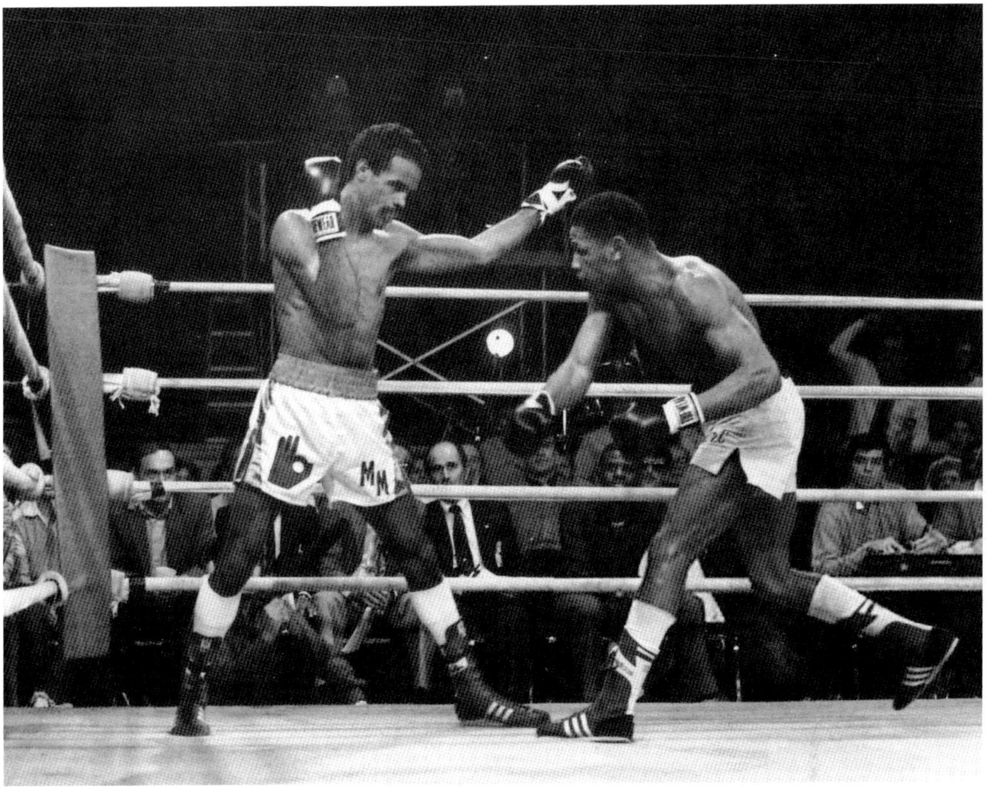

BATTLE OF PUNCHERS. Although Earl Hargrove had knocked out all 24 of his previous opponents, it was Mark Medal (left) who scored a fifth-round TKO in their punch-out for the first IBF junior middleweight title on March 11, 1984, at the Sands. Hargrove started quickly, but Medal survived the storm and staggered Hargrove in round five. Referee Paul Venti stepped in to save Hargrove from any further punishment. (Photograph by Pete Goldfield.)

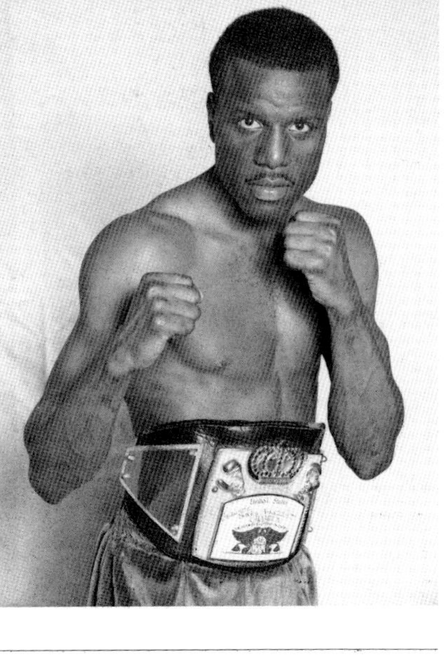

PHILLY SOUTHPAW. Junior welterweight Gary Hinton fought in AC 18 times. During a career that spanned from 1978 to 1989, Hinton held the IBF title from April to October 1986. In his most notable AC fights, Hinton won the USBA title against Jerome Kinney in 1984 and the WBC Continental Americas title against Darryl Fuller in 1985 and made his first attempt at the world title against Aaron Pryor in 1985. (Photograph by Pete Goldfield.)

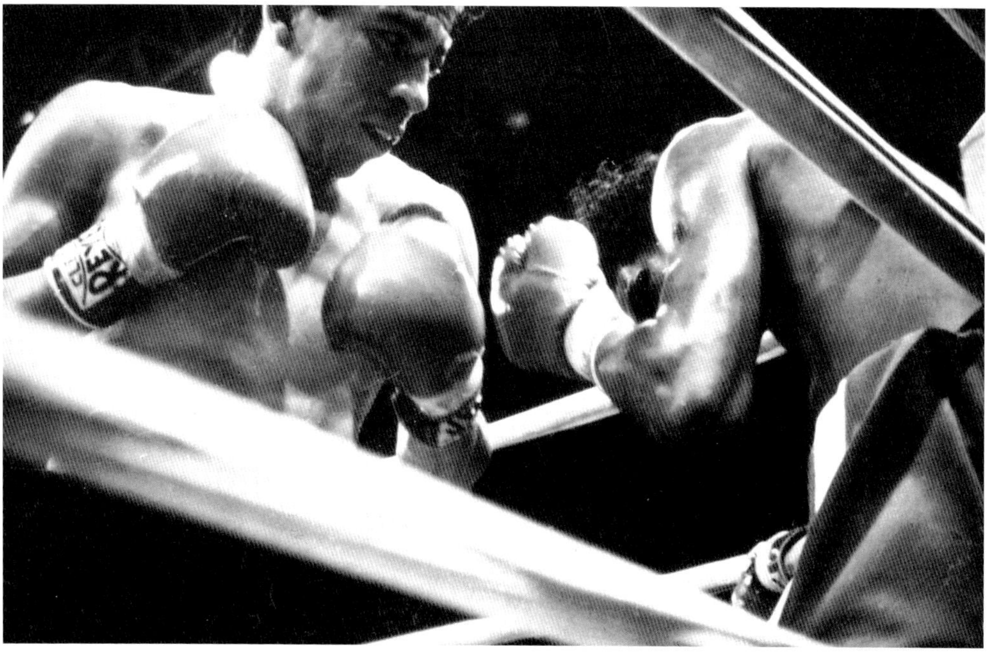

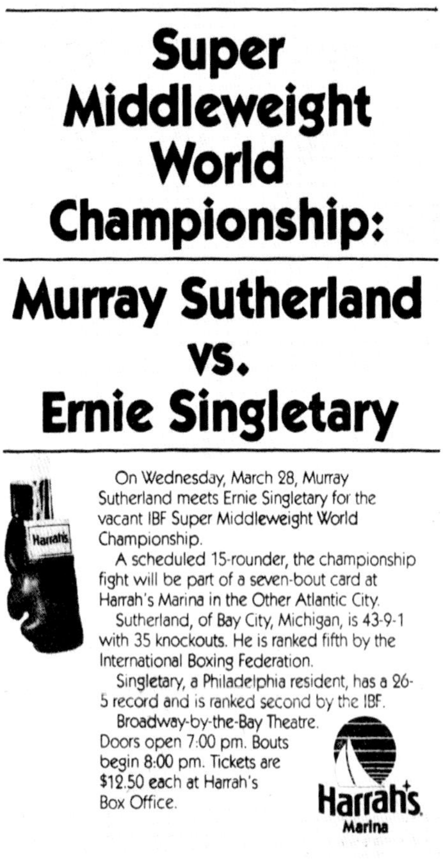

CHANDLER DETHRONED. After nearly four years as champion, Jeff Chandler was dethroned in his 10th defense by Californian Richie Sandoval on April 7, 1984, at the Sands. Sandoval dictated most of the fight, dropped Chandler for the only time in his career in round 11, and won the WBA bantamweight title by TKO in round 15. Sandoval successfully defended the title twice. Chandler retired after this fight due to cataracts. (Photograph by Pete Goldfield.)

THIRD TIME'S A CHARM. Scottish contender Murray Sutherland finally won a world title in his third try when he faced Ernie Singletary at Harrah's Marina on March 28, 1984. Sutherland previously lost two light heavyweight championship bids by knockout to Matthew Saad Muhammad in 1981 and Michael Spinks in 1982. However, after moving down to super middleweight, Sutherland earned the vacant IBF title with a unanimous decision victory over Singletary. (Author's collection.)

"CHOO CHOO" DERAILED. Harry Arroyo stepped in as a late substitute and upset IBF lightweight champion Charlie "Choo Choo" Brown by 14th-round technical knockout on April 15, 1984, at the Sands. Arroyo hurt Brown with two right hands in round 14 and pounded away until referee Larry Hazzard halted the bout. Youngstown, Ohio's Arroyo defended the title twice before losing it to Jimmy Paul in AC. (Photograph by Pete Goldfield.)

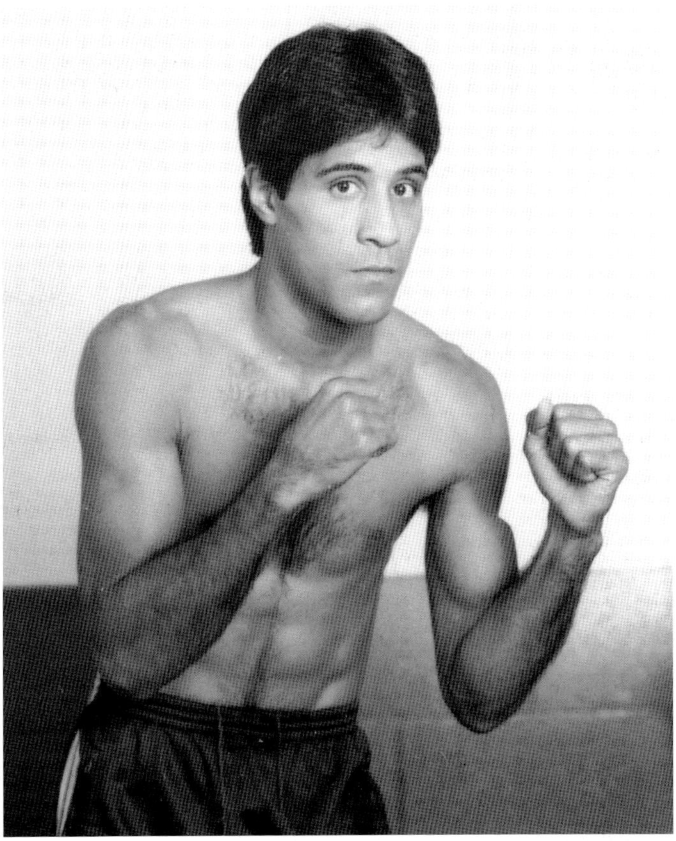

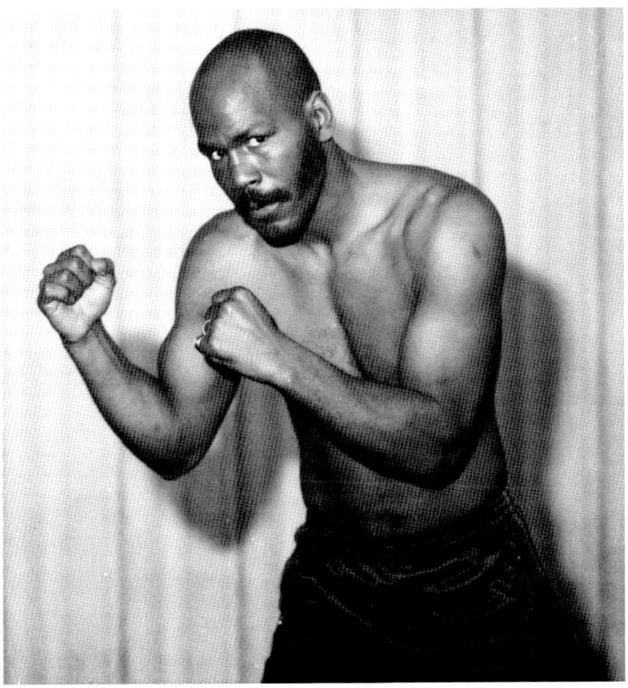

"POPS" JOHNSON. After two reigns as world light heavyweight champion, Marvin "Pops" Johnson came to Resorts and the Sands for seven fights between 1980 and 1985. Johnson won six of them, including victories over brothers Johnny and Eddie Davis, Junior Royster, Eddie Gonzales, and Jerome Clouden. After this rebuilding stage, Johnson went on to win a third world title in 1986. His only AC loss was by knockout to Michael Spinks. (Photograph by Pete Goldfield.)

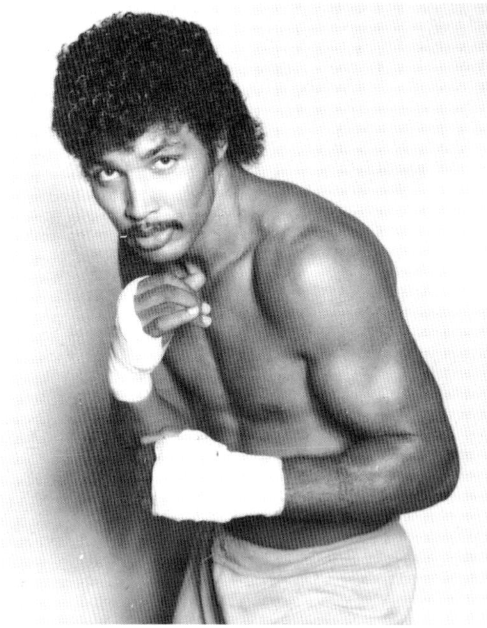

Eight-Second KO. On December 11, 1984, cruiserweight Ricky Parkey scored a technical knockout over Broderick Mason after only eight seconds at the Tropicana. Parkey stormed out and immediately hit Mason with an overhand right. The punch landed with such force that referee Vincent Rainone instantly stopped the fight. It remains one of the quickest knockouts in boxing history. Parkey won the IBF title two years later. Mason retired after this bout. (Photograph by Pete Goldfield.)

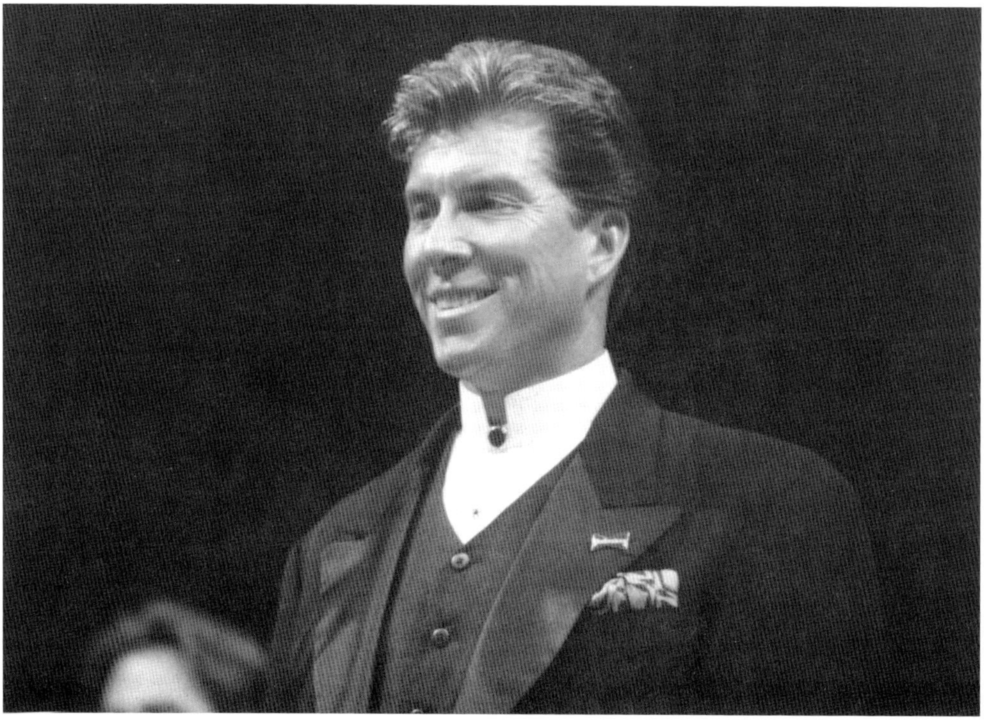

Ready to Rumble. The voice of Michael Buffer is recognizable to boxing and non-boxing fans alike thanks to his catchphrase, "Let's Get Ready to Rumble." The Philadelphia-area native began as a ring announcer in 1982 and became the most famous emcee in boxing history. Buffer worked at all of the Trump-owned casinos during AC's heyday and also announced many of the most important bouts all over the world. (Photograph by Ray Bailey.)

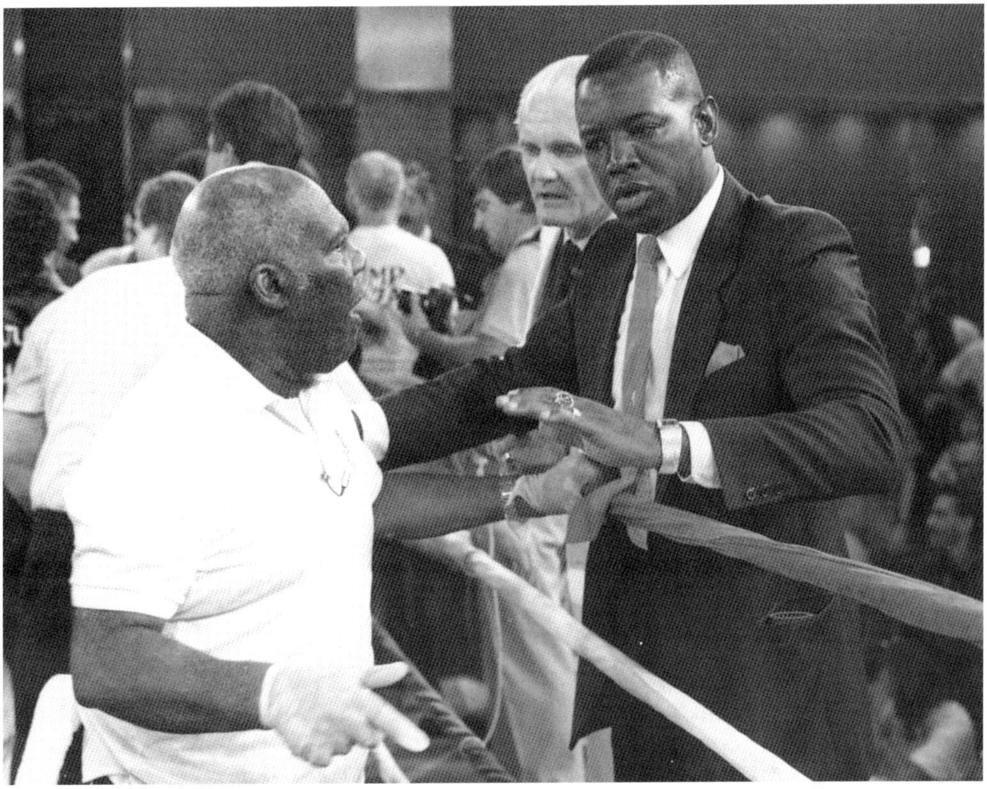

The Boss. Larry Hazzard Sr. (pictured with trainer Sam Solomon) was one of the most prominent referees in Atlantic City from 1979 to 1985. In 1985, Hazzard was appointed commissioner of the New Jersey State Athletic Control Board, a position he held for 22 years. In 2014, after pursuing other opportunities in and out of the sport, Hazzard returned for a second stint as commissioner, a position he still holds today. (Photograph by Pete Goldfield.)

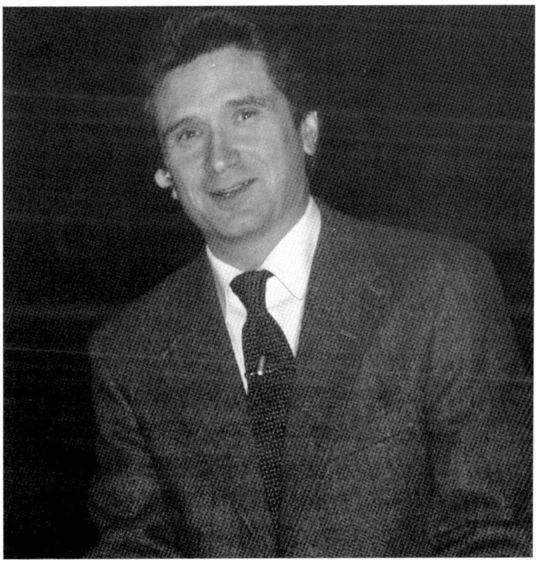

Writer and Broadcaster. Florham Park, New Jersey, native Dave Bontempo was a writer for the *Press of Atlantic City* during the 1980s when he began commentating on fights for television in 1985. He left the newspaper in 1991 to pursue broadcasting full-time and worked for a number of prestigious networks during his career. In 1997, Bontempo won the Boxing Writers Association of America's Sam Taub Award for excellence in broadcasting. (Photograph by Pete Goldfield.)

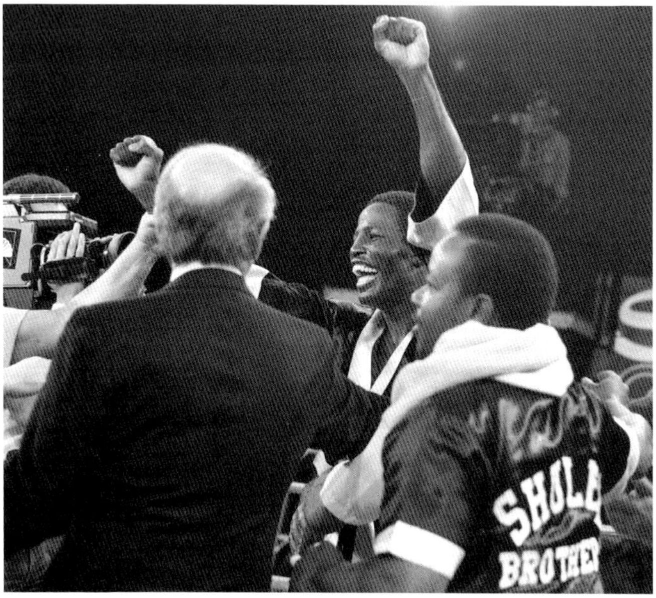

Tragic Contender. James "Black Gold" Shuler fought 11 of his 23 career bouts in Atlantic City, including a defense of his NABF middleweight title against James Kinchen on February 16, 1985, at the Sands. Shuler won by a 12-round split decision. He returned in his next fight to defeat Jerry Holly at Resorts. Tragically, Shuler died in a motorcycle accident on March 17, 1986, two months shy of his 27th birthday. (Photograph by Bill Baron.)

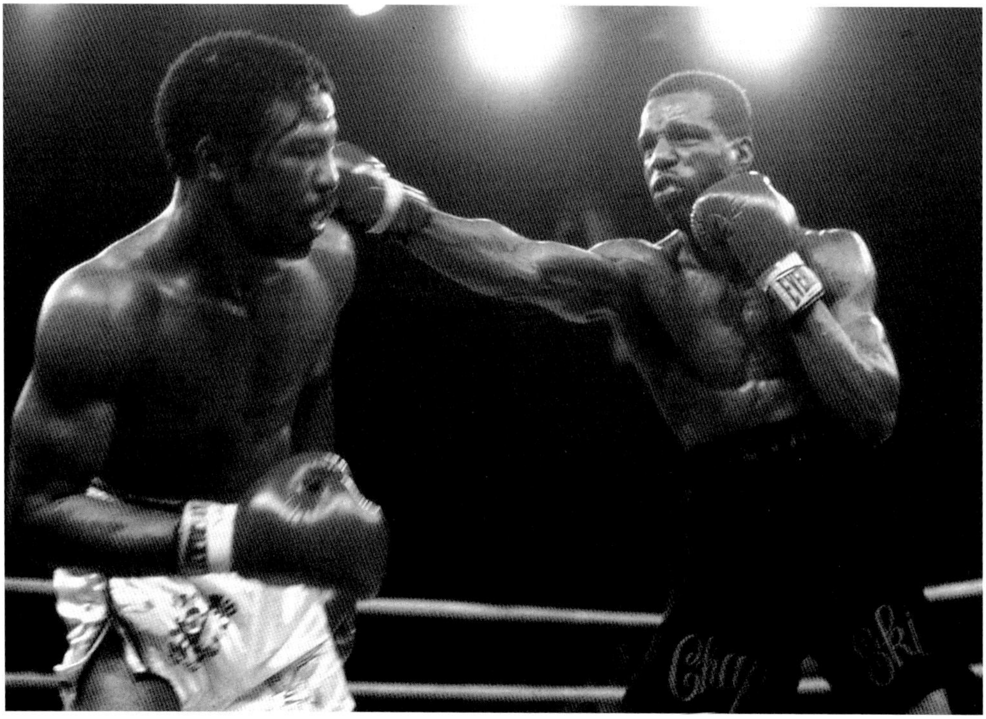

Pryor's Last Defense. Aaron Pryor (left) defended his junior welterweight championship for the last time with a close 15-round decision victory over Gary Hinton on March 2, 1985, at the Sands. Hinton proved to be difficult, but Pryor salvaged his title with a late-round knockdown. Although he escaped with his undefeated record intact, Pryor appeared to be on the decline in the last of his three AC fights. Hinton became world champion two years later. (Photograph by Pete Goldfield.)

4

ZENITH

1986–1989

AC experienced a sharp decline in the number of fights beginning in 1986, with only 80 shows at Resorts, Trump Plaza, the Sands, Tropicana, and Harrah's. In 1987, the total number fell further, but important future AC bouts were developing. In 1986, Mike Tyson defeated Jose Ribalta to extend his undefeated record to 26-0. Although the fight itself was a relatively small event, it pushed Tyson closer to the heavyweight title. Two bouts later, he became the youngest heavyweight champion in history.

AC staple Michael Spinks, who had won a share of the heavyweight title in 1985, relinquished his belt but continued his heavyweight campaign with a 1987 knockout of Gerry Cooney at Convention Hall. As both Tyson and Spinks extended their undefeated runs, it became clear that their eventual showdown would be one of the biggest fights ever. Luckily for AC fans, that fight would eventually happen on the Boardwalk.

In the meantime, AC venues hosted other important boxers in significant fights. Hector Camacho, Evander Holyfield, Virgil Hill, Bert Cooper, Pernell Whitaker, Bobby Czyz, and Doug DeWitt all fought at the shore.

Mike Tyson defended his world title at Convention Hall against Tyrell Biggs late in 1987 and then dispatched former champion Larry Holmes early in 1988. The Tyson era was heating up, and fans were eager for him to face Spinks, a man some felt was still the *real* champion. Only a contest between the two would settle the debate. Their fight, AC's biggest ever, came on June 27, 1988. It only lasted 91 seconds and is widely considered Tyson's peak performance.

Other key championship fights during the late 1980s featured Meldrick Taylor, Edwin Rosario, Julio Cesar Chavez, Michael Moorer, Calvin Grove, Orlando Canizales, and in a historic win, Roberto Duran, who took the middleweight title from Iran Barkley in 1989.

Tyson capped the decade with one more title defense, a one-round knockout of Carl Williams. Although it seemed Tyson's impact on Atlantic City might go on for years, he lost the championship in 1990. Atlantic City boxing was never quite the same.

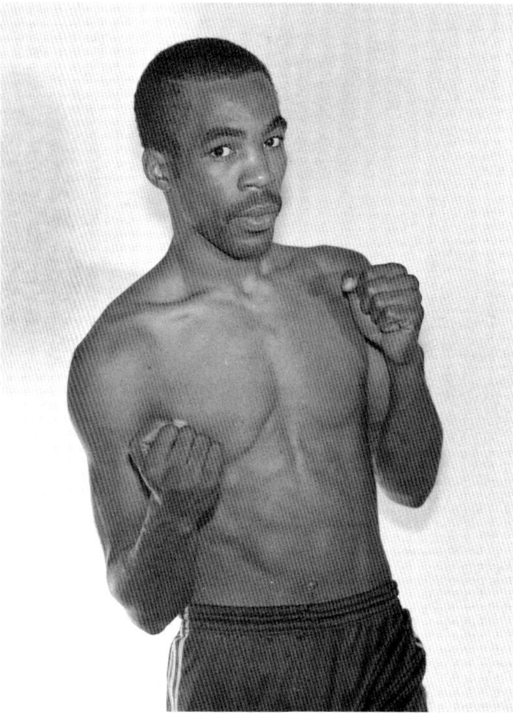

UPSET-MINDED UNDERSTUDY. Detroit's Jimmy Paul replaced an injured Robin Blake as the challenger to IBF lightweight champion Harry Arroyo on April 6, 1985, at Bally's. In an upset, Paul scored three knockdowns and won a decisive 15-round decision to take Arroyo's title and issue the champ his first loss. Arroyo made 12 AC appearances, including three title bouts. Paul also defeated Freddie Pendleton, Darryl Tyson, and Jerome Artis in AC. (Photograph by Pete Goldfield.)

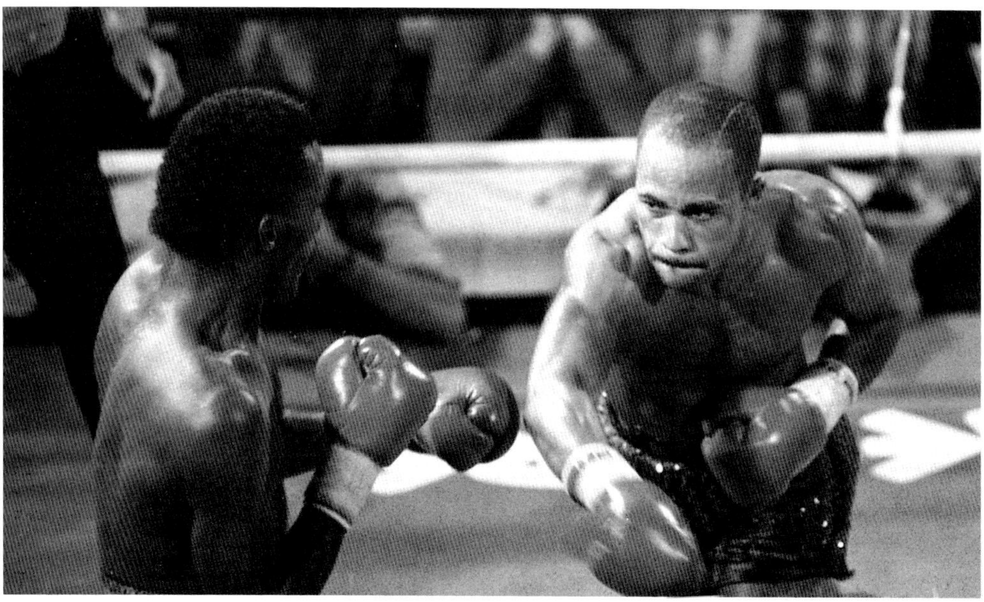

SHOCKER AT CAESARS. Donald Curry was the undisputed world welterweight champion, 25-0, and eight bouts into his championship reign when he faced Londoner Lloyd Honeyghan on September 27, 1986, at Caesars. Honeyghan was 27-0, the British and European champion, and ranked first by the WBC, but few gave him a chance. However, Honeyghan upset the odds when Curry gave up in his corner after round six. It was the biggest upset of the year. (Photograph by Bill Baron.)

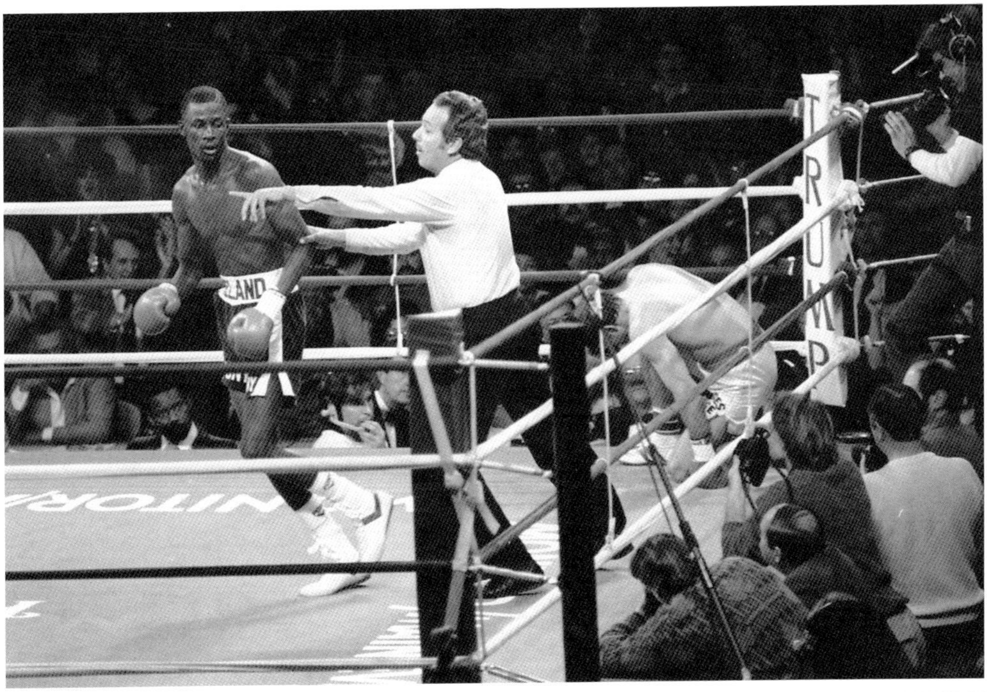

Breland Becomes Champion. Mark Breland was one of the most celebrated amateurs, with five New York Golden Gloves titles and a Gold Medal at the 1984 Olympics. On February 6, 1987, Breland won his first professional title with a seventh-round TKO of Harold Volbrecht at Trump Plaza (pictured). In 1989, after losing and regaining the WBA title, Breland defended it with a fifth-round TKO of Rafael Pineda at Trump Castle. (Photograph by Bill Baron.)

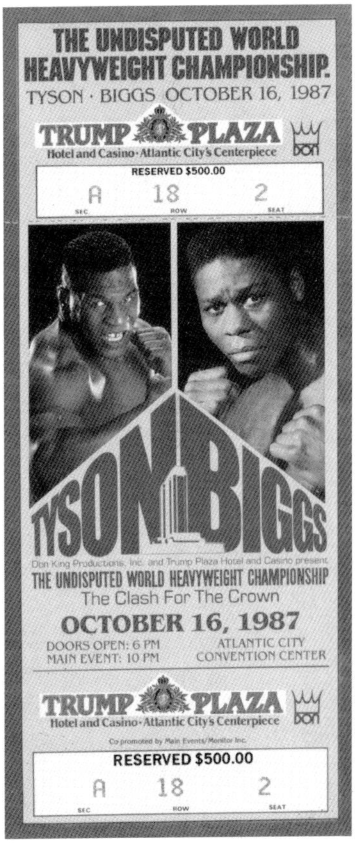

Tyson Halts Biggs. In the first of four heavyweight title defenses at Convention Hall, Mike Tyson defeated top contender Tyrell Biggs on October 16, 1987. The champion pummeled the undefeated Biggs, a 1984 Olympic Gold Medalist, from the opening bell and stopped him in round seven of their scheduled 15-round fight. Tyson's fourth title defense improved his record to 32-0, with 28 KOs. A crowd of 7,419 attended the event. (Author's collection.)

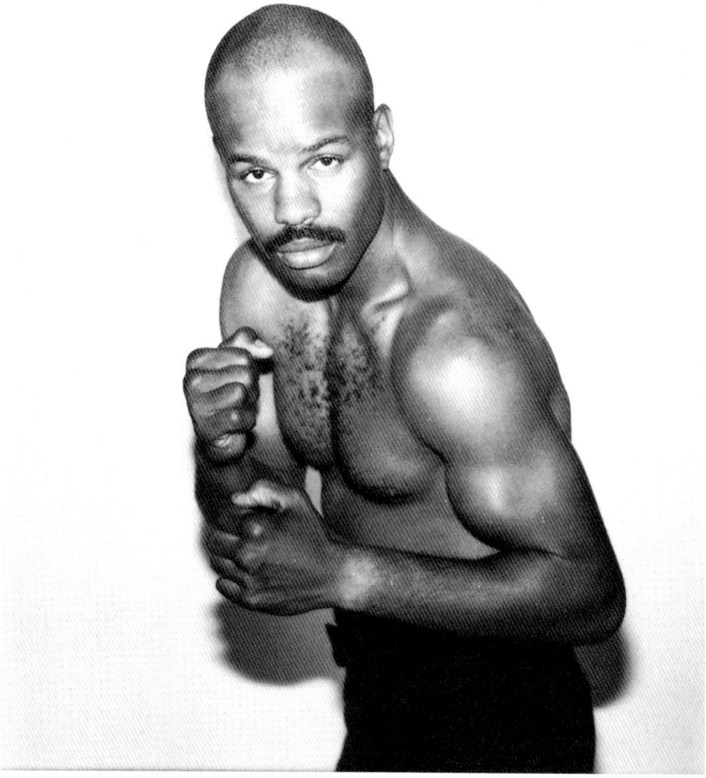

TIE-BREAKER. After 12 rounds at the Sands, the USBA middleweight title fight between Tony Thornton and Doug DeWitt was scored a draw. However, a brand new experimental rule was used to break the tie. The boxers were required to immediately fight a 13th round. In the sudden-death session, DeWitt won the round and earned the official decision on November 6, 1987. Thornton (pictured) lost for the first time. (Photograph by Pete Goldfield.)

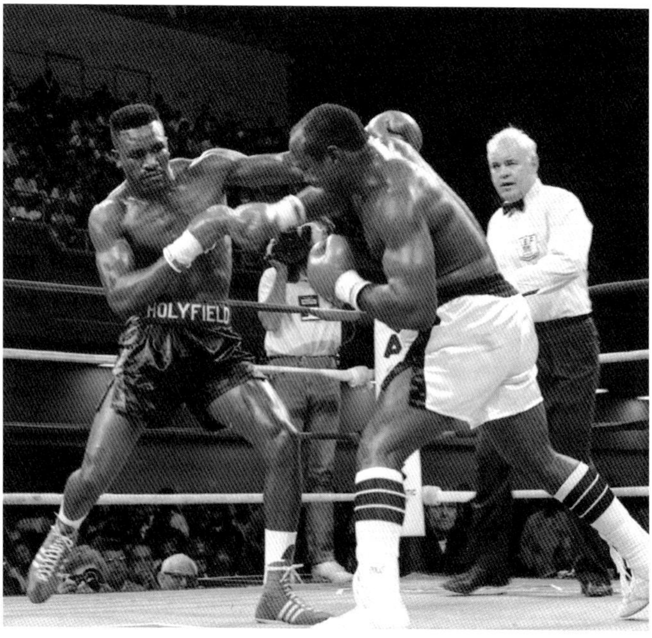

HOLYFIELD KAYOS QAWI. In 1986, Evander Holyfield won his first world championship with a grueling decision over Dwight Muhammad Qawi in Atlanta. The rematch on December 5, 1987, at Convention Hall was much easier for the champion. Holyfield floored Qawi twice and knocked him out in round four. It was Holyfield's fourth cruiserweight title defense and the first time Qawi had ever been stopped. (Photograph by Pete Goldfield.)

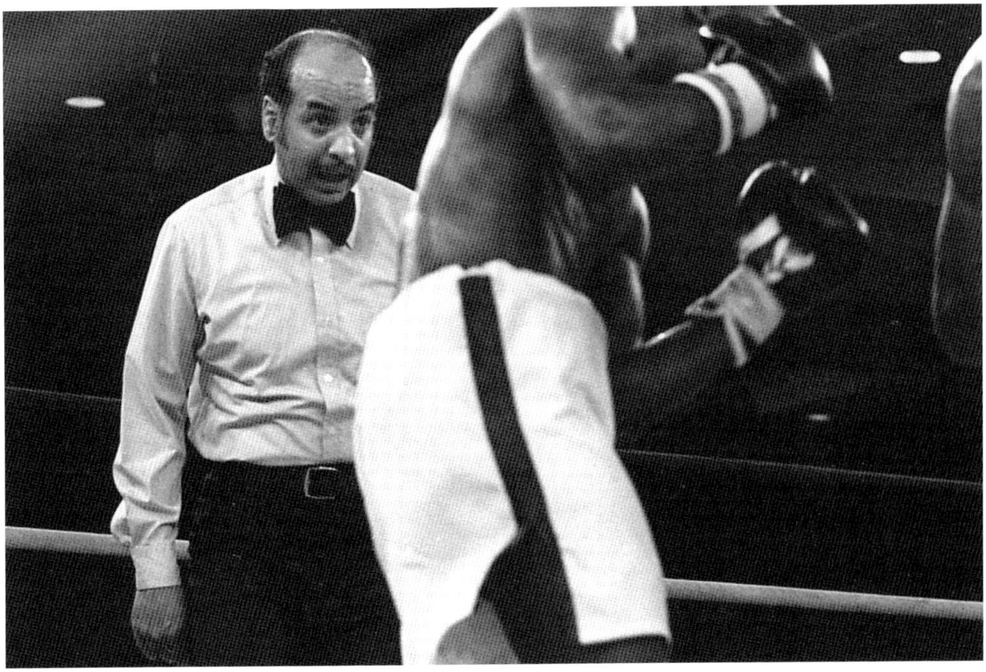

FAIR BUT FIRM. Two years into his career as a referee, Joe Cortez made his Atlantic City debut in 1981. In 1982, he refereed his first world title bout, Aaron Pryor versus Miguel Montilla at the Playboy. Cortez continued to be a busy referee in AC and eventually officiated big bouts like Tyson versus Holmes and Duran versus Barkley. He relocated to Las Vegas, where his catchphrase, "I'm fair, but I'm firm," became famous. (Photograph by Pete Goldfield.)

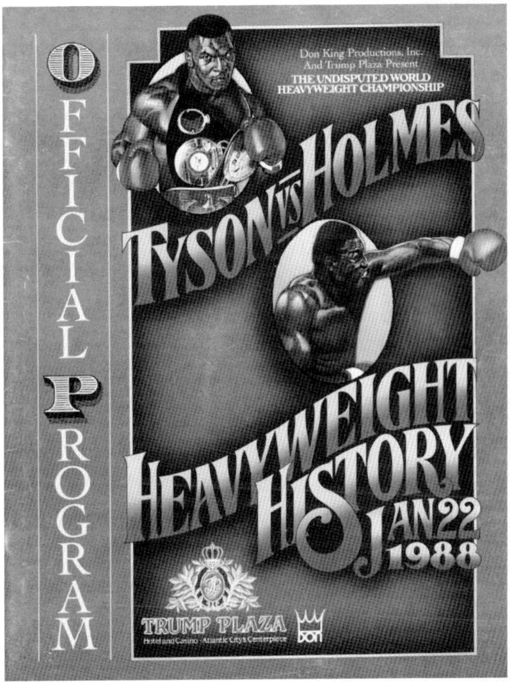

TYSON FLATTENS FORMER CHAMP. Mike Tyson continued his Atlantic City era with a fourth-round technical knockout of former champion Larry Holmes at Convention Hall on January 22, 1988. A booming right by Tyson caused the first knockdown in round four. After Holmes went down two more times, referee Joe Cortez stopped the fight. Tyson, 17 years younger than Holmes, defended his title for the fifth time. More than 16,000 fans attended. (Author's collection.)

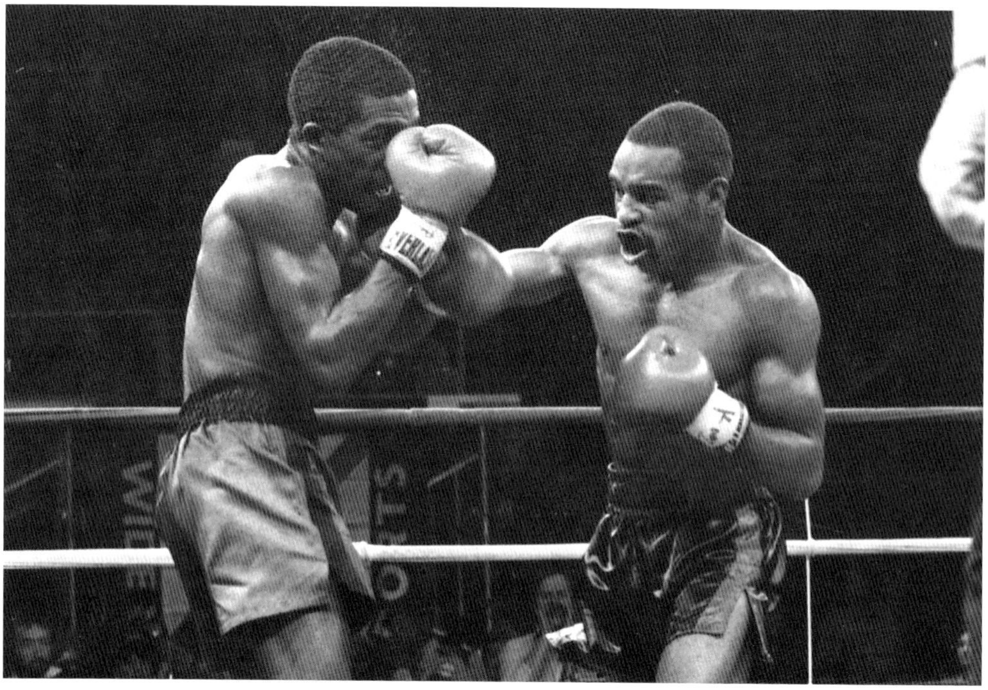

LOCKRIDGE DEFENDS TITLE. Rocky Lockridge made the second defense of his IBF junior lightweight title with a 15-round decision victory over Harold Knight on April 2, 1988, at the Sands. Knight, the number-one contender, fought well, but the champion was faster and more skillful. Lockridge won easily on points in the last of his 11 Atlantic City bouts. Knight, who fought 15 of his 20 bouts in AC, retired after this fight. (Photograph by Pete Goldfield.)

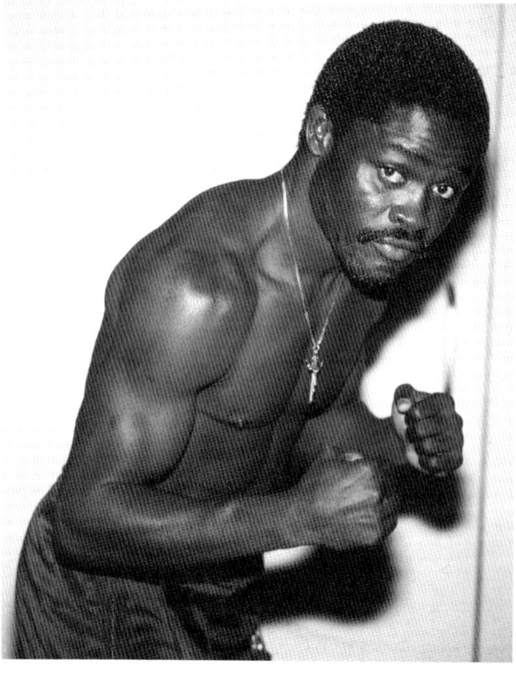

"THE PROFESSOR." Azumah Nelson of Ghana defended his WBC junior lightweight title with a ninth-round technical knockout of Texan Lupe Suarez at the Trump Plaza on June 25, 1988. Nelson hurt Suarez badly near the end of round eight and finished him off 27 seconds into the ninth round. This was Nelson's first defense of his second divisional title and his only appearance in Atlantic City. (Photograph by Pete Goldfield.)

BADDEST MAN ON THE PLANET. Mike Tyson and Michael Spinks finally faced off at Convention Hall on June 27, 1988, in a highly anticipated heavyweight championship fight. Both men had a legitimate claim to the title, but it only took Tyson 91 electrifying seconds to prove that he was the "Baddest Man on the Planet." A crowd of 21,785 attended Atlantic City's biggest fight ever. (Author's collection.)

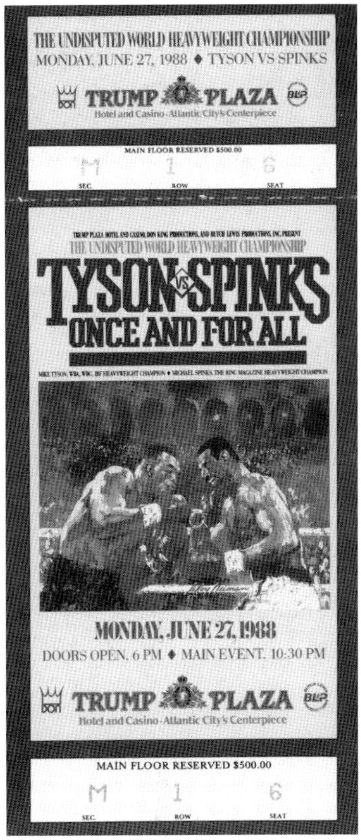

THE TWO KINGS. When AC's boxing scene peaked with fights that made the world stop and take notice, Donald Trump and Don King were pulling the strings. In the late 1980s, when they staged four Mike Tyson championship bouts, Convention Hall, Trump Plaza, Don King Promotions, and Tyson's career were all booming. Both Trump and King were involved with numerous other fights at the shore, but these events were undoubtedly the pinnacle. (Author's collection.)

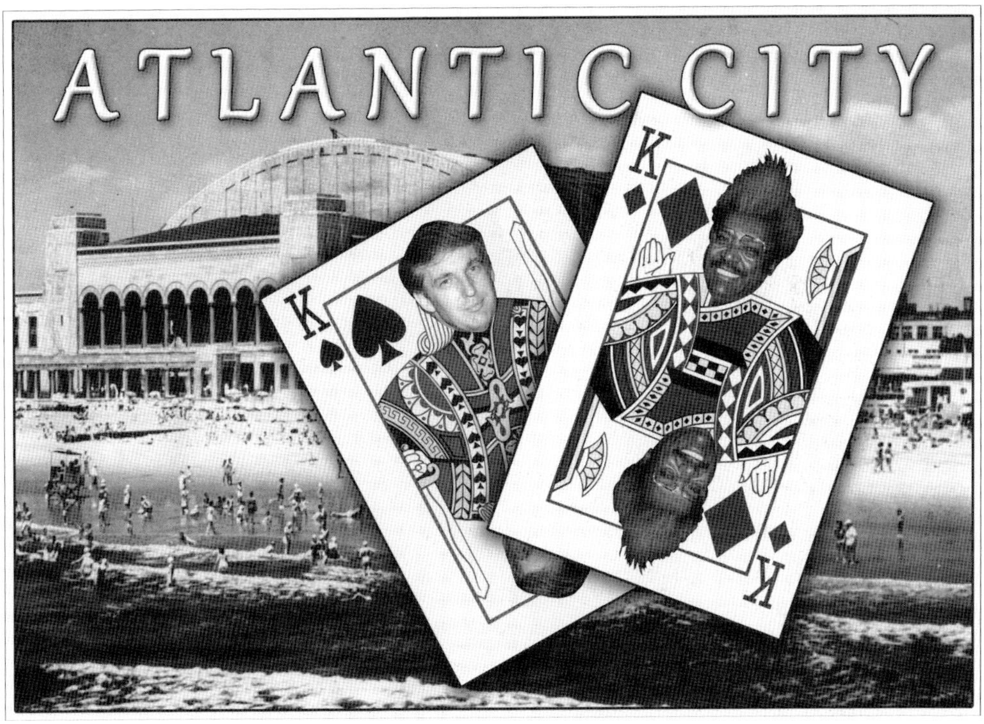

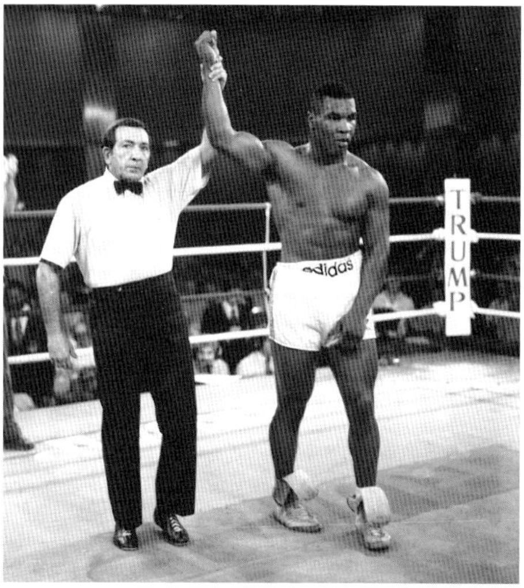

THIRD MAN IN THE RING. Referee Frank Cappuccino was one of the top officials during Atlantic City's boom years. He refereed numerous fights in the city, including bouts involving Arturo Gatti, Hector Camacho, Pernell Whitaker, Johnny Tapia, Dwight Muhammad Qawi, and major events, including Tyson versus Spinks, Lewis versus Briggs, and Spinks versus Cooney. (Photograph by Pete Goldfield.)

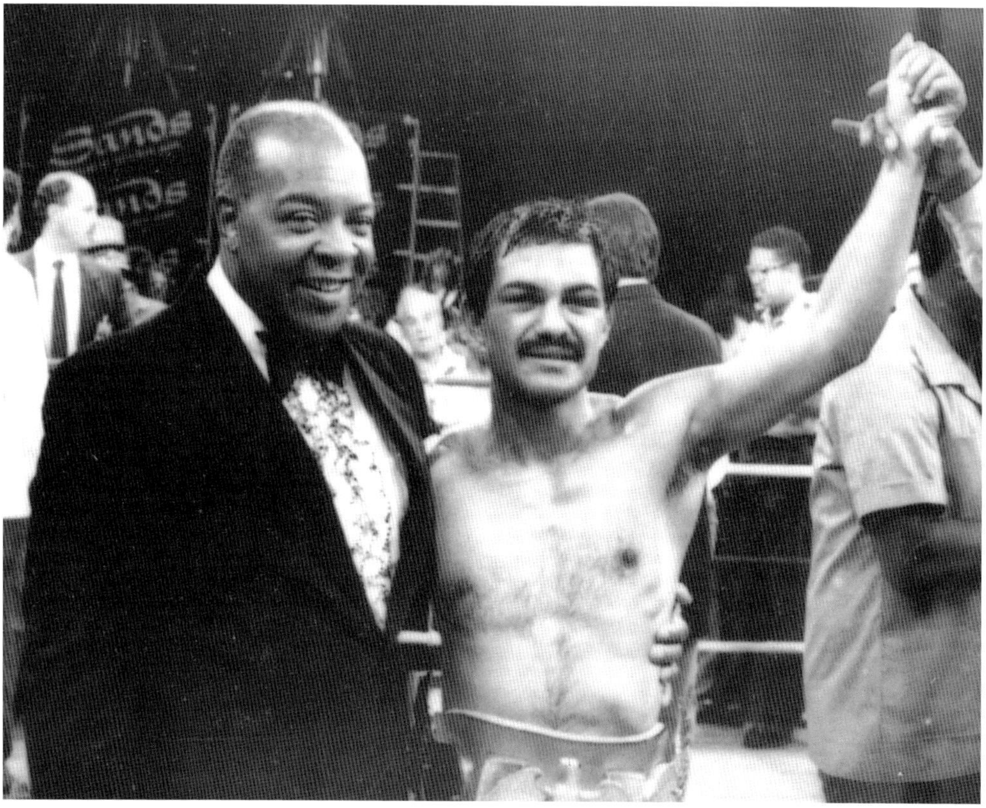

DON'T MESS WITH TEXAS. Texan Orlando Canizales won the IBF bantamweight championship with a 15th-round technical knockout of Kelvin Seabrooks at the Sands on July 9, 1988. He made 16 successful defenses, including another TKO of Seabrooks (the following year at Harrah's Marina) during his hall-of-fame career. Orlando is pictured with Bob Lee, founder of the IBF. Lee previously held positions as the president of the WBA and New Jersey State athletic commissioner. (Photograph by Pete Goldfield.)

"THE HAWK" RETAINS TITLE TWICE. Julian "The Hawk" Jackson scored two of his best career victories in AC. On July 30, 1988, Jackson made the first defense of his WBA junior middleweight title with a third-round technical knockout of former world champion Buster Drayton in a slugfest at Harrah's Marina. The following year, Jackson stopped future world champion Terry Norris in round two for his third defense on July 30, 1989, at Convention Hall. (Author's collection.)

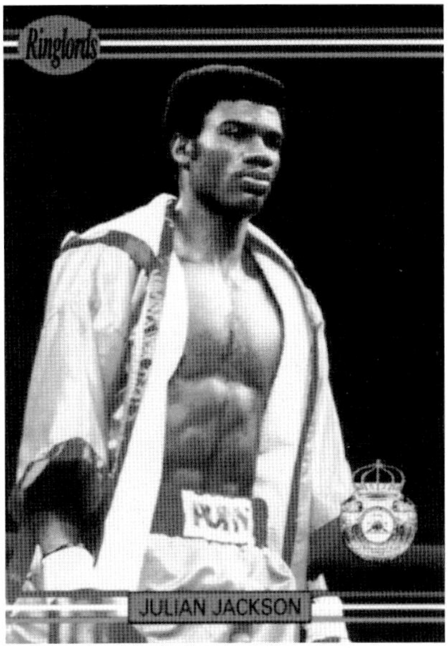

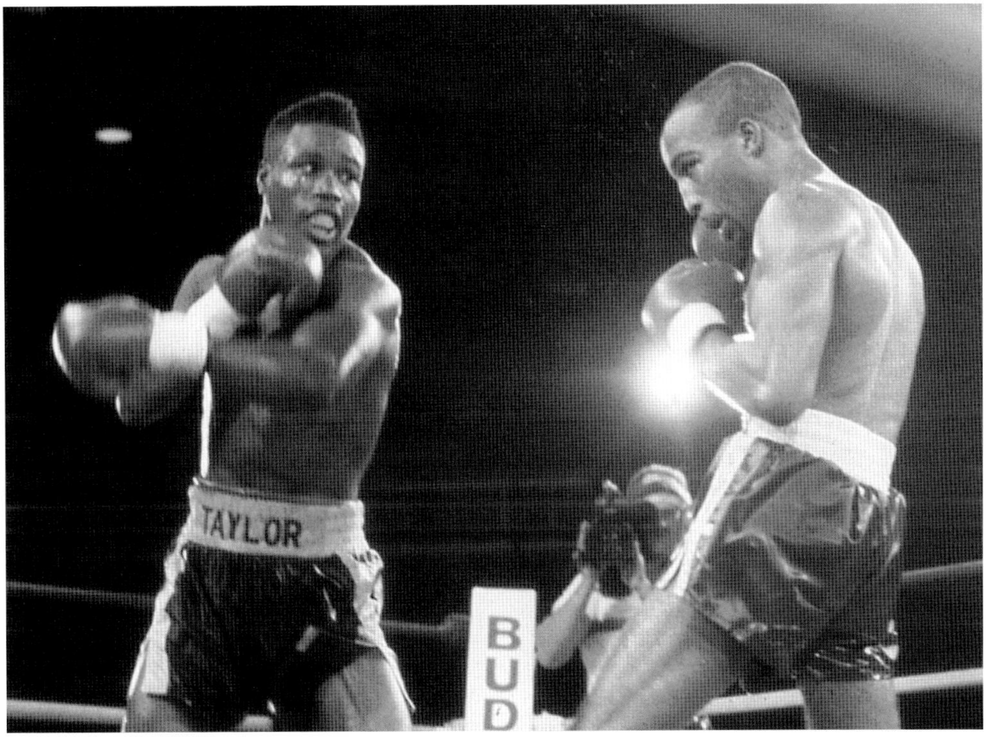

TAYLOR BECOMES IBF CHAMPION. Olympic Gold Medalist Meldrick Taylor won his first professional championship with a 12th-round TKO of James "Buddy" McGirt (pictured) on September 3, 1988, at Harrah's Marina. Taylor also made two successful title defenses in AC against John Wesley Meekins and Courtney Hooper. After losing the belt to Julio Cesar Chavez, Taylor returned to AC to win the IBF welterweight title against Aaron Davis at Convention Hall in 1991. (Photograph by Pete Goldfield.)

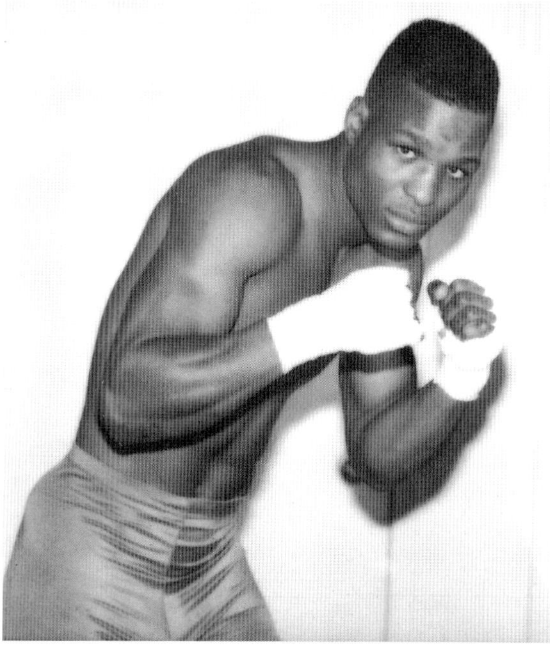

NO ALIEN TO AC. Bernard Hopkins fought professionally from 1988 to 2016 and held world titles as a middleweight and light heavyweight. Known as "The Executioner" and later "The Alien," Hopkins fought until he was 51 years old. His 19 AC appearances began with his debut loss to Clinton Mitchell and included notable title fight wins against Bo James, Simon Brown, William Joppy, and Karo Murat. Hopkins went 16-3 in AC. (Photograph by Pete Goldfield.)

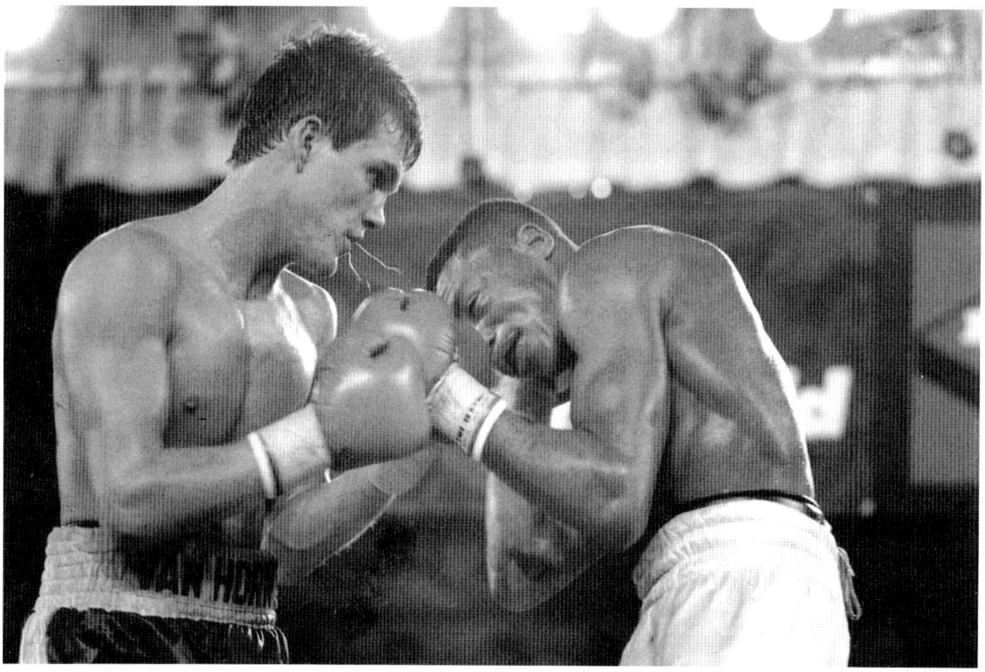

THE "SCHOOLBOY" EARNS AN A PLUS. Darrin Van Horn upset IBF junior middleweight champion Robert Hines by a 12-round decision on February 5, 1989, at Trump Castle. Lexington's Van Horn played up his "Schoolboy" nickname by wearing the University of Kentucky's letters on his trunks. Van Horn lost the title at Trump Castle in his next bout but later won the IBF super middleweight title in another of his four AC fights. Hines appeared 19 times in AC. (Peltz Boxing Promotions.)

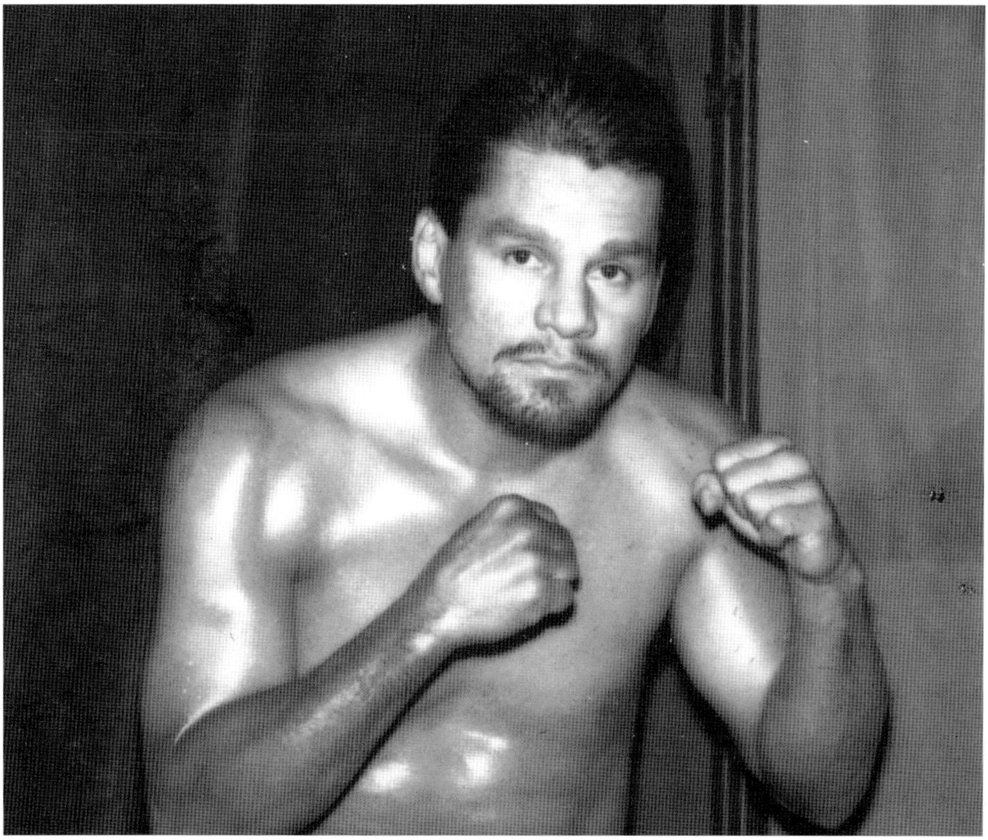

Champion Again. Ring legend Roberto Duran was considered too old for the fearsome Iran Barkley, the WBC middleweight champion. However, Duran turned back the clock and defeated Barkley by a 12-round split decision in an exciting battle. Duran's knockdown of Barkley in round 11 sealed the victory and made Duran a four-division champion. A strongly pro-Duran crowd braved snowy conditions to watch the upset at Convention Hall on February 24, 1989. (Photograph by Pete Goldfield.)

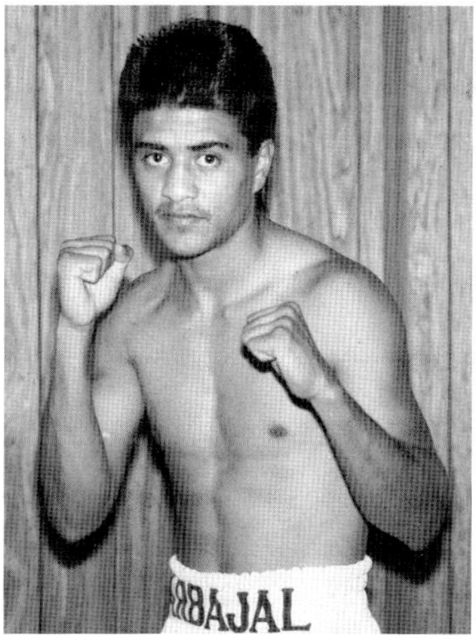

Auspicious Debut. After winning a silver medal at the 1988 Olympics, future world junior flyweight champion Michael Carbajal made his pro debut with a four-round decision victory over Will Grigsby at Convention Hall on February 24, 1989. Also debuting that night were Olympians Ray Mercer, Kennedy McKinney, Andrew Maynard, and Robert Wangila. These bouts were part of the undercard of the Roberto Duran versus Iran Barkley world title fight. (Photograph by Pete Goldfield.)

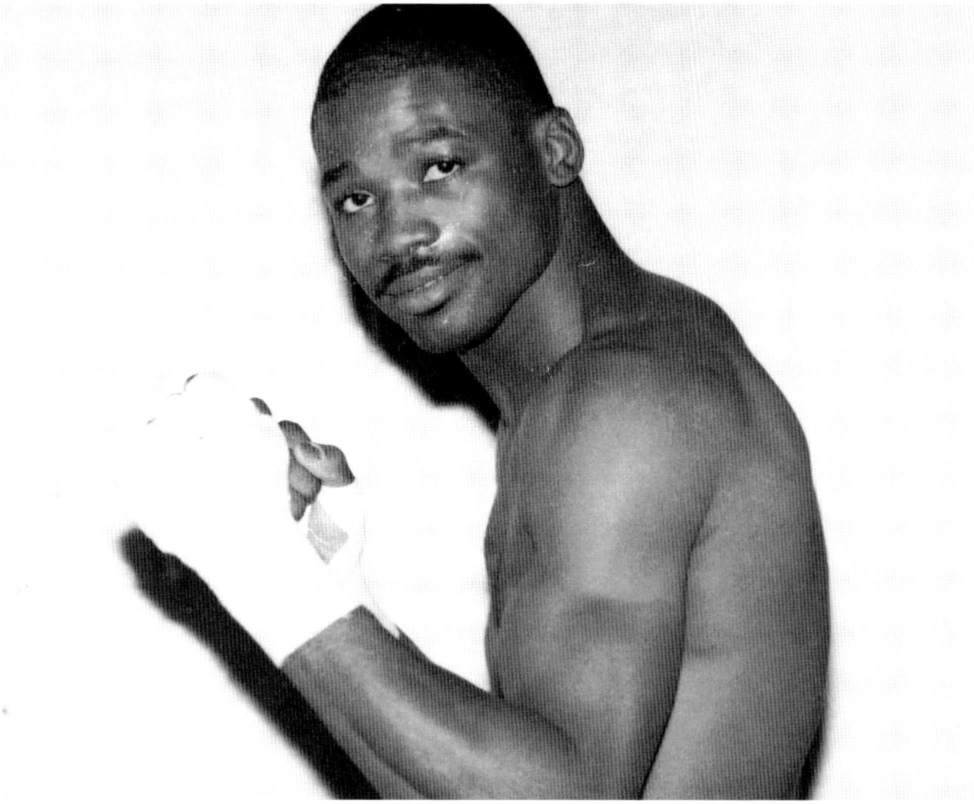

MAGIC MAN. Welterweight Marlon Starling fought nine AC bouts, including two losses to Donald Curry, one for a world title. He won regional title bouts against Lupe Aquino, Floyd Mayweather Sr., and Simon Brown. He also defended his WBA world title against Fujio Ozaki on February 5, 1988. Tomas Molinares knocked Starling out cold with a blow he landed after the bell on July 29, 1988, at Convention Hall. The fight was ruled a no-contest, and Starling retained his belt. (Photograph by Pete Goldfield.)

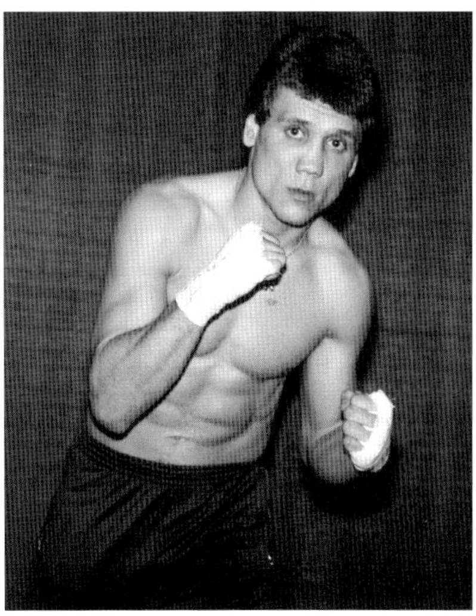

DEWITT WINS WBO TITLE. Doug DeWitt won the very first middleweight title sanctioned by the WBO with a 12-round split decision victory over Robbie Sims on April 18, 1989, at the Showboat. The fight came near the end of DeWitt's career and finally earned the persistent contender a world title. DeWitt fought in Atlantic City 22 times, while Sims made 11 appearances. (Photograph by Pete Goldfield.)

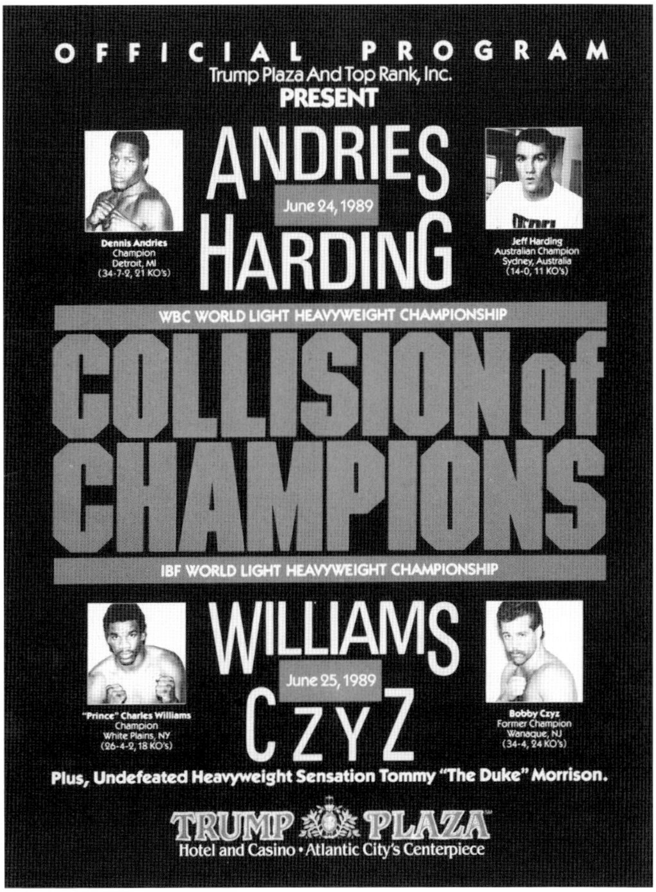

LIGHT HEAVYWEIGHT TRILOGY. Between 1989 and 1991, Australian Jeff Harding and Guyanese Londoner Dennis Andries swapped the WBC light heavyweight title in a trilogy that kicked off in AC on June 24, 1989, at Convention Hall. Harding came from behind to win the title by technical knockout in round 12. Andries won the rematch in Australia by knockout in round seven. Finally, Harding won the rubber match by decision in the United Kingdom. (Author's collection.)

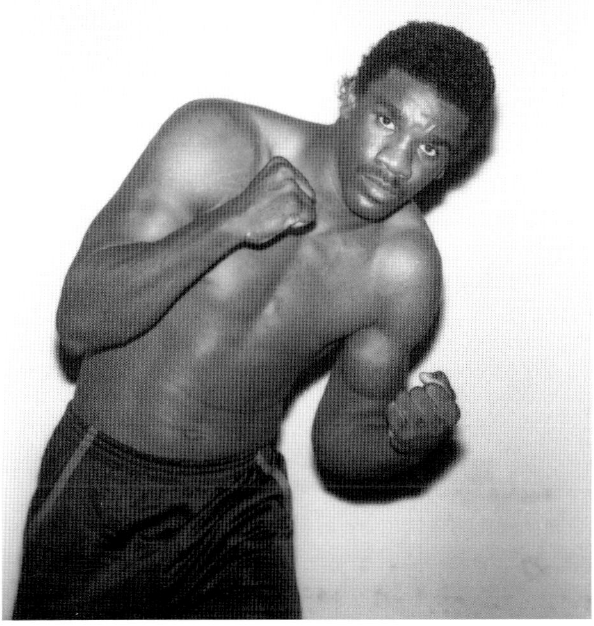

PRINCE TOPS CZYZ AGAIN. IBF light heavyweight champion "Prince" Charles Williams and Bobby Czyz fought a rematch on June 25, 1989, at Convention Hall. As in their first fight, Williams closed Czyz's eye with right-hand power shots. After 10 rounds, Bobby's eye was so badly swollen that the fight was stopped in his corner. This was one of 10 AC appearances by Williams and one of 18 by Czyz. (Photograph by Pete Goldfield.)

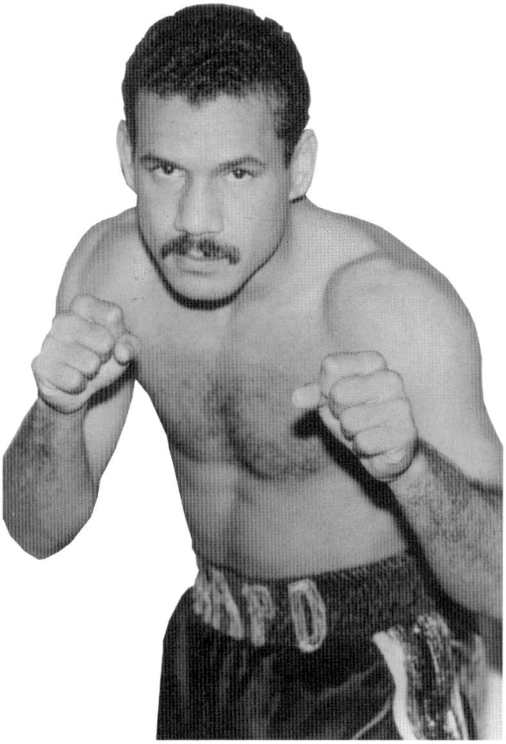

"Chapo" Wins Another Title. In Edwin "Chapo" Rosario's third and final stop in AC, he won the lightweight world title for the third time. Rosario stopped Anthony Jones in round six to claim the vacant WBA title on July 9, 1989, at the Showboat. A devastating right hand floored Jones in round six. He managed to pull himself up from the mat, but after three more punches by "Chapo," referee Tony Orlando stopped it. (Photograph by Pete Goldfield.)

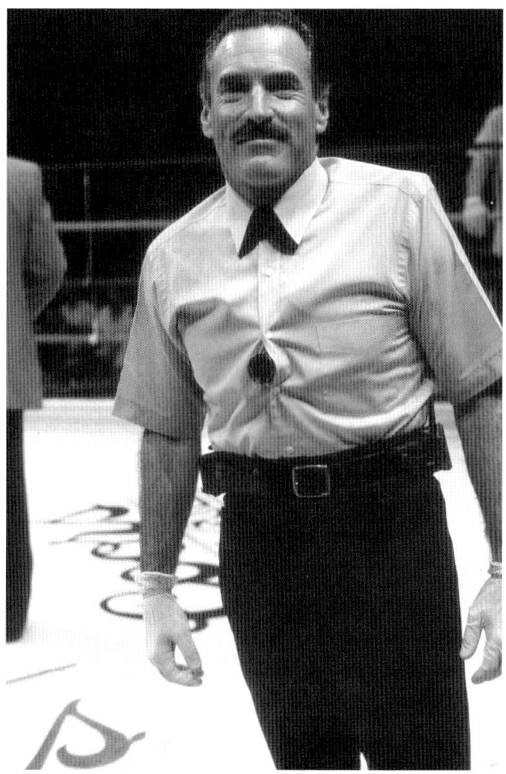

World-Class Referee. Steve Smoger is a world-traveled referee who has worked in more states and more countries than any other referee in boxing history. His work in AC began in 1982 under then-Commissioner Jersey Joe Walcott. To date, he has refereed more than 200 world title bouts involving the very biggest ring stars. Outside the sport, Smoger is an Air Force veteran and has served as an attorney and a judge. (Photograph by Pete Goldfield.)

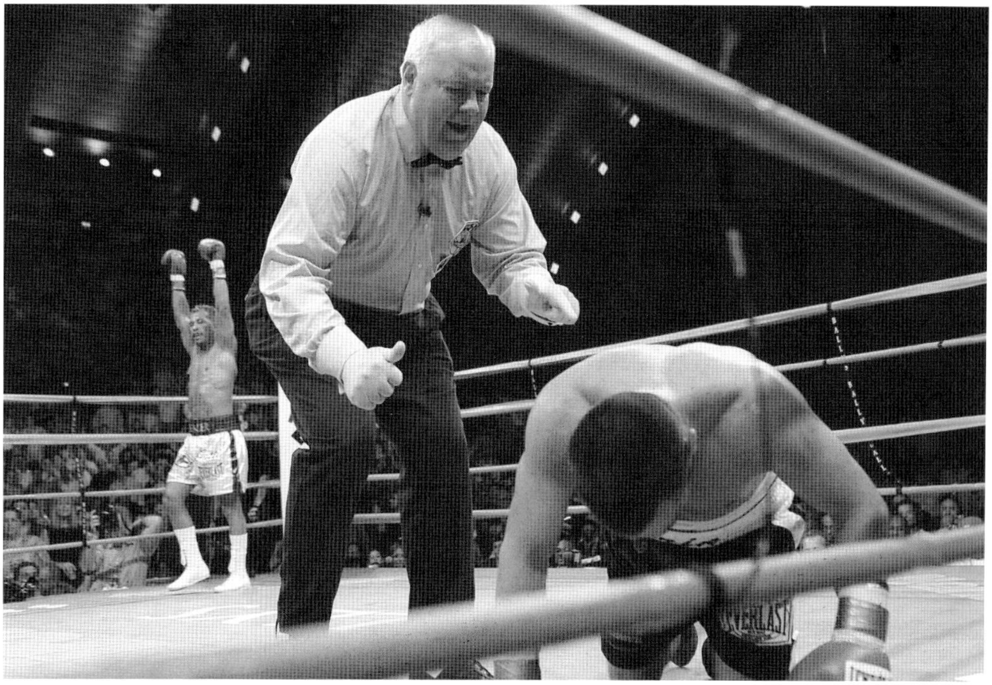

JERSEY GUY WORE MANY HATS. Boxer, referee, judge, financial advisor, writer, and actor are some of the job titles associated with former New Jersey heavyweight champion Randy Neumann. Although he never boxed in AC during his pro career (1969–1977), Neumann made up for it with a distinguished career as a referee. His nearly 200 AC assignments included several world title fights. Neumann also had a cameo in the HBO series *Boardwalk Empire*. (Photograph by Ray Bailey.)

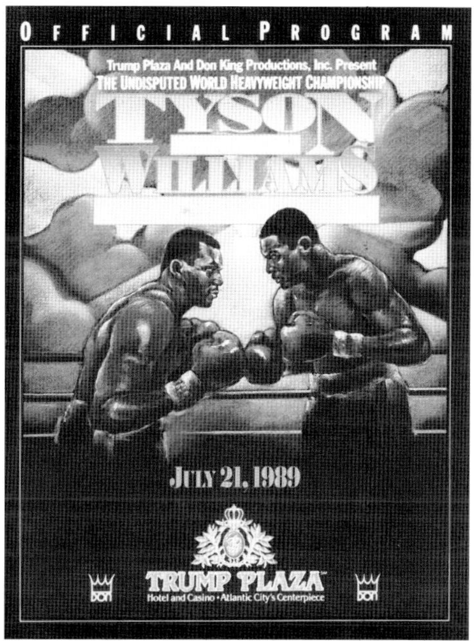

ANOTHER QUICKIE. Heavyweight champion Mike Tyson defended his world title for the ninth time with a 93-second technical knockout of Carl "The Truth" Williams before 11,000 fans on July 21, 1989, at Convention Hall. Despite Williams's high ranking, it only took one Tyson left hook to send him to the canvas. Williams got up, but referee Randy Neumann stopped the fight. Tyson shockingly lost his crown in his next bout. (Author's collection.)

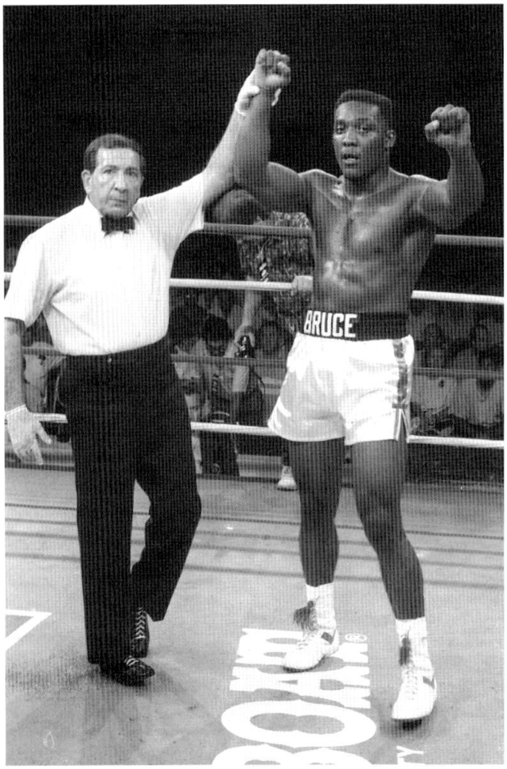

"THE ATLANTIC CITY EXPRESS." Hometown hero Bruce Seldon won his pro debut at the Atlantis Casino in 1988. It was the first of 23 starts in AC. On April 8, 1995, he captured the WBA heavyweight title by defeating Tony Tucker in Las Vegas and made one successful title defense before falling to Mike Tyson in 1996. Seldon's notable AC fights included victories over David Bey, Jose Ribalta, Jesse Ferguson, and Alexander Popov. Seldon was trained by Carmen Graziano, Bruce Blair, and Diego Rosario during his career. (Photograph by Pete Goldfield.)

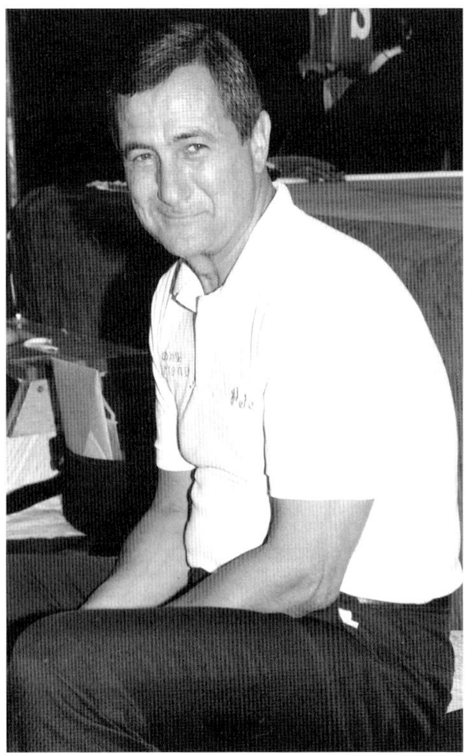

LENS MAN. Pete Goldfield was a South Jersey photographer (and insurance agent) who vibrantly documented the local boxing scene, especially in Atlantic City during the 1980s and 1990s. Although Goldfield shot numerous fights in AC, he was especially masterful in his classic portraits of boxers. Many of these photographs appeared on the fight posters and programs of the day. His work, both action and posed shots, are featured throughout this book. (Photograph by Bill Baron.)

5

Sustaining

1990–1999

Despite a sharp decline in the number of fights during the 1990s, AC's boxing relevance continued with some of the sport's biggest stars appearing along the Boardwalk. Without Mike Tyson to attract fans, the scene still continued to thrive with big names sharing star billing. Thomas Hearns, James Toney, Michael Moorer, Pernell Whitaker, Felix Trinidad, Hector Camacho, Roberto Duran, Vinny Pazienza, and others all fought major fights at the shore. In addition, heavyweights continued to be key attractions, with Evander Holyfield, Lennox Lewis, George Foreman, Bruce Seldon, Tommy Morrison, Riddick Bowe, and Tim Witherspoon leading the pack.

HBO Boxing also made its mark on AC during this decade, with the network airing more than 60 fights from the city. The April 19, 1991, world heavyweight championship fight between Evander Holyfield and George Foreman was broadcast on TVKO, HBO's pay-per-view arm, and grossed approximately $55 million from pay-per-view purchases. "The Battle of the Ages" was also a winner at the live box office, with 19,000 people paying $8 million at the gate.

Stars like Nigel Benn, David Reid, and Junior Jones started their championship reigns in AC, while all-time greats "Sugar" Ray Leonard and George Foreman closed out their boxing days in the city.

Convention Hall held nearly 40 shows during the 1990s, including many of the top fights of the decade, but the Taj Mahal's Etess Arena, Harrah's, Resorts, Bally's, and Tropicana remained busy and important venues. In 1997, Diane Lee Fischer promoted a show at the Tropicana, where she also ran a hair salon. Although Nancy Sciacca preceded her with a single show in 1980, Fischer was the more prominent female promoter in AC, where she staged several boxing shows over the next two decades.

Arturo Gatti engaged in his first classic rivalry when he lost two 10-round contests against Ivan Robinson in 1998, both televised by HBO. Their first bout was named the "Fight of the Year," and Gatti, who scored the "Knockout of the Year" in 1997, began to emerge as a box office favorite. His series with Robinson foreshadowed an even bigger rivalry that would unfold the following decade.

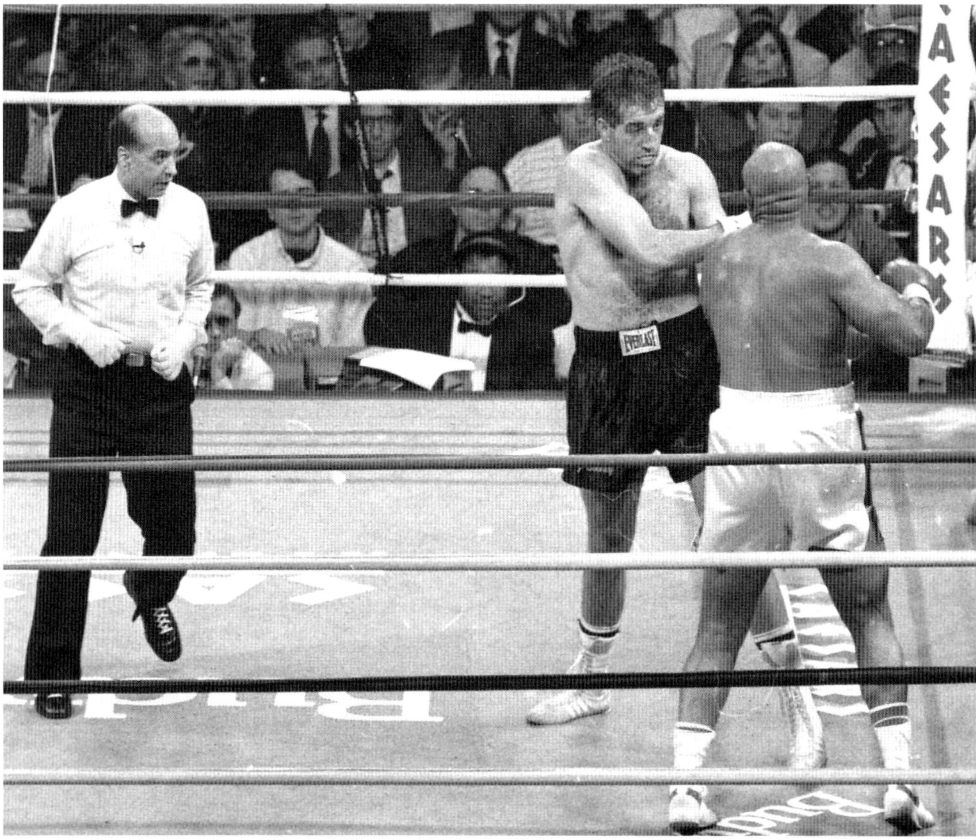

BATTLE OF THE GIANTS. Former heavyweight champion George Foreman continued his remarkable comeback campaign with a second-round TKO of former world title challenger Gerry Cooney on January 15, 1990, at Convention Hall. Foreman and Cooney were two of the biggest and most popular heavyweights of their era, but it was Foreman who proved that he was still a contender. Another heavyweight title was in Foreman's future, while Cooney retired after this defeat. (Photograph by Ray Bailey.)

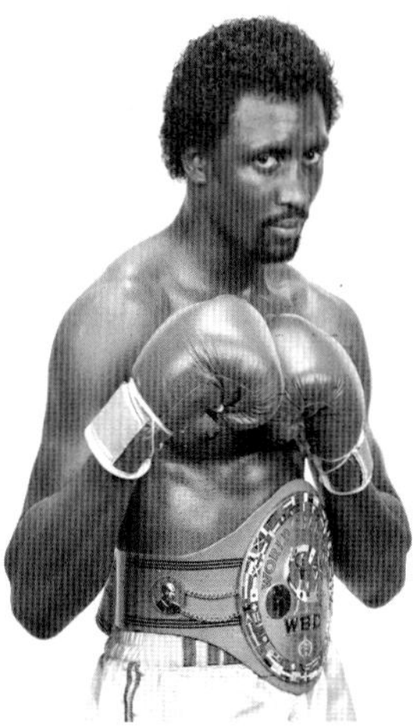

"HITMAN" HEARNS. Coming off a rematch with "Sugar" Ray Leonard, Thomas Hearns made one of only two career stops in Atlantic City on April 28, 1990, when he defended his WBO super middleweight title against Michael Olajide at the Taj Mahal. Hearns dominated the fight and easily won the decision. In 1991, Hearns moved up to light heavyweight and won his fifth weight division title. Olajide retired after his next bout. (Photograph by Pete Goldfield.)

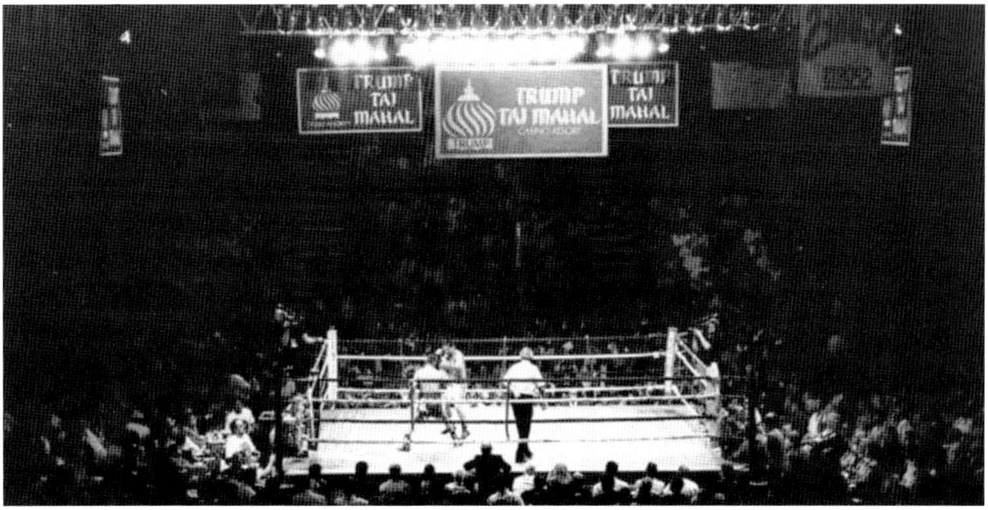

ETESS ARENA. Mark Grossinger Etess, the president and chief operating officer of Trump Plaza, died in a helicopter crash near Lacey Township, New Jersey, on October 10, 1989. Etess, traveling between New York City and Atlantic City, was killed with four others in the crash. In memory of his contributions to the Trump Organization, the Etess Arena was opened in the Taj Mahal and named in his honor in April 1990. (Photograph by John DiSanto.)

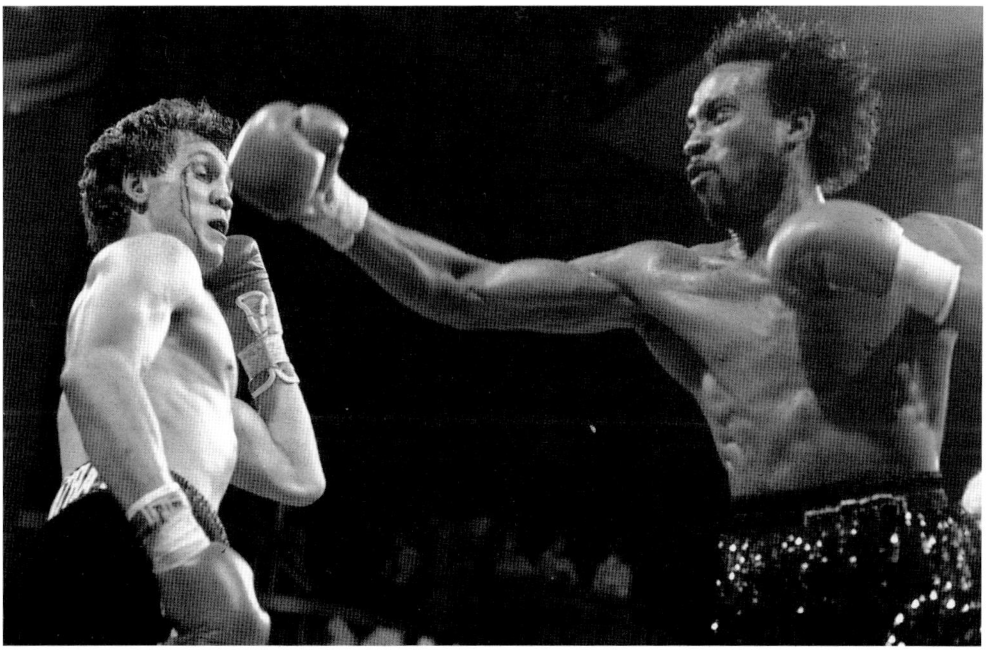

"THE DARK DESTROYER." Londoner Nigel Benn, "The Dark Destroyer," took the WBO middleweight title from Doug DeWitt with an eighth-round technical knockout on April 29, 1990, at Caesars. The heavy-handed Benn came off the floor in round two, dropped DeWitt in round three, and finished the job with three knockdowns in round eight. With the win, Benn became the first world champion from England in 10 years. (Photograph by Ray Bailey.)

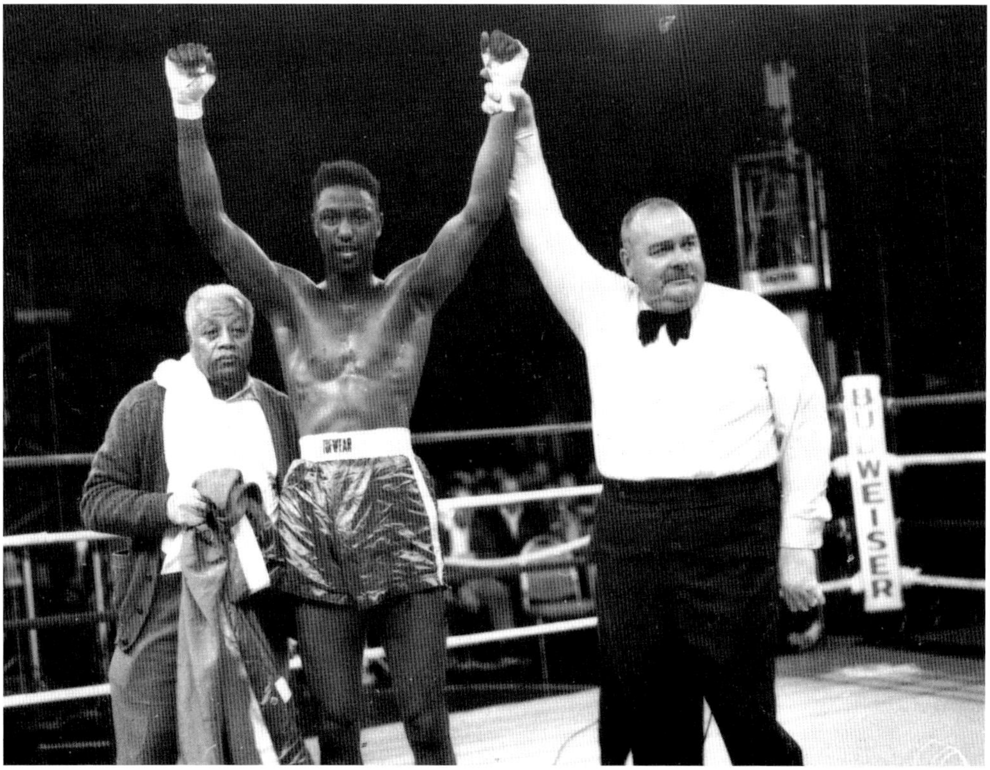

REFEREE JOE O'NEILL. Joe O'Neill was a familiar referee to Atlantic City boxing fans. O'Neill worked at the shore between 1981 and 1993, officiating hundreds of fights, including bouts featuring Mike Tyson, Dwight Muhammad Qawi, Buster Douglas, Mark Breland, Iran Barkley, Rocky Lockridge, and many others. One of his most memorable fights was Michael Moorer versus Bert Cooper in 1992. (Photograph by Pete Goldfield.)

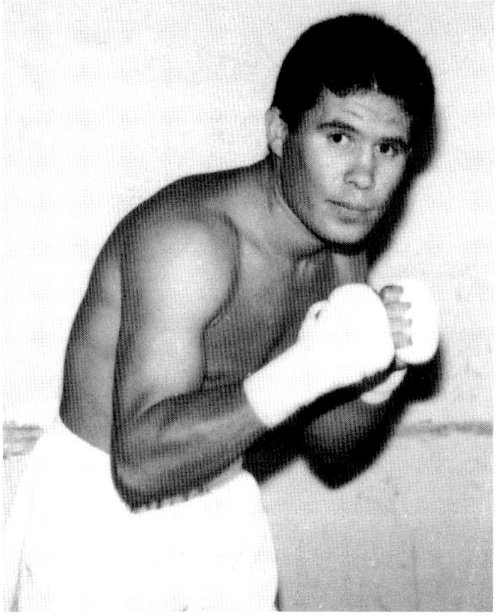

"J.C. SUPERSTAR." All-time great Julio Cesar Chavez made his second and final trip to AC on December 8, 1990. He defended his WBC and IBF junior welterweight title against South Korean Kyung Duk Ahn at Convention Hall. Despite a number-one ranking by the WBC, Ahn offered little resistance, hitting the canvas three times before the fight ended in round three. Chavez improved his record to 73-0 with the win. Ahn never fought again. (Photograph by Pete Goldfield.)

Dynamic Duo. Old-school writers Jack "KO-JO" Obermayer and Jeff Jowett (wearing a tie) traveled the country together to cover as many fight cards as they could. Both were on the boxing beat in Atlantic City for decades. They helped to document the fight game at the shore, attending countless boxing shows all along the Boardwalk. With a specific eye for details including weights, times, dates, and colorful descriptions, their work appeared in various boxing publications and later on the Internet. (Photograph by Pete Goldfield.)

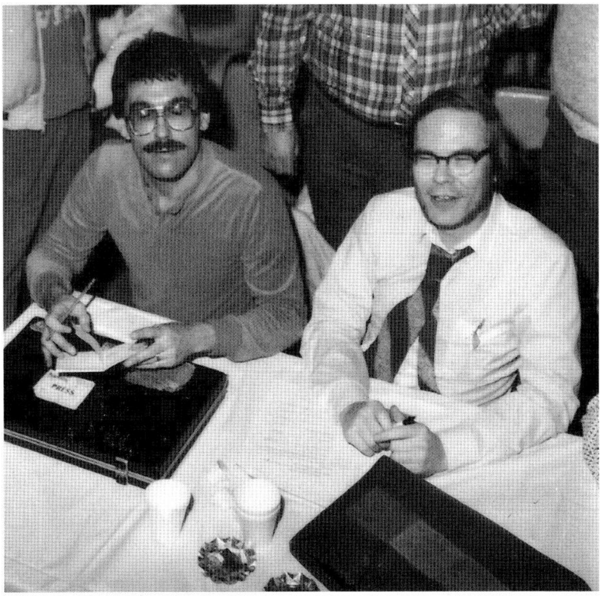

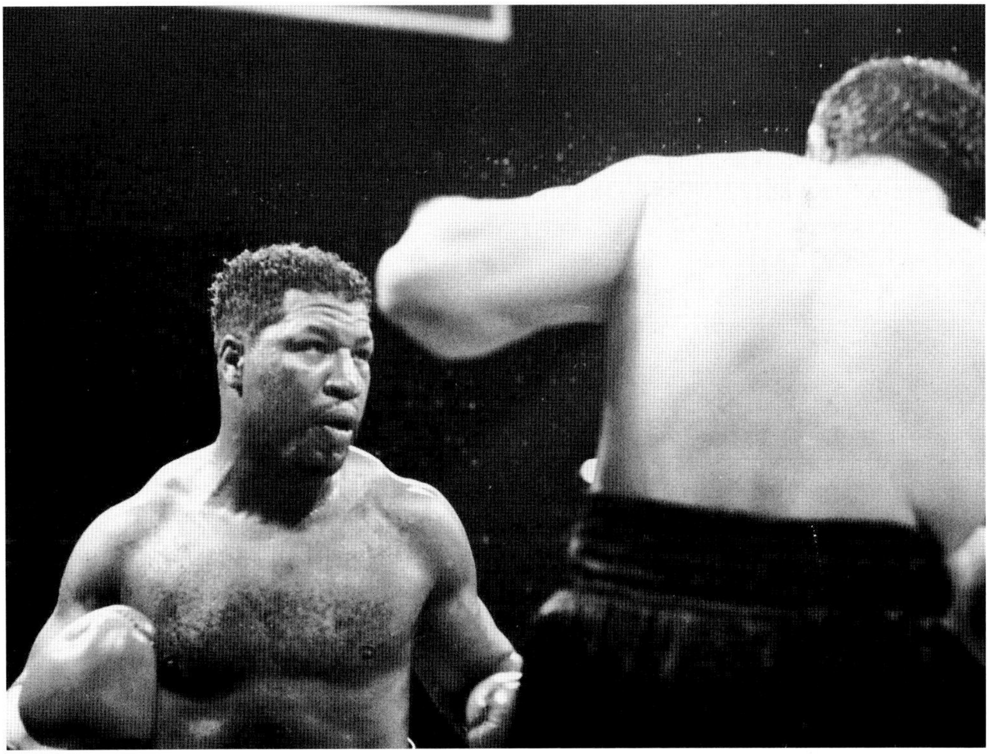

Mercer Takes Title. In a battle of undefeated heavyweights, Ray Mercer knocked out Francesco Damiani to win the WBO championship on January 11, 1991, at the Taj Mahal. With Damiani leading on all three scorecards, Mercer cracked the Italian with a left uppercut in round nine that broke Damiani's nose and put him on the canvas for referee Rudy Battle's full 10-count. (Photograph by Ray Bailey.)

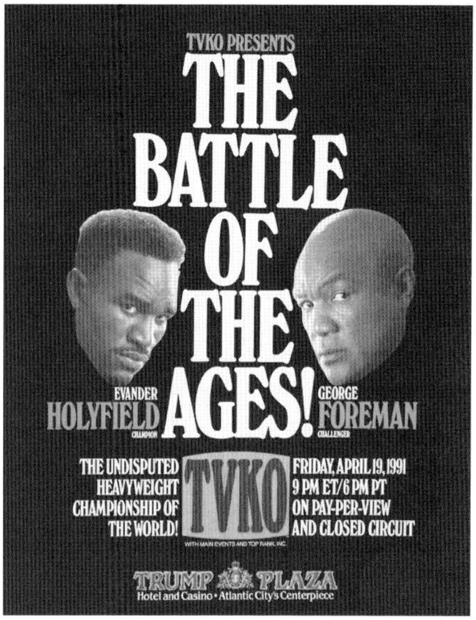

HOLYFIELD TOPS FOREMAN. In one of AC's biggest bouts ever, undisputed heavyweight champion Evander Holyfield made his first defense against 42-year-old George Foreman on April 19, 1991, at Convention Hall. Former champion Foreman was the sentimental favorite, but sentiment could not conquer a prime Holyfield, who handled Foreman's size and power. Evander outworked George to win by unanimous decision. In time, Foreman would regain the heavyweight championship at the unprecedented age of 45. (Author's collection.)

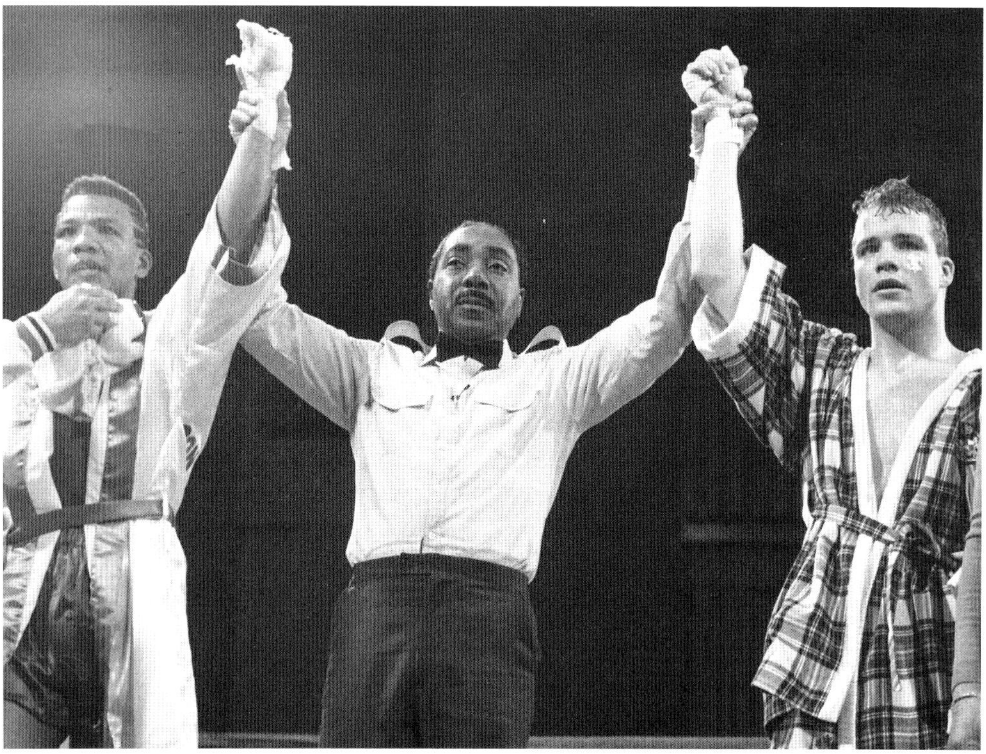

BATTLE TESTED. Referee Rudy Battle was a fixture in AC rings during the 1980s and 1990s. He worked important fights like Aaron Pryor versus Gary Hinton, Donald Curry versus Marlon Starling, Ray Mercer versus Francisco Damiani, and Mike Tyson versus Jose Ribalta. Battle also refereed bouts with Roberto Duran, Bernard Hopkins, Micky Ward, and Bobby Czyz. His biggest local assignment was the 1991 Holyfield versus Foreman heavyweight title fight. Battle eventually became the Pennsylvania boxing commissioner. (Photograph by Pete Goldfield.)

FRIGHTENING FINISH. In a Convention Hall brawl on October 18, 1991, Ray Mercer scored a fifth-round technical knockout over Tommy Morrison to defend his WBO heavyweight title. Morrison started fast, hurting Mercer with heavy punches, but he couldn't stop "Merciless" Ray from coming forward. In round five, Mercer caught Morrison with a right hand that sent Tommy to the ropes and then brutally pounded away until referee Tony Perez stopped the fight. (Photograph by Pete Goldfield.)

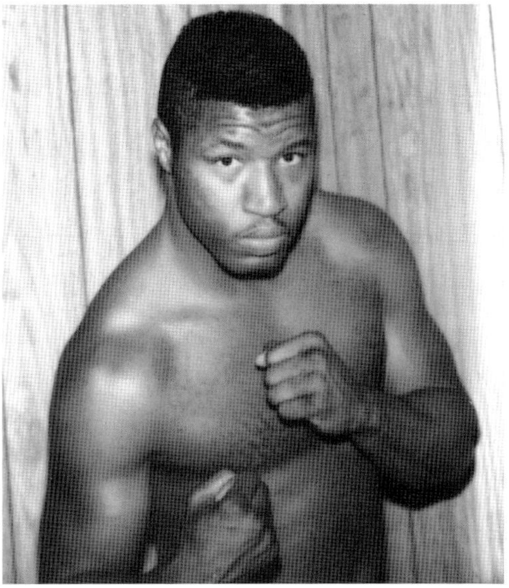

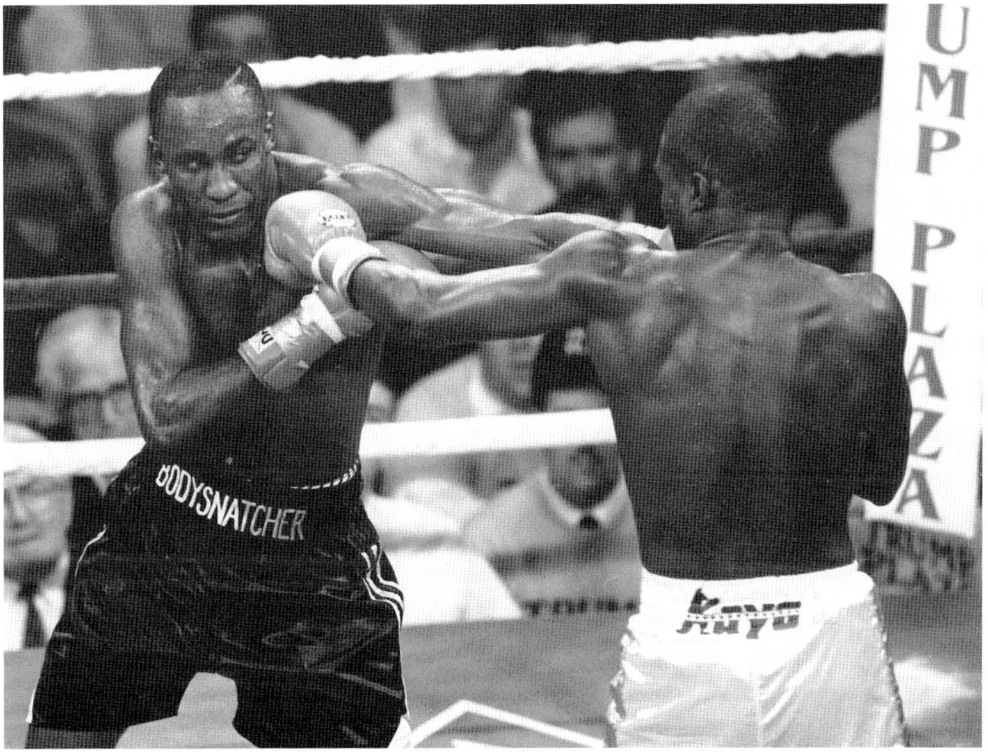

TRILOGY ACROSS FOUR WEIGHT CLASSES. Mike McCallum (left) and James Toney fought a trilogy that spanned six years and four weight classes. The first installment, a world middleweight title fight, ended in a split decision draw at Convention Hall on December 13, 1991 (pictured). The following August, Toney defeated McCallum by majority decision in another middleweight championship bout in Reno. In 1997, Toney was the victor in the final installment, a cruiserweight bout. (Photograph by Ray Bailey.)

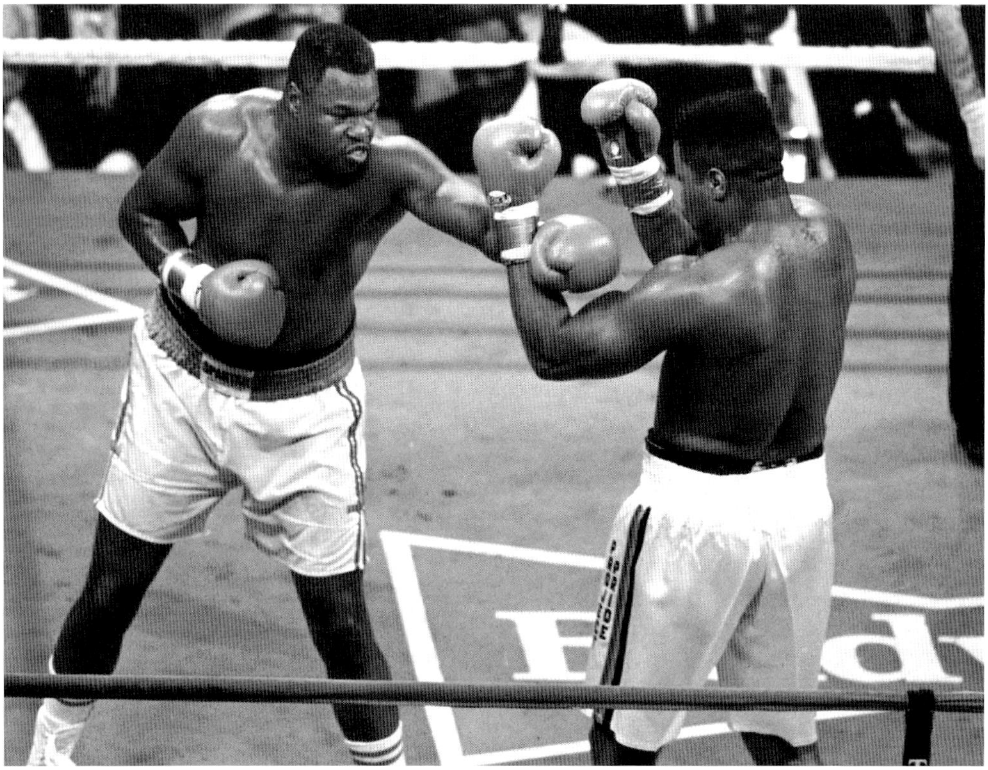

OLD MASTER EARNS TITLE SHOT. Former champion Larry Holmes (left) kept his career going with a 12-round decision over Ray Mercer at Convention Hall on February 7, 1992. Despite his 18-0 record, Mercer fell victim to the experienced veteran. This was Holmes's third and final appearance in Atlantic City, and it earned him his final shot at the title, which came next against Evander Holyfield. Mercer returned to AC another nine times. (Photograph by Ray Bailey.)

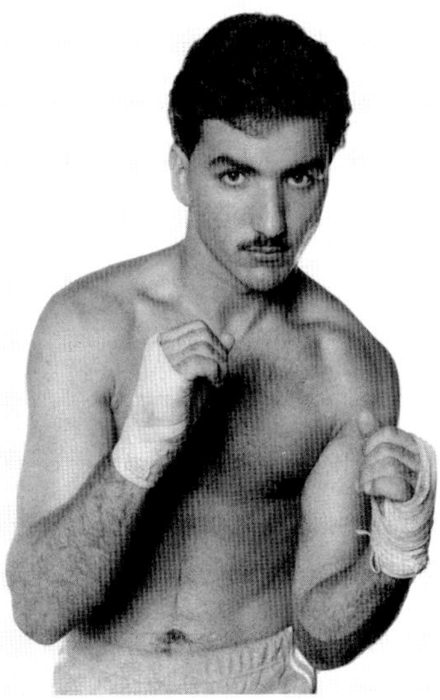

RETIRED IN PROTEST. On February 8, 1992, James Toney retained his IBF middleweight championship with a highly controversial decision over Dave Tiberi at the Taj Mahal. The decision was one of the most contested results in boxing history. Tiberi was so outraged by the verdict that he immediately retired in protest. He refused lucrative rematch offers and never fought again. Toney fought for another 25 years. (Photograph by Pete Goldfield.)

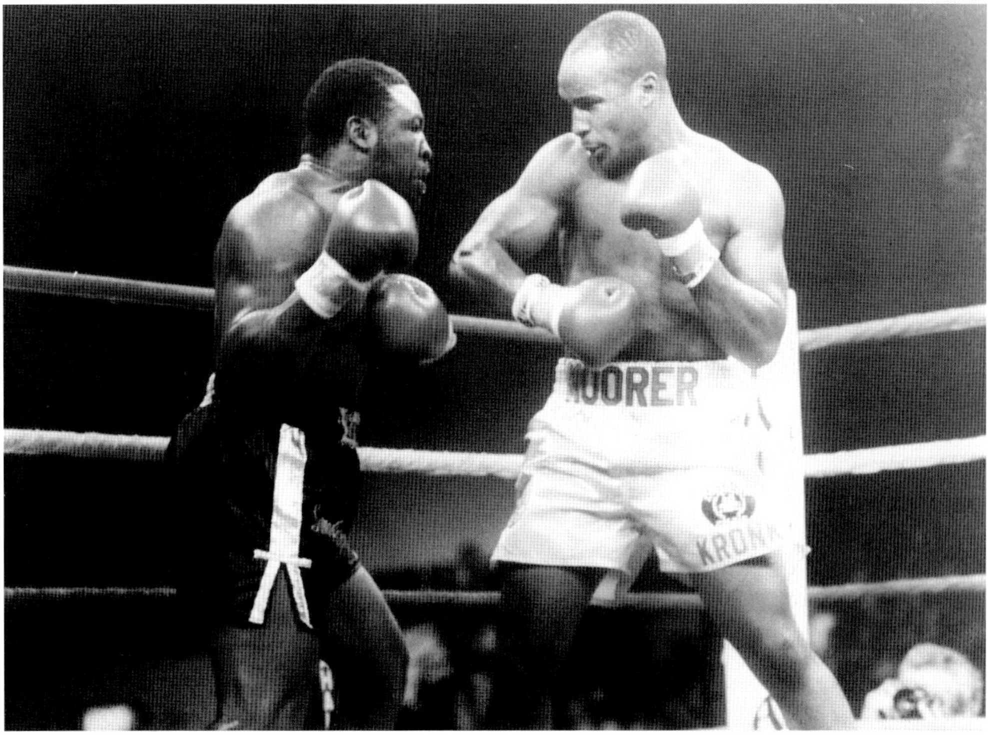

Bombs Away! Michael Moorer won the vacant WBO heavyweight title with a fifth-round TKO of Bert Cooper at the Taj Mahal on May 15, 1992. In this great punch-out, both fighters hit the canvas twice before it was over. Moorer was down in the first and third, while Cooper went down in the first and fifth. Cooper was still on his feet when referee Joe O'Neill stopped the classic slugfest. This was one of nine AC fights for Moorer, including four defenses by knockout of his WBO light heavyweight title, and his first bout as a heavyweight. Cooper fought 21 battles in AC. (Photograph by Ray Bailey.)

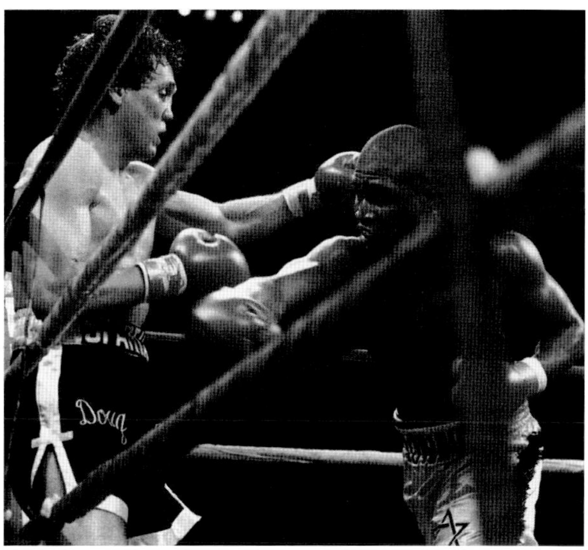

Moving on Up. IBF middleweight champion James Toney moved up to the super middleweight division with a sixth-round technical knockout of former WBO middleweight champion Doug DeWitt on December 5, 1992, at the Taj Mahal. This was the final bout of DeWitt's career, while the unbeaten Toney took the IBF super middleweight title in his next bout. Gradually, Toney would move all the way up to the heavyweight division. (Photograph by Ray Bailey.)

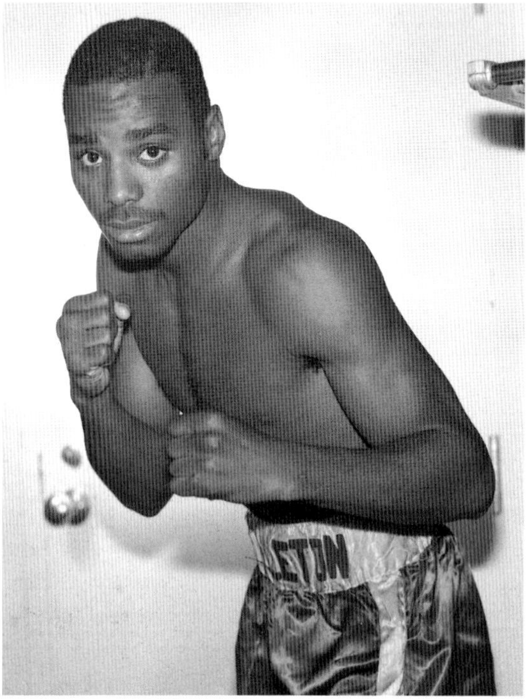

NEVER GIVE UP. Lightweight Freddie Pendleton was a tough competitor, but his dream of becoming champion seemed like a long shot. However, after toiling for years, "Fearless Freddie" finally won the IBF lightweight crown in his 54th career bout against Tracy Spann on January 10, 1993, at Harrah's Marina. Pendleton fought in AC 26 times, including fights with Pernell Whitaker, Frankie Randall, Anthony Fletcher, Jimmy Paul, and Livingstone Bramble. (Photograph by Pete Goldfield.)

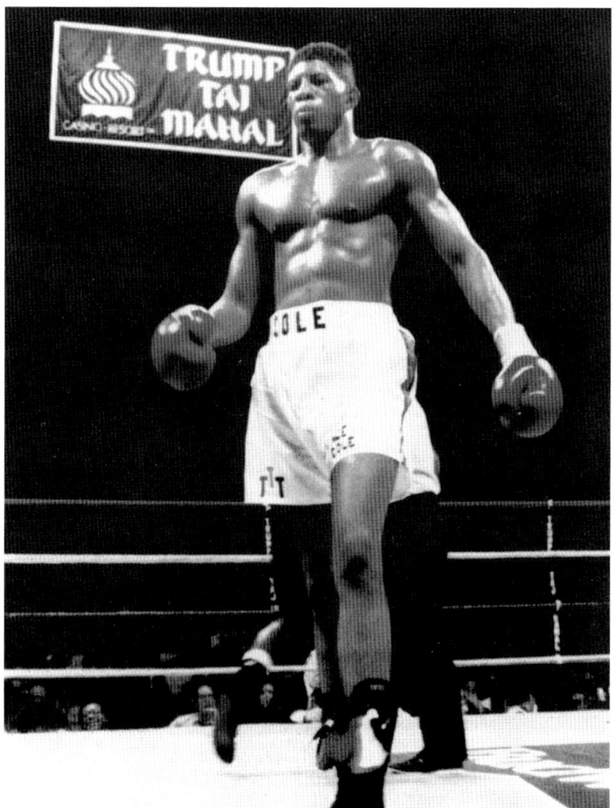

ICE-HOT IN AC. Born in AC and raised in Spring Valley, New York, Al "Ice" Cole won the IBF cruiserweight title against James Warring on July 30, 1992, in Stanhope, New Jersey. He held the title from 1992 to 1995. Cole fought 17 times in AC, including three title defenses against Uriah Grant twice (in 1993 and 1995) and Vincent Boulware in 1993. (Photograph by Ray Bailey.)

POISONOUS PUNCHER. Brooklyn's Junior "Poison" Jones fought 17 times in AC as a professional. A career highlight for Jones in the city came on October 23, 1993, when he captured his first world title at the Sands, defeating Jorge Eliecer Julio for the WBA bantamweight title via unanimous decision. Jones held the title until the following April, when he was defeated by John Michael Johnson in Las Vegas. (Photograph by Pete Goldfield.)

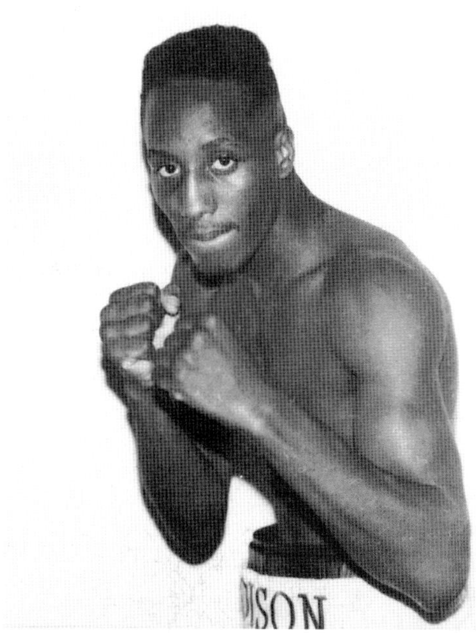

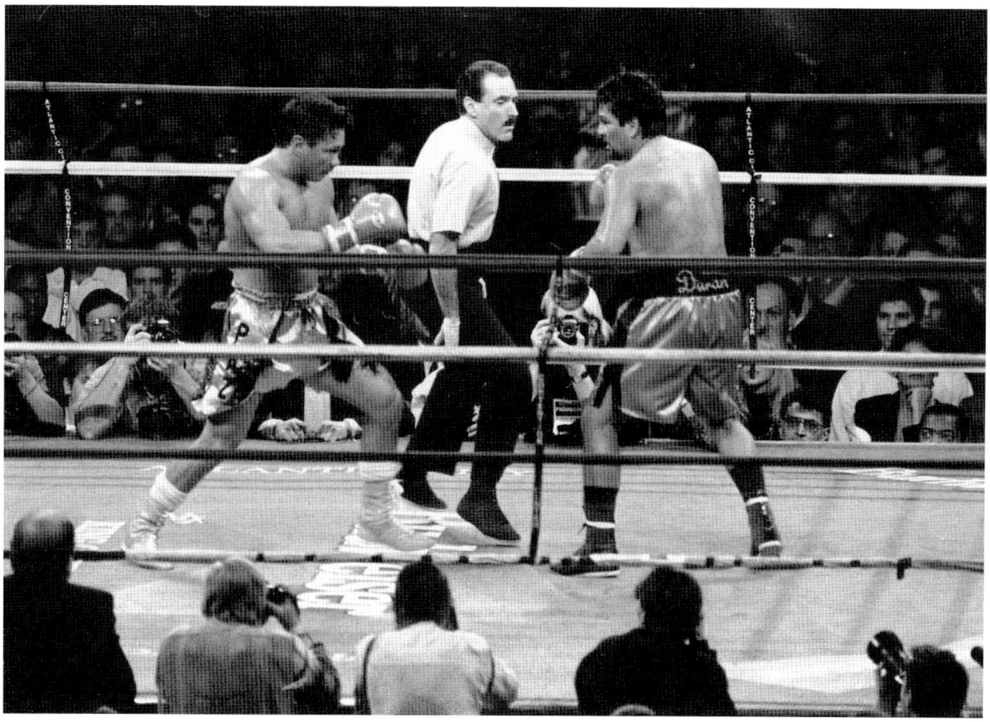

PAZIENZA REPEATS. Six months after he defeated Roberto Duran in Las Vegas, Vinny Pazienza repeated the feat at Convention Hall with another 12-round unanimous decision victory on January 14, 1995. Unlike the questionable result of their first bout, Pazienza won the rematch by a comfortable margin. The fight drew a live crowd of 10,382. This was one of twenty appearances in AC for Pazienza and one of five for Duran. (Photograph by Ray Bailey.)

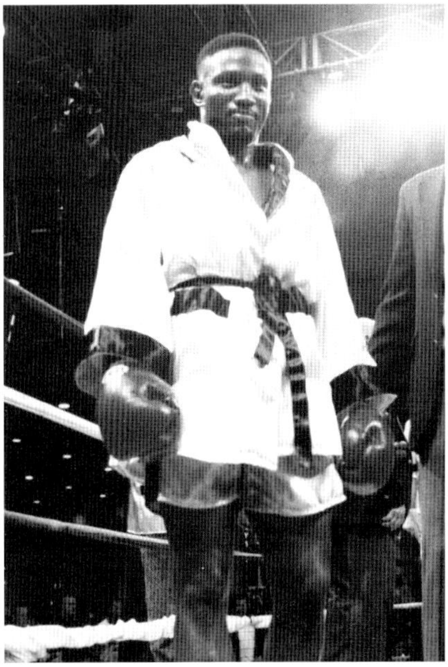

"SWEET PEA." Four-division champion Pernell "Sweet Pea" Whitaker fought in AC seven times, including five title bouts at Convention Hall. In 1990, he defended his WBC and IBF lightweight title with a decision over Freddie Pendleton. In 1995, Whitaker defended his WBC welterweight championship twice against Gary Jacobs and Jake Rodriguez and won the WBA junior middleweight championship against Julio Cesar Vasquez. In 1997, Whitaker dramatically knocked out Diosbelys Hurtado to defend his WBC welterweight title. (Photograph by Ray Bailey.)

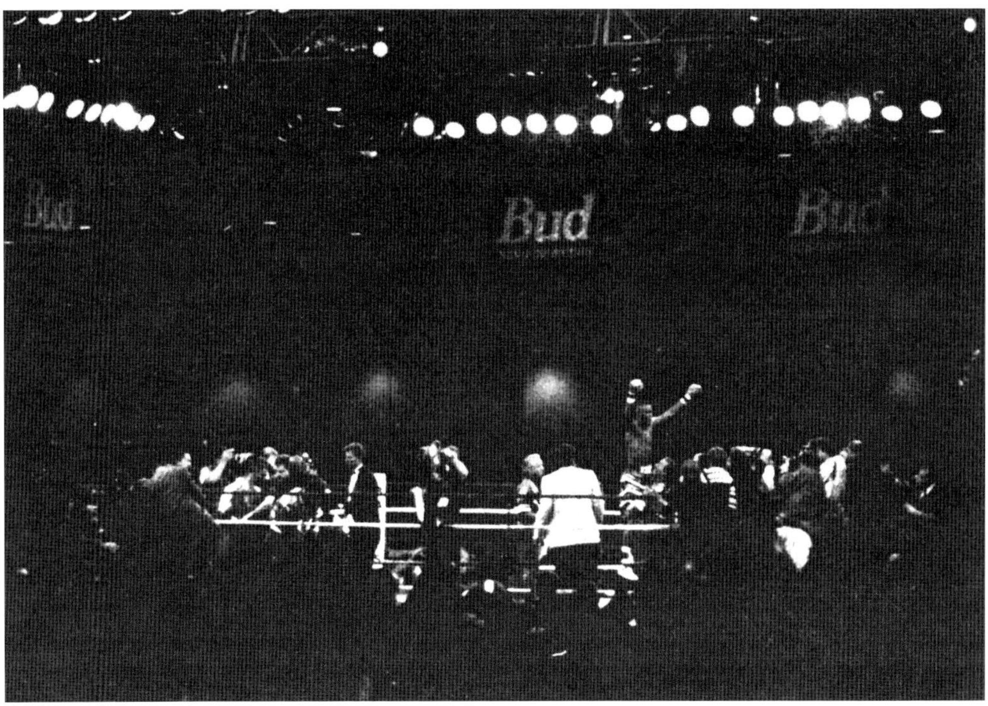

"TITO" TRINIDAD. IBF welterweight champion Felix "Tito" Trinidad made his lone Atlantic City appearance on November 18, 1995, with a fourth-round technical knockout of number-one contender Larry Barnes at Convention Hall. It was the seventh defense of his title. Trinidad ended the bout with a devastating body shot that dropped Barnes in round four. Trinidad shared the bill with WBC champion Pernell Whitaker, who also won that night. (Photograph by John DiSanto.)

Legends Meet. Ring icons Hector Camacho and Roberto Duran faced off in a 12-round fight at the Taj Mahal's Mark Etess Arena on June 22, 1996. Camacho, the younger man by 11 years, built an early lead using his superior speed. Duran, 45, rallied down the stretch to make the fight close, but the unanimous decision went to Camacho. Although considered a "turn back the clock" event, both veterans went on to fight for years to come. (Author's collection.)

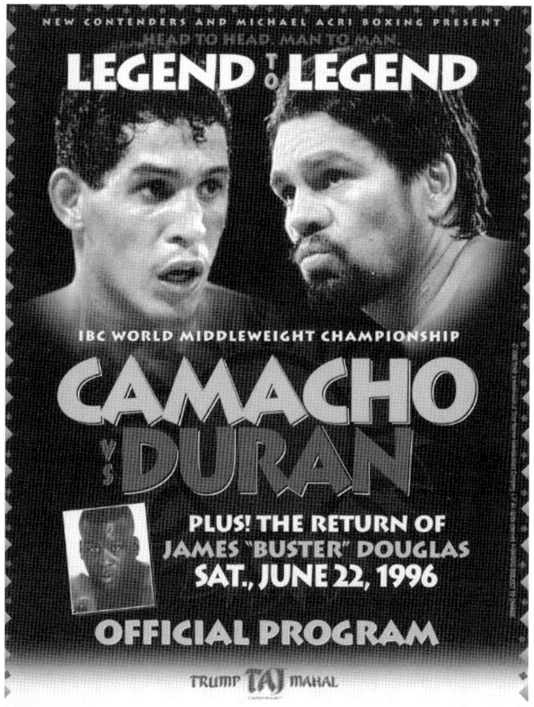

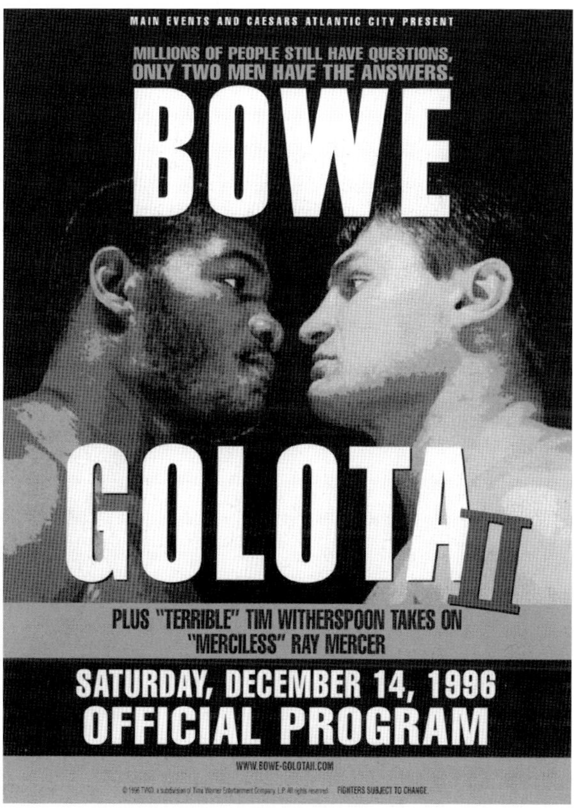

Foul Out. Heavyweight Andrew Golota was disqualified for a second time against Riddick Bowe for repeated low blows on December 14, 1996, at Convention Hall. Despite a lead in the fight, Golota unraveled after Bowe knocked him down in round four. Golota survived but began employing dirty tactics, including several low blows. Finally, after he floored Bowe in the ninth round with another punch below the belt, referee Eddie Cotton disqualified Golota. (Author's collection.)

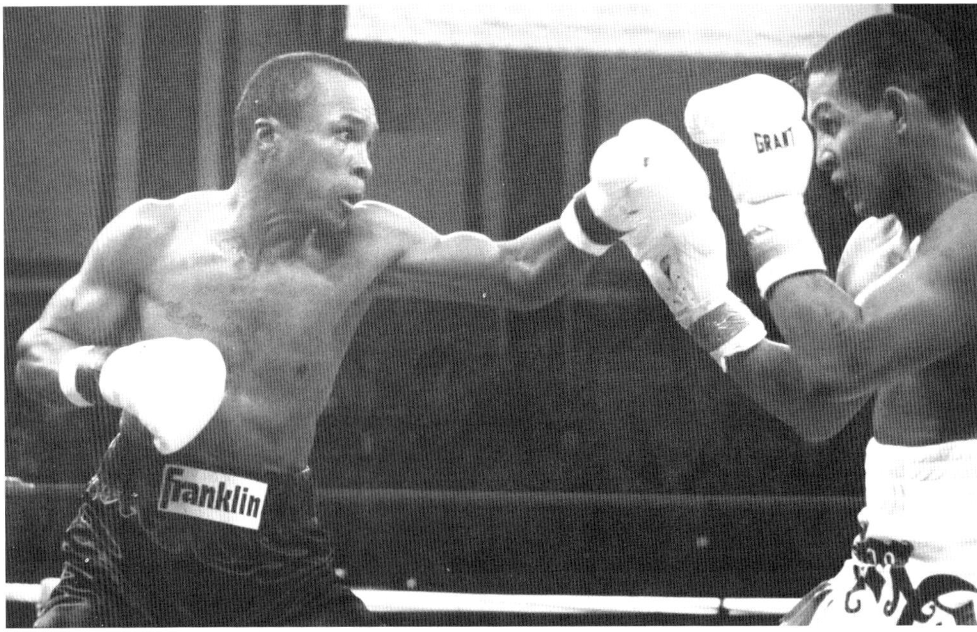

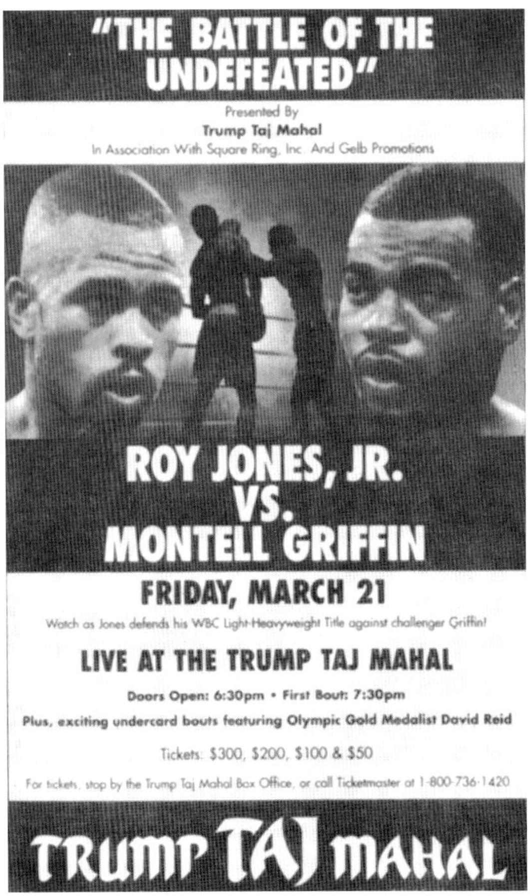

Father Time Wins Again. On March 1, 1997, Father Time caught up with "Sugar" Ray Leonard in his fight with Hector Camacho at Convention Hall. Camacho dominated the fight and knocked Leonard down in the fifth round. Ray beat the count, but Camacho pounded away until referee Joe Cortez stopped it. The crowd of 10,324 was shocked, almost as much as Leonard. Ray never fought again. It was his only AC appearance. (Photograph by Ray Bailey.)

Disqualified. In a surprising upset, Montell Griffin won the WBC light heavyweight title by disqualification over Roy Jones Jr. on March 21, 1997, at the Taj Mahal. Jones dropped Griffin to one knee in round nine and added a pair of punches while the challenger was down. Jones was disqualified for the infraction, and Griffith won the belt. Five months later, Jones regained the title with a first-round knockout of Griffin. (Author's collection.)

PHILLIPS STUNS TSZYU. Vince Phillips ignored the odds when he faced undefeated IBF champion Kostya Tszyu on May 31, 1997, at the Taj Mahal. Most fans expected Tszyu to win and move on to fight Oscar De La Hoya. However, Phillips scored a stunning 10th-round TKO to take the title. He defended it once in AC. Tszyu eventually won more titles but never returned to the shore or fought De La Hoya. (Photograph by Pete Goldfield.)

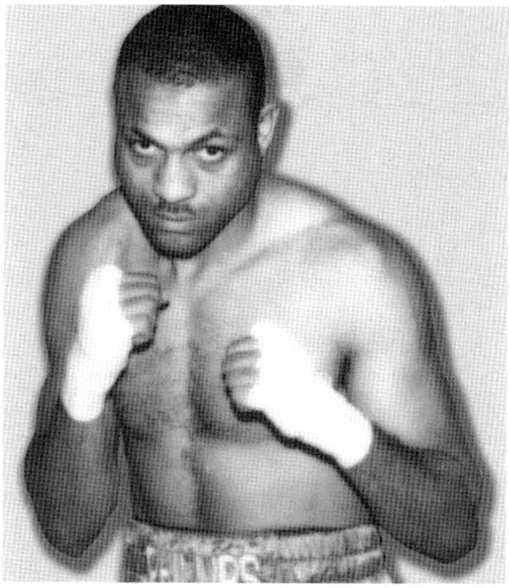

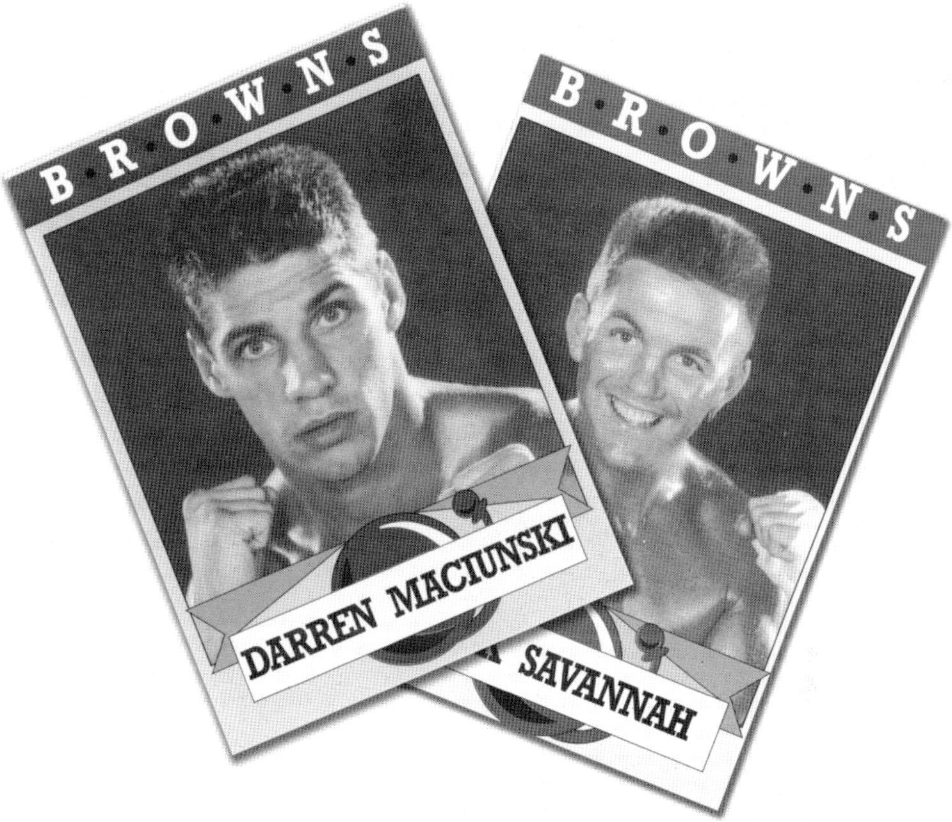

JERSEY SHORE TALENT. The venues of AC served as a showcase for fighters from the Jersey Shore area. Forked River's "Irish" Teddy Mann, Little Silver's Chris "Shamrock Express" Reid, Brick's Frank Savannah and Daniel Pasciolla, May Landing's Antowyan Aikens, Somers Point's Isiah Seldon, Middletown's Johnny Molnar, Toms River's Chris Thomas, and Little Egg Harbor's Brendan Barrett all fought in AC. On August 22, 1998, Toms River's Darren Maciunski fought future world champion Fernando Vargas at Convention Hall. (Peltz Boxing Promotions.)

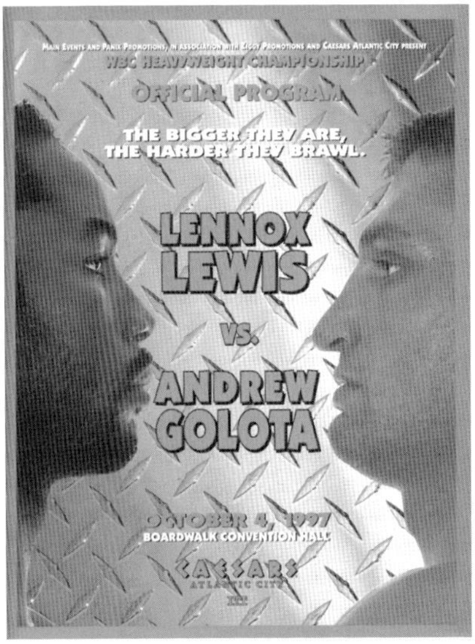

STEAMROLLED. Despite losing by disqualification to Riddick Bowe in his two previous bouts, Andrew Golota still received a shot against WBC heavyweight champion Lennox Lewis. On October 4, 1997, before 13,889 fans at Convention Hall, Golota froze in his tracks at the opening bell, and Lewis steamrolled him in just 95 seconds. Lewis returned to AC once more in his next bout. This was Golota's eighth of 12 Atlantic City appearances. (Author's collection.)

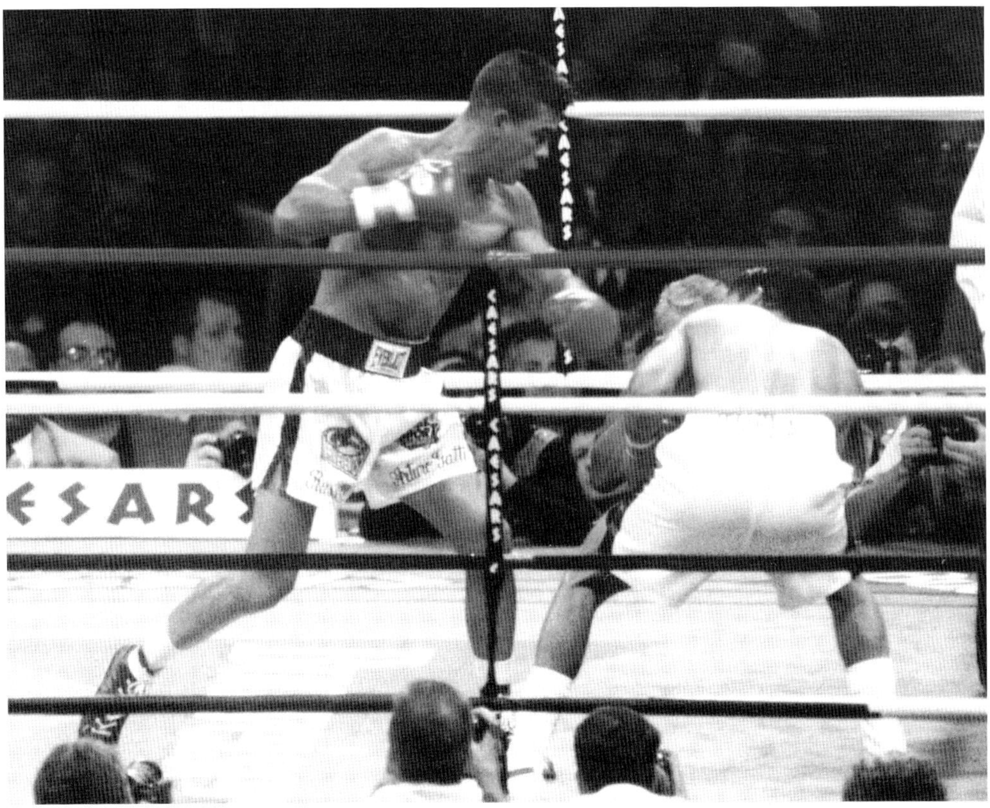

KNOCKOUT OF THE YEAR. Arturo Gatti defended his IBF junior lightweight title against Gabriel Ruelas at Convention Hall on October 4, 1997. Both fighters were hurt badly in round four, but Gatti landed a left hook in the fifth round that floored Ruelas. Gabe made it to his feet, but referee Benjy Esteves Jr. stopped the fight. The bout was named both the "Knockout of the Year" and the "Fight of the Year" by *The Ring*. (Photograph by Ray Bailey.)

FOREMAN CLOSES CAREER. Two-time heavyweight champion George Foreman finished his boxing career in 1997 with two AC performances against Lou Savarese (April 26 at Convention Hall) and Shannon Briggs (November 22 at the Taj Mahal). In a bruising battle, the ageless Foreman defeated Savarese by split decision. Seven months later, before 5,220 fans, Foreman, two months shy of his 49th birthday, lost a close decision to Briggs and never fought again. (Photograph by Pete Goldfield.)

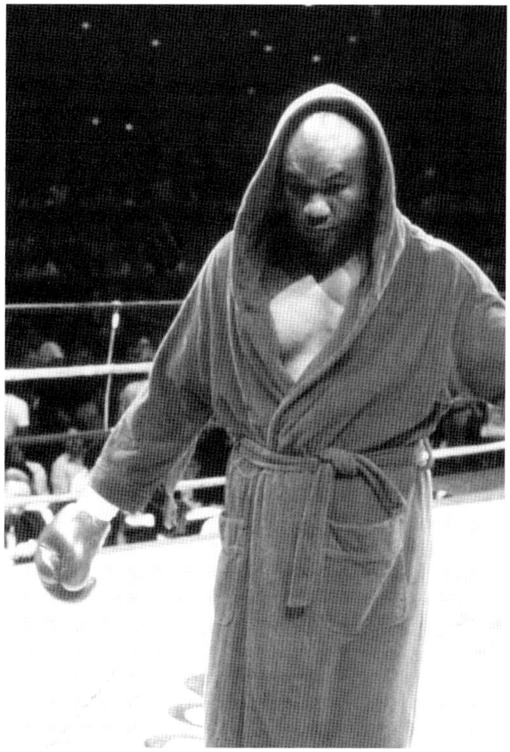

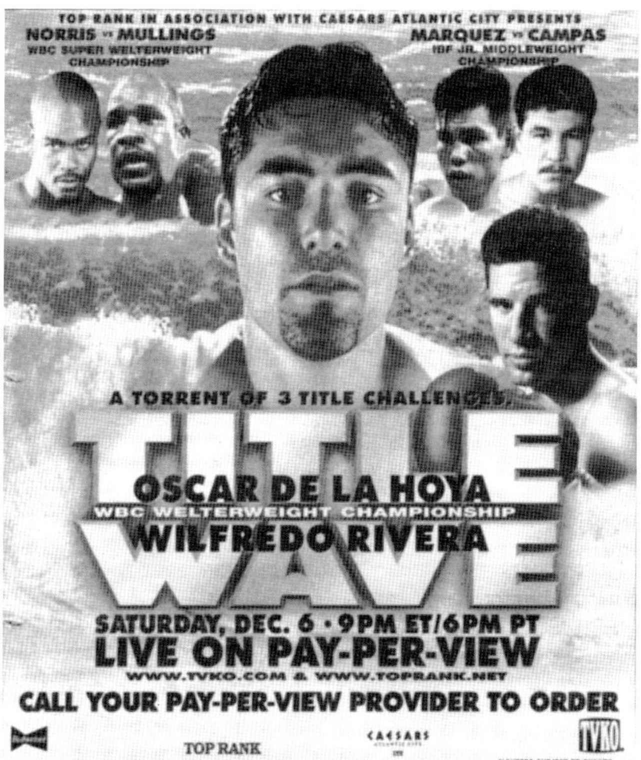

"THE GOLDEN BOY" BATTERS RIVERA. On December 6, 1997, Wilfredo Rivera challenged Oscar De La Hoya for the WBC welterweight title at Convention Hall in front of a crowd of 11,271. "The Golden Boy" battered Rivera so badly that referee Joe Cortez called a stop to the action at the 2:48 mark of the eighth round. This was De La Hoya's only appearance as a professional in Atlantic City. (Author's collection.)

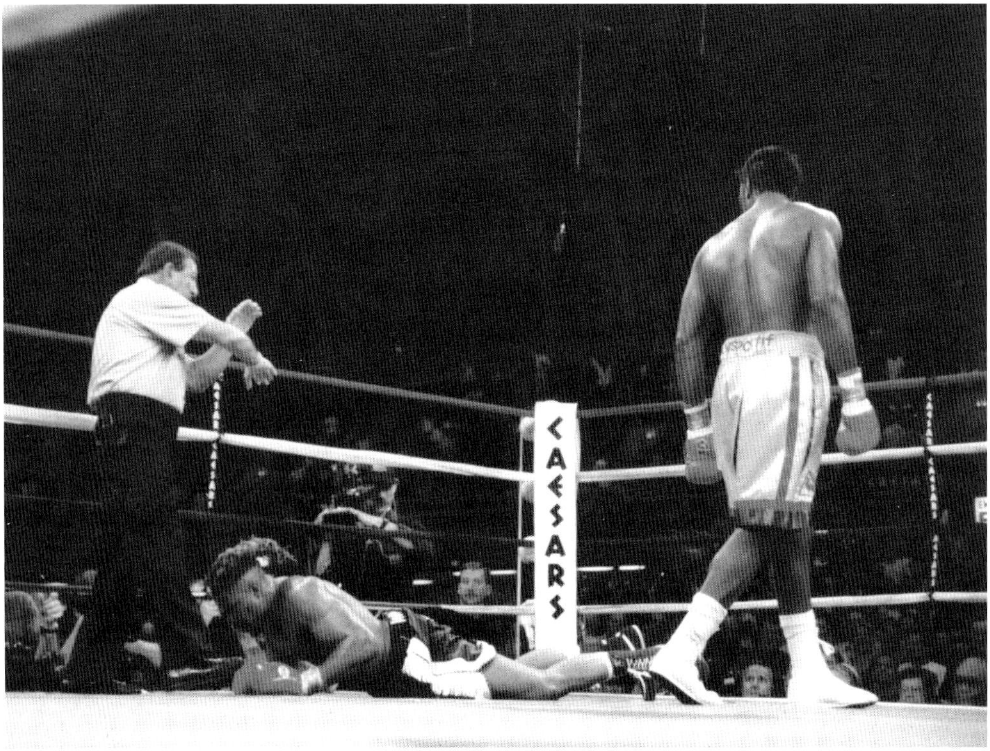

LEWIS TOPPLES BRIGGS. Shannon Briggs started fast against Lennox Lewis in a fight for the WBC heavyweight title on March 28, 1998, at Convention Hall. Briggs shook the champ early on, but Lewis regained control, and Briggs began to tire. Lewis put Briggs down in the fourth round and then finished him midway through the fifth round. A crowd of 9,173 was in attendance. (Photograph by Ray Bailey.)

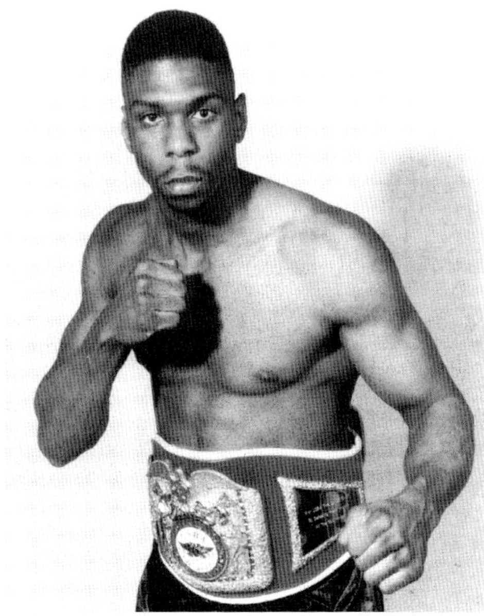

"THE HATCHET." Charles "The Hatchet" Brewer was IBF super middleweight champion from 1997 to 1998 and compiled a career record of 40-11, 28 KOs. An exciting fighter who fought all over the world during his 16 years in the ring, Brewer made 17 appearances in Atlantic City, including his second professional bout and his second title defense on March 28, 1998, against Herol Graham at Convention Hall. The fight was on the Lewis versus Briggs undercard. (Peltz Boxing Promotions.)

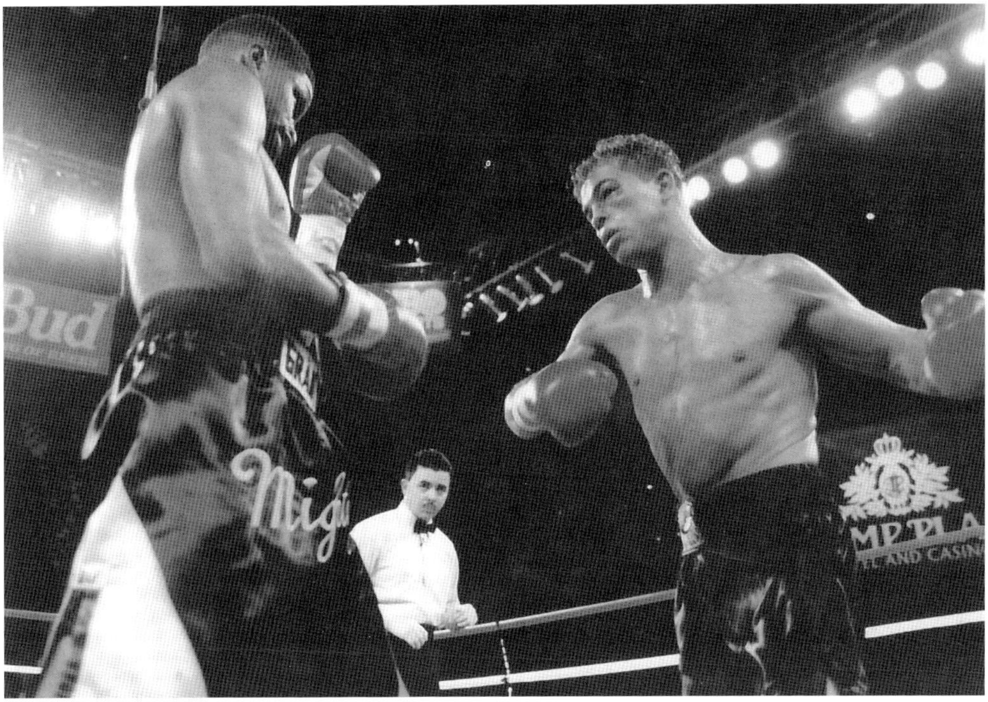

Mighty Good Showing. Philadelphia's Ivan "Mighty" Robinson (left) fought eight of his 46 professional bouts in AC, including two victories over Arturo Gatti. On August 22, 1998, at Convention Hall, Robinson won a 10-round split decision that was later named "Fight of the Year" and "Upset of the Year" by *The Ring*. Robinson won their rematch (pictured) again by close 10-round decision, this time at the Taj Mahal on December 12, 1998. Robinson also faced Phillip Holiday and Angel Manfredy during his career. (Photograph by Ray Bailey.)

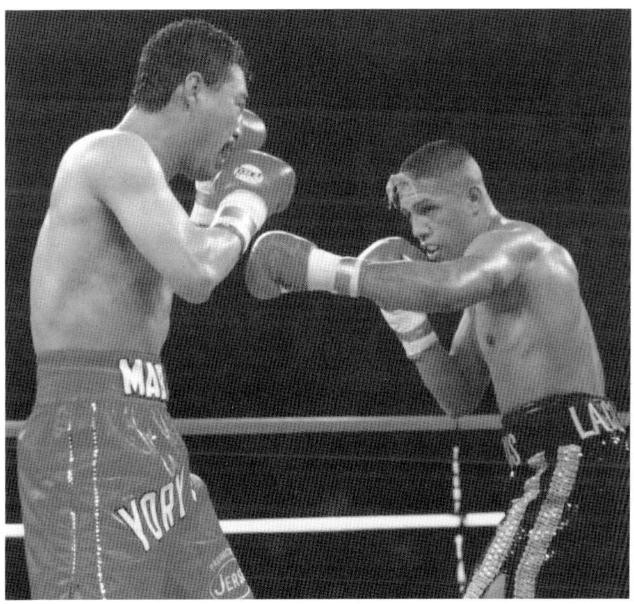

Vargas Claims Title. In his 15th professional bout, Fernando Vargas won the IBF junior middleweight title from 75-bout veteran Yori Boy Campas by seventh-round TKO on December 12, 1998, at the Taj Mahal. After Campas suffered a broken nose, cut lip, and swollen eye, he surrendered in his corner. Vargas went on to defend the title five times. Campas fought 52 more bouts, including title fights against Oscar De La Hoya and Oba Carr. (Photograph by Ray Bailey.)

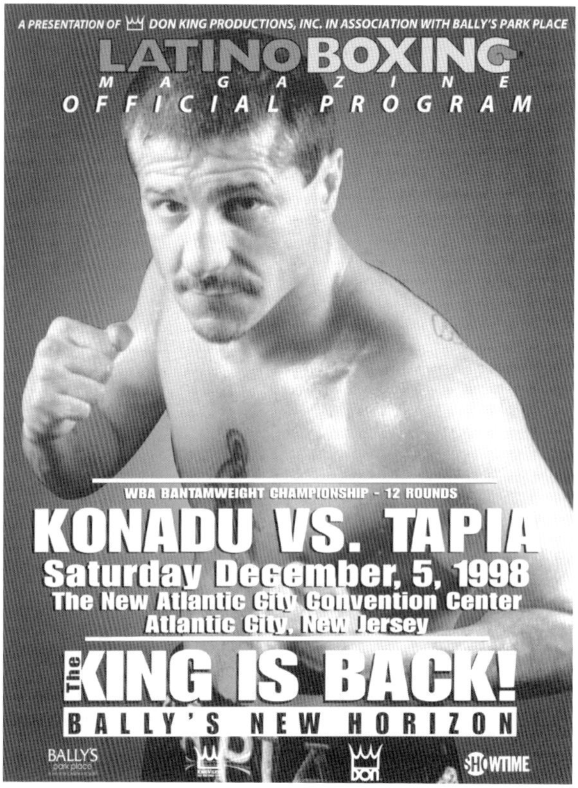

Two-Time Champ. Johnny Tapia won the WBA bantamweight championship with a 12-round decision over Nana Konadu at the new Convention Center on December 5, 1998. In Tapia's only Atlantic City visit, he earned a title in a second weight division and extended his unbeaten streak to 45-0-2. The Convention Center, located a few blocks off the Boardwalk, hosted some boxing shows but never became a major fight venue. (Author's collection.)

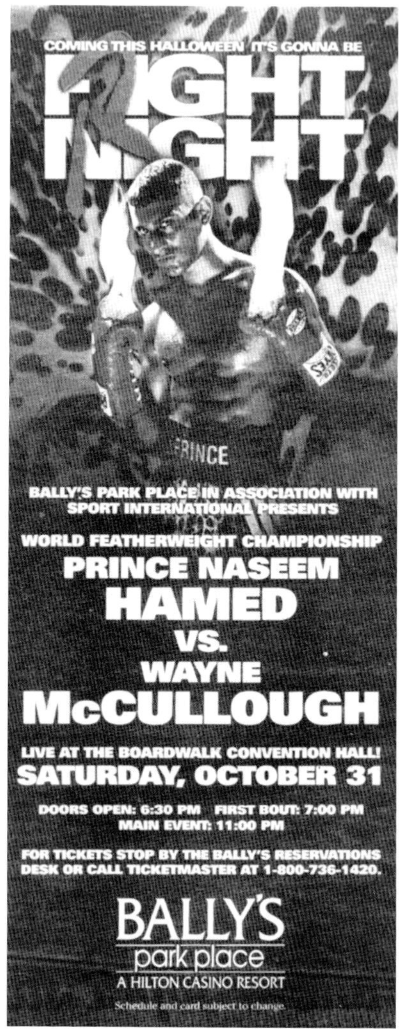

Halloween Thriller. In what was billed as a "Halloween Fright Night," "Prince" Naseem Hamed defeated former world champion Wayne McCullough to defend his WBO and linear featherweight titles at Convention Hall on October 31, 1998. Hamed, who entered the ring to Michael Jackson's hit single "Thriller," outpointed McCullough by unanimous decision. Although Hamed won easily, his 18-bout knockout streak ended with this fight. (Author's collection.)

REID WINS PROFESSIONAL GOLD. A 1996 Olympic Gold Medalist, David Reid added a professional world championship to his resume on March 6, 1999, when he took the WBA junior middleweight title from Laurent Boudouani by unanimous decision at Convention Hall. Reid remained champion for one year and made two successful title defenses. Reid made eight total appearances in AC, including his pro debut and his first defense. Boudouani retired after this fight. (Author's collection.)

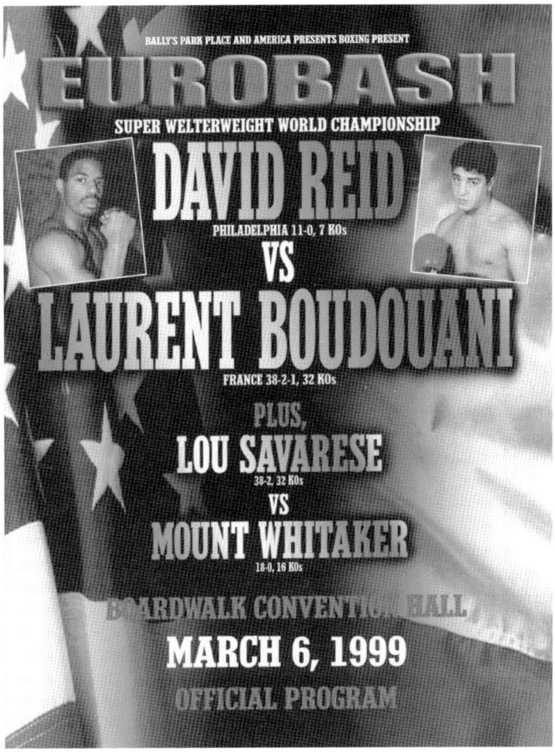

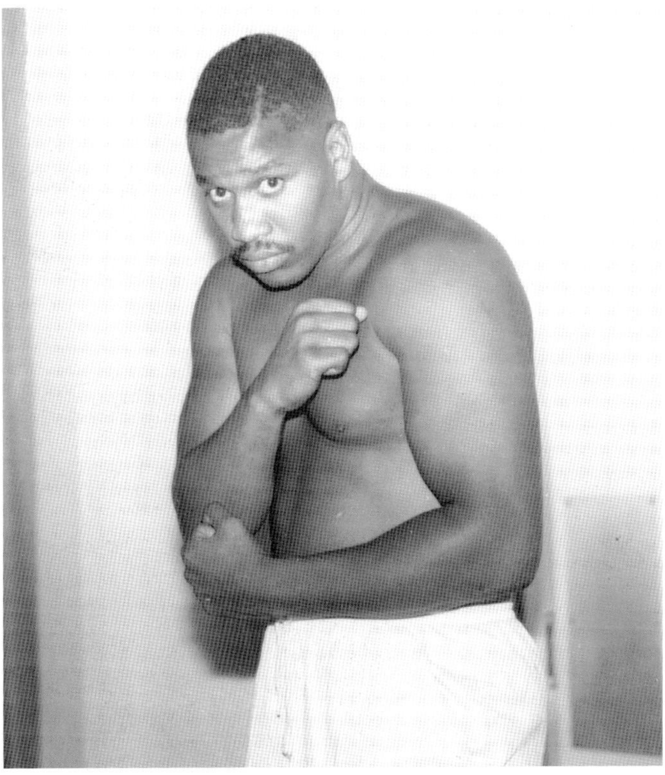

"TERRIBLE" TIM. Two-time heavyweight champion "Terrible" Tim Witherspoon made 15 appearances in Atlantic City during his 24-year career. Witherspoon beat good heavyweights, including Marvin Stinson, Alfonzo Ratliff, Jeff Sims, and Anders Eklund. His biggest win at the shore was a 1991 twelve-round decision over Carl Williams at the Taj Mahal to win the USBA title. He won all of his AC fights except his defeat to Ray Mercer in 1996. (Photograph by Pete Goldfield.)

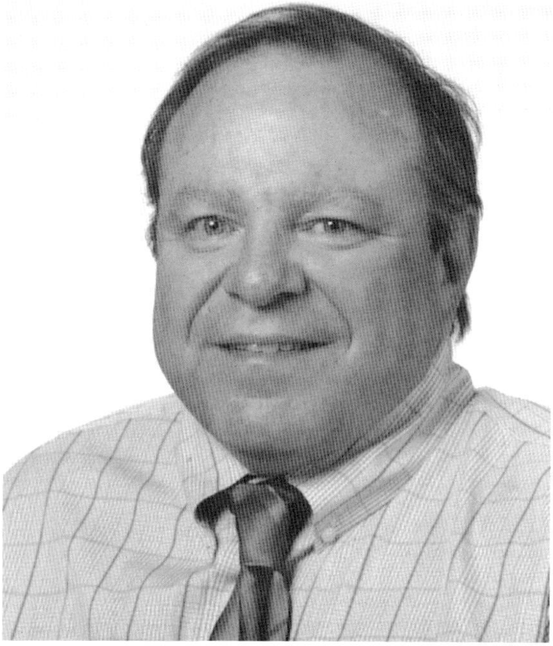

Boxing Scribe. Sportswriter David Weinberg worked the AC boxing beat for the *Press of Atlantic City* from 1986 to 2019. A journalist who covered a wide variety of sports, Weinberg is especially well respected as a boxing writer. Having covered all of the major fights in the city throughout his career, Weinberg lists Tyson versus Spinks, Holyfield versus Foreman, Mercer versus Morrison, and Gatti versus Ward III as some of his most memorable assignments. (New Jersey Boxing Hall of Fame.)

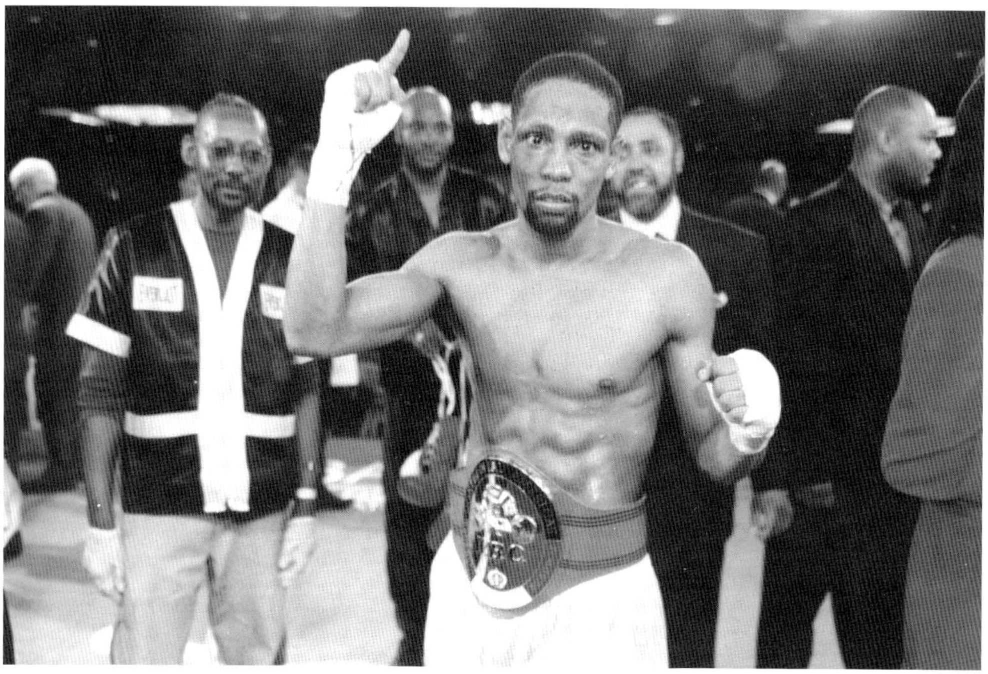

Tragic Prince. With his father, Bill Johnson, in his corner as head trainer (background left), AC-born Leavander Johnson fought at home 17 times. Johnson's biggest AC win was an eighth-round TKO over Ray Minus for a regional title on March 31, 2001, at the Taj Mahal. Johnson became IBF lightweight champion in 2005, but tragedy struck in his first defense: a TKO loss to Jesus Chavez. Johnson suffered a subdural hematoma and died on September 22, 2005. (Photograph by Ray Bailey.)

6

DECLINE

2000–2020

In the first decade of the 21st century, it became clear that AC boxing's best days were over. Activity continued to slip with less than 120 shows between 2000 and 2009. This sharp decline came as AC's casino and gaming industry diminished due to competition from new casinos in Pennsylvania and New York as well as the emergence of online gambling. The AC boxing scene hit a low point in 2007, when there were only six fight cards in the city that once hosted more than 20 times that number in a single year.

In 2002 and 2003, Arturo Gatti and Micky Ward clashed in the last two installments of their epic trilogy. Ward had won the out-of-town opener, but Gatti prevailed in both AC fights and continued to be the main drawing card in the city throughout the decade. Fans packed Convention Hall for the final nine bouts of his legendary career. This string of sellouts ended with Gatti's 2007 retirement.

Other highlights in the 2000s included the rise of hometown hero Leavander Johnson, who won a regional title in AC in 2001 before becoming a world champion and then tragically dying in Las Vegas from ring injuries sustained in his first title defense in 2005.

Between 2010 and 2020, there were around 100 shows in the city, with Bally's and Convention Hall being the busiest venues. Sergio Martinez and Bernard Hopkins were standouts, while Jacqui Frazier-Lyde and Claressa Shields each made strides in female boxing. In 2019, Shields headlined the last Convention Hall show to date. With AC boxing activity slumping in the final few years of the decade, Rising Star Promotions emerged as the most consistent promoter in town, running shows at the Claridge and Showboat. Main Events, Top Rank, and a few other promoters came with occasional marquee fights, but AC boxing almost completely dried up by the end of the decade. A ray of hope for renewed interest in AC's boxing scene came when Ray McCline founded the Atlantic City Boxing Hall of Fame and inducted its star-studded first class in 2017.

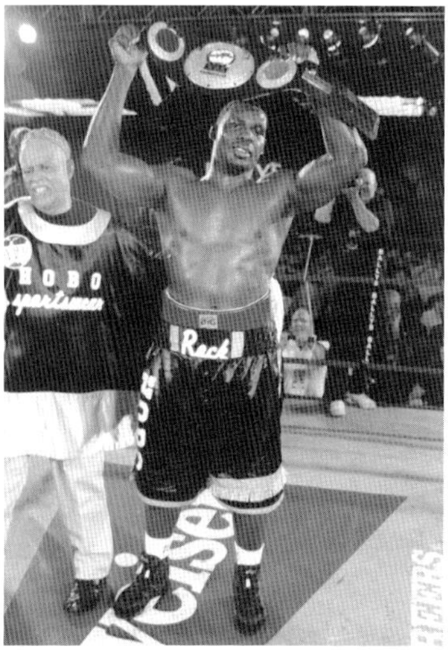

"The Rock." Hasim Rahman, once world heavyweight champion, made 10 colorful stops in AC, including wins over Trevor Berbick, Jesse Ferguson, and Corrie Sanders. "The Rock" was knocked out of the ring by Oleg Maskaev in 1999 and lost by technical decision to Evander Holyfield in 2002. Rahman also lost a 12-round decision to John Ruiz for the vacant WBA title and, in his final appearance in AC, fought to a draw with James Toney in a WBC title fight. (Photograph by Ray Bailey.)

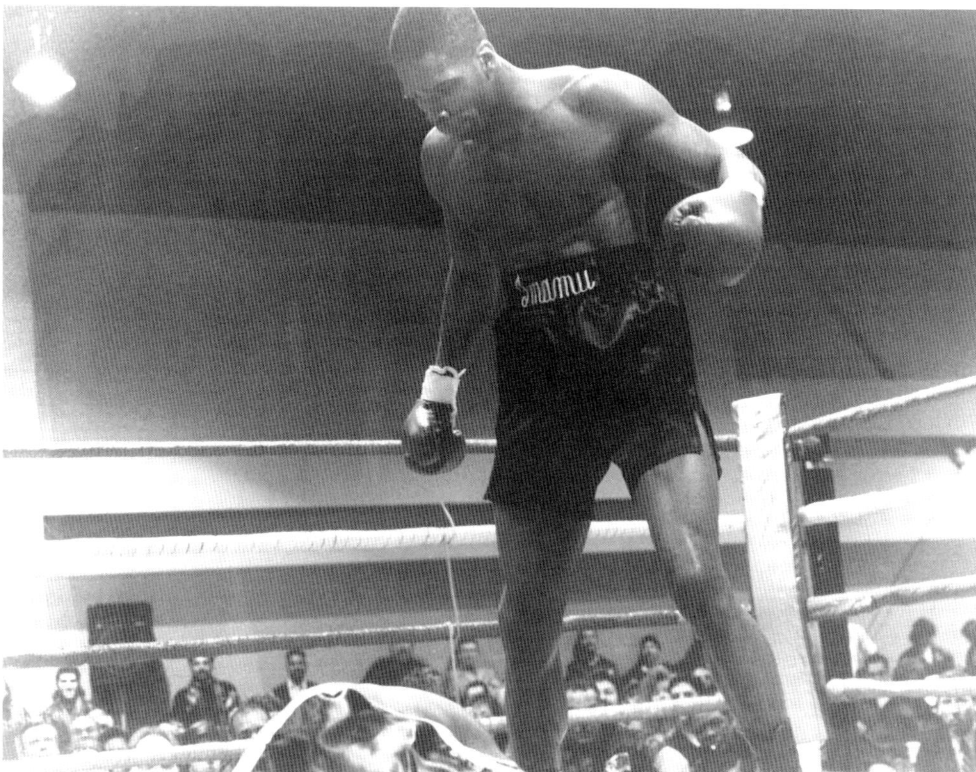

Imamu Mayfield. Freehold, New Jersey's Imamu Mayfield held the IBF cruiserweight title between 1997 and 1998. He fought in Atlantic City four times, including his most notable shore bout, a 10th-round technical knockout of Gary Wilcox at the Taj Mahal to win the USBA cruiserweight title on June 30, 2001. Mayfield returned to AC late in his career for three fights promoted by Rising Star Promotions at the Claridge in 2016 and 2017. (Photograph by Ray Bailey.)

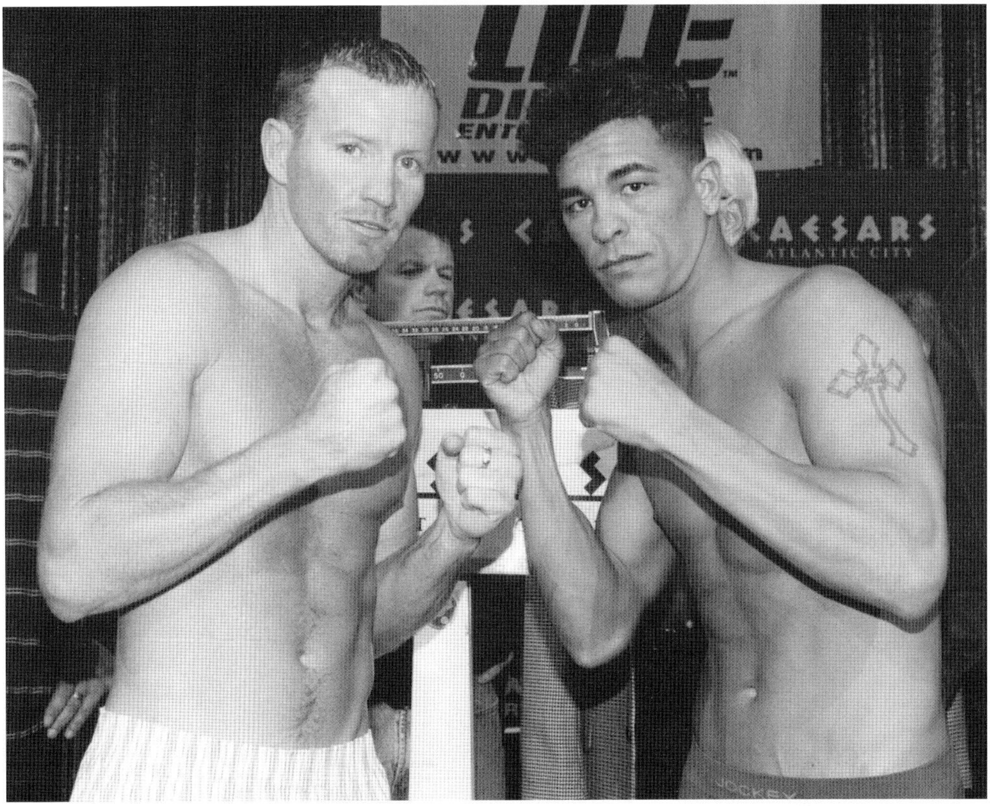

Classic Rivalry. Two-thirds of one of boxing's most celebrated trilogies occurred at Convention Hall in 2002 and 2003. After losing the opener of their series, Arturo Gatti (right) defeated archrival Micky Ward twice "at home" on the AC Boardwalk. The classic rivalry produced three battles that fans still consider some of the best fights in history. All three bouts went the distance, and the first and third installments were named the "Fight of the Year" by *The Ring.* (Photograph by Ray Bailey.)

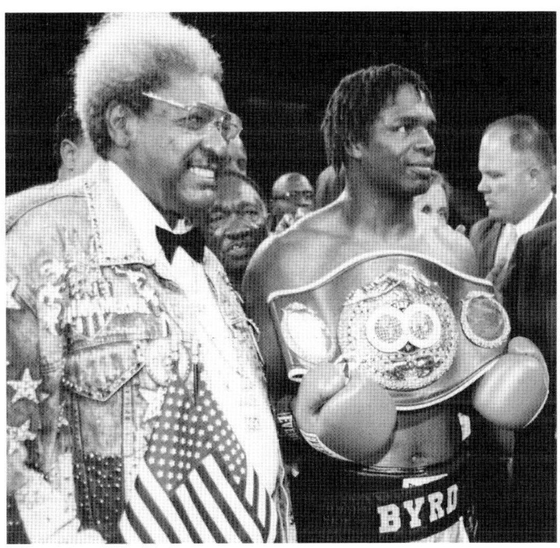

Changing of the Guard. Evander Holyfield, a former undisputed champion in both the heavyweight and cruiserweight divisions, fought 11 times under the lights of Atlantic City's venues. In his final bout at the seaside resort, an aging Evander lost by unanimous decision to younger and faster Chris Byrd (right, shown with Don King) in a fight for the vacant IBF heavyweight title on December 14, 2002, at Convention Hall. Byrd held the IBF title until 2006. (Photograph by Ray Bailey.)

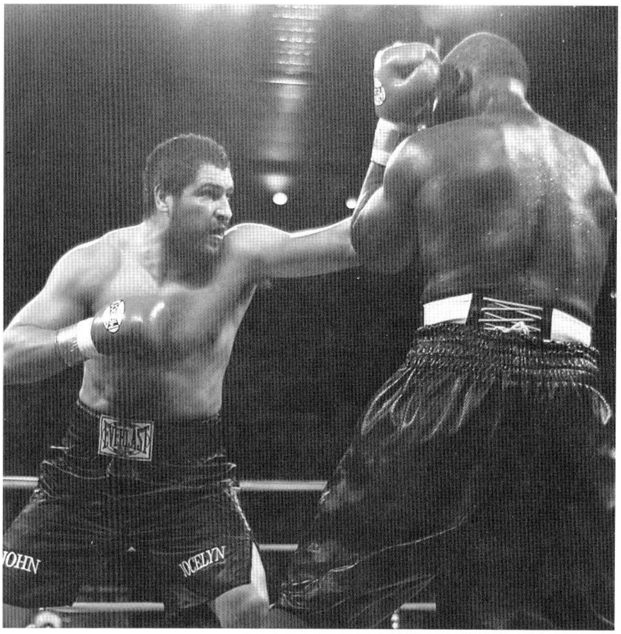

MONSTER CARD. On December 13, 2003, Don King presented a gigantic card at Convention Hall featuring eight world title bouts. John Ruiz won the vacant WBA heavyweight title with a decision over Hasim Rahman (pictured). Cory Spinks unified the world welterweight title with a 12-round decision over Ricardo Mayorga. World middleweight champion Bernard Hopkins made his 17th defense with a win over William Joppy. Zab Judah also defended his title that night. (Photograph by Ray Bailey.)

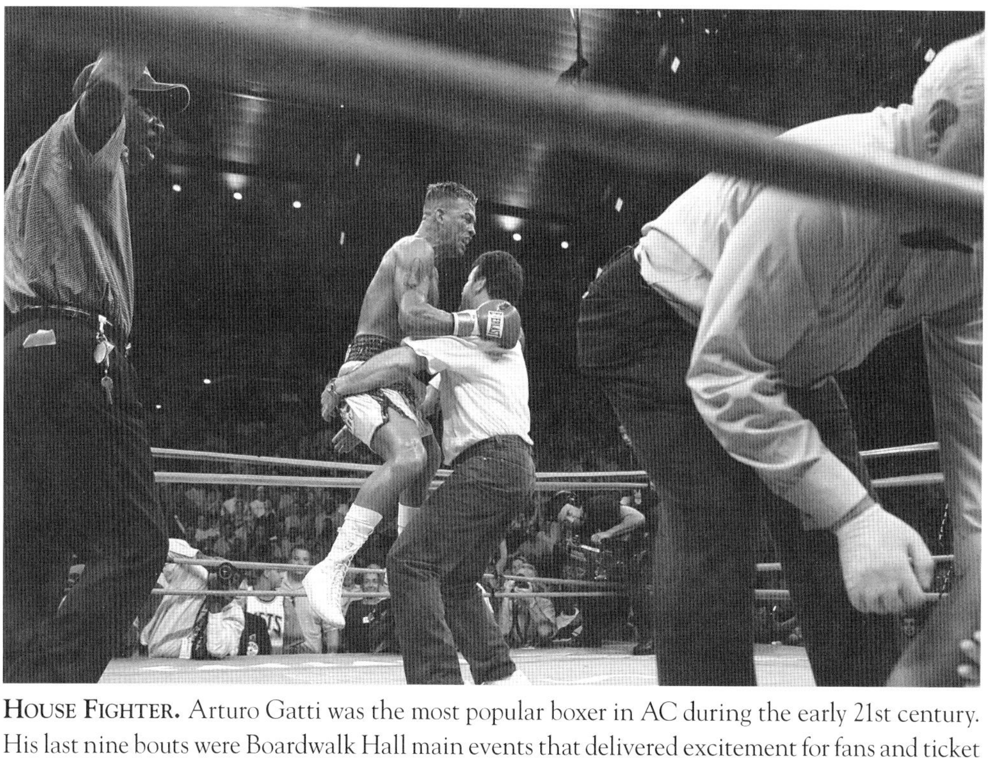

HOUSE FIGHTER. Arturo Gatti was the most popular boxer in AC during the early 21st century. His last nine bouts were Boardwalk Hall main events that delivered excitement for fans and ticket sales for promoters. His box office appeal earned him a new nickname, the "Bruce Springsteen of Boardwalk Hall." Some of his final opponents included Gianluca Branco, Leonard Dorin, Jesse James Leija, Thomas Damgaard, Carlos Baldomir, and Alfonso Gomez. (Photograph by Ray Bailey.)

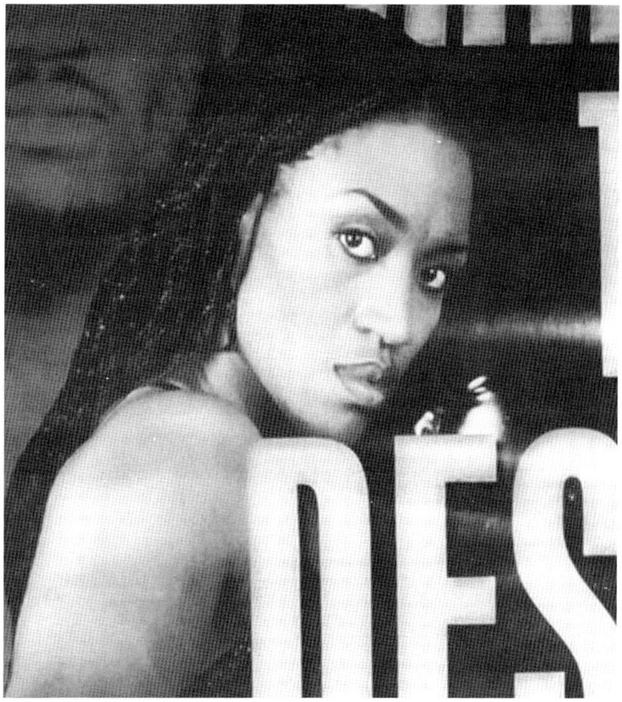

Sister Smoke. Jacqui Frazier-Lyde, the daughter of "Smokin'" Joe Frazier, fought her final career bout on September 10, 2004, at the Tropicana. "Sister Smoke," the former super middleweight and light heavyweight female champion, defeated Mary Ann Almager, a former two-division champion herself, by unanimous 10-round decision to win the women's heavyweight championship. Almager knocked Jacqui down twice, but Frazier-Lyde still swept the judges' scorecards. The fight was promoted by Diane Lee Fischer's Dee Lee Promotions. (Author's collection.)

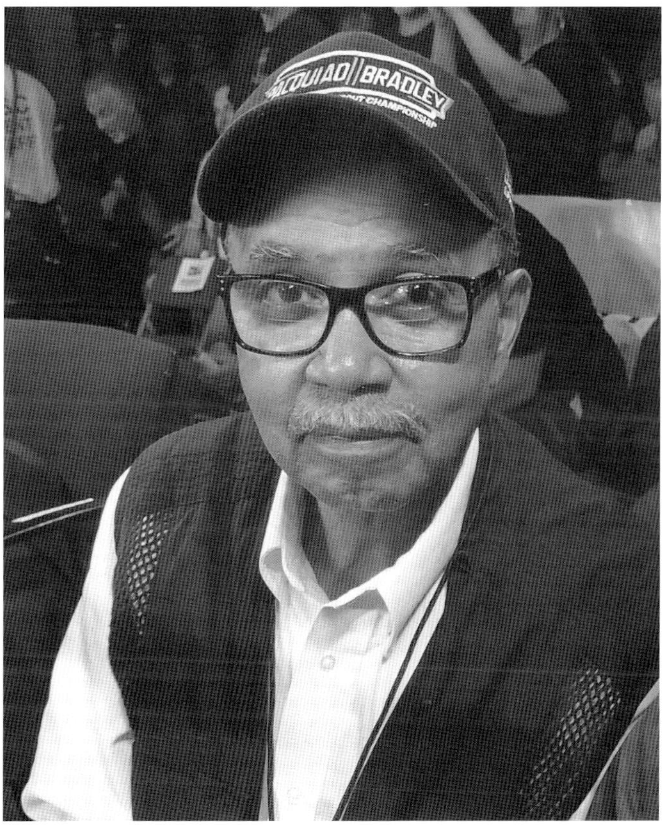

Ringside Photographer. Ray Bailey began photographing fights around 1990 and remains active today. Bailey's lens captured many greats over the past three decades, including Arturo Gatti, Evander Holyfield, George Foreman, Larry Holmes, James Toney, Roberto Duran, Ray Leonard, Hector Camacho, Lennox Lewis, Floyd Mayweather, Bernard Hopkins, and Andre Ward. His work earned him spots in the New Jersey and Atlantic City Halls of Fame, and his photographs are featured throughout this book. (Photograph by Ray Bailey.)

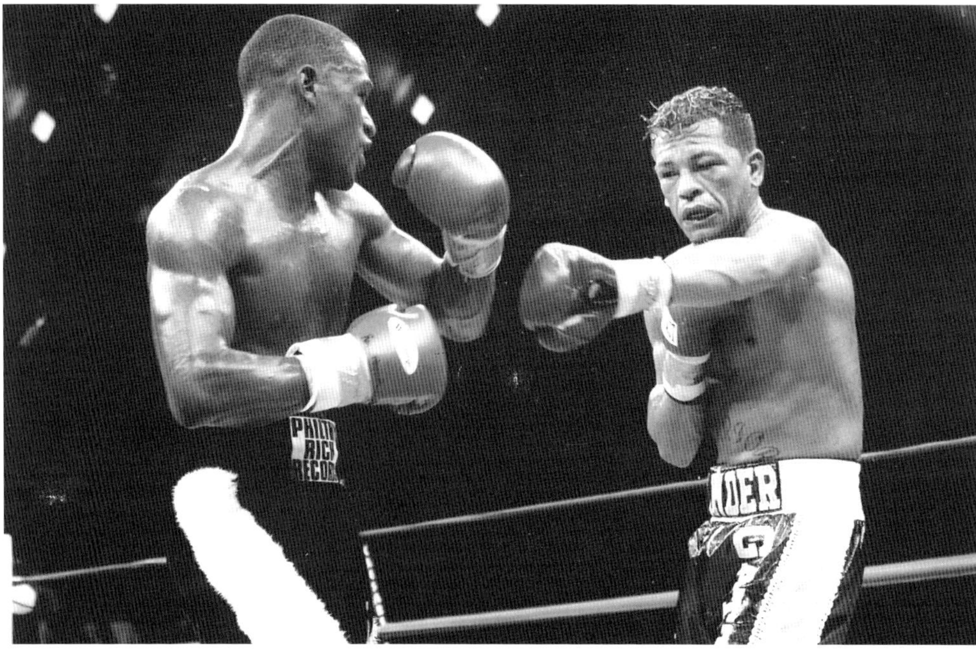

On the Money. Floyd "Money" Mayweather Jr. fought four times in Atlantic City, including a win over DeMarcus Corley in a title eliminator. His biggest AC bout came against WBC junior welterweight champion Arturo Gatti on June 25, 2005, at Convention Hall. Headlining his first ever pay-per-view event, Mayweather (left) stopped Gatti after six rounds to win his third division title before a crowd of 12,675. Mayweather improved to 34-0 with the win. (Photograph by Ray Bailey.)

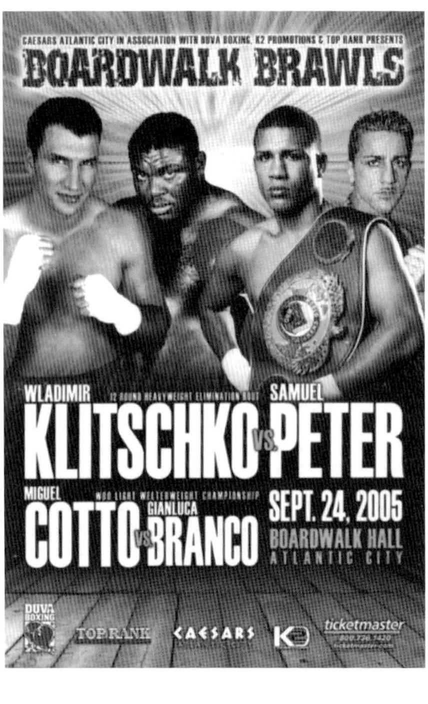

Pride of Ukraine. Over the course of his 20-year professional career, Wladimir Klitschko fought in AC on two occasions. The first came on June 29, 2002, when the Ukrainian defeated Ray Mercer by sixth-round technical knockout at the Taj Mahal to defend his WBO heavyweight title. Klitschko returned to the city on September 24, 2005, when he defeated Sam Peter by unanimous decision in an important title elimination bout at Convention Hall. (Author's collection.)

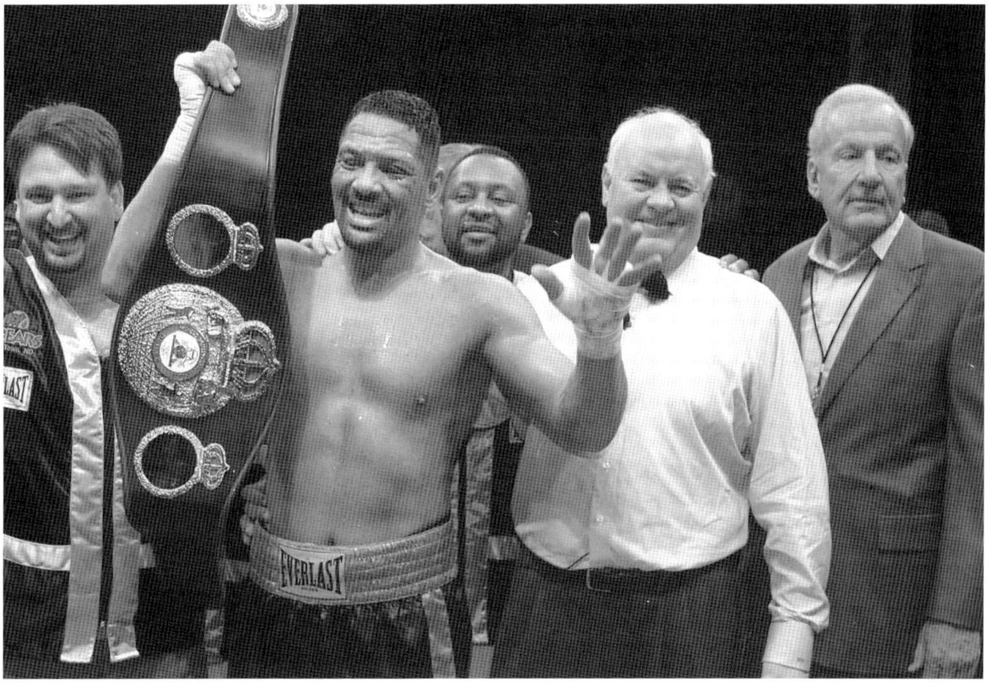

Only a Number. Forty-two-year-old former two-division champion Virgil Hill won a statement victory and proved that "age is only a number" on January 27, 2006, at the Tropicana. Hill decisively defeated 29-year-old Valery Brudov for the vacant WBA cruiserweight title. This was not the first time Hill won a world title in AC. In 1987, he captured the WBA light heavyweight title by defeating Leslie Stewart at Trump Plaza. (Photograph by Ray Bailey.)

Conventional Hall Knockouts. All three of Miguel Cotto's Atlantic City fights were knockouts at Convention Hall. Cotto came off the floor to stop Ricardo Torres in the seventh round of a WBO junior welterweight title defense on September 24, 2005. On December 2, 2006, Cotto halted Carlos Quintana in five rounds to win the vacant WBA welterweight title (pictured). Cotto also stopped Alfonso Gomez in five rounds on April 12, 2008. (Photograph by Ray Bailey.)

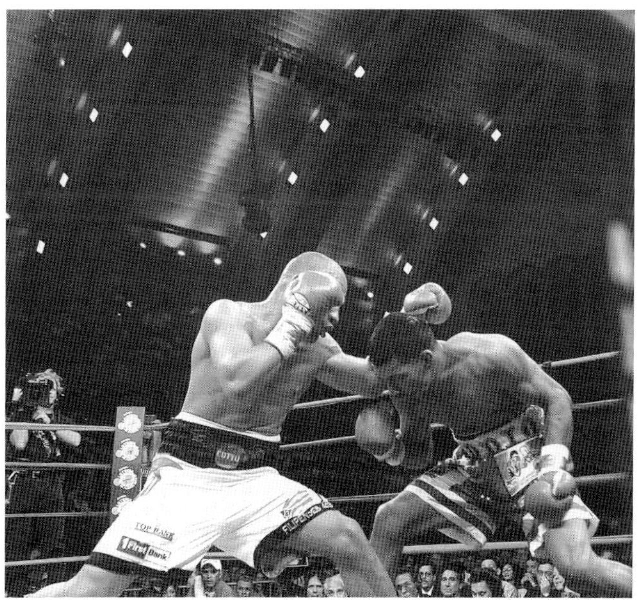

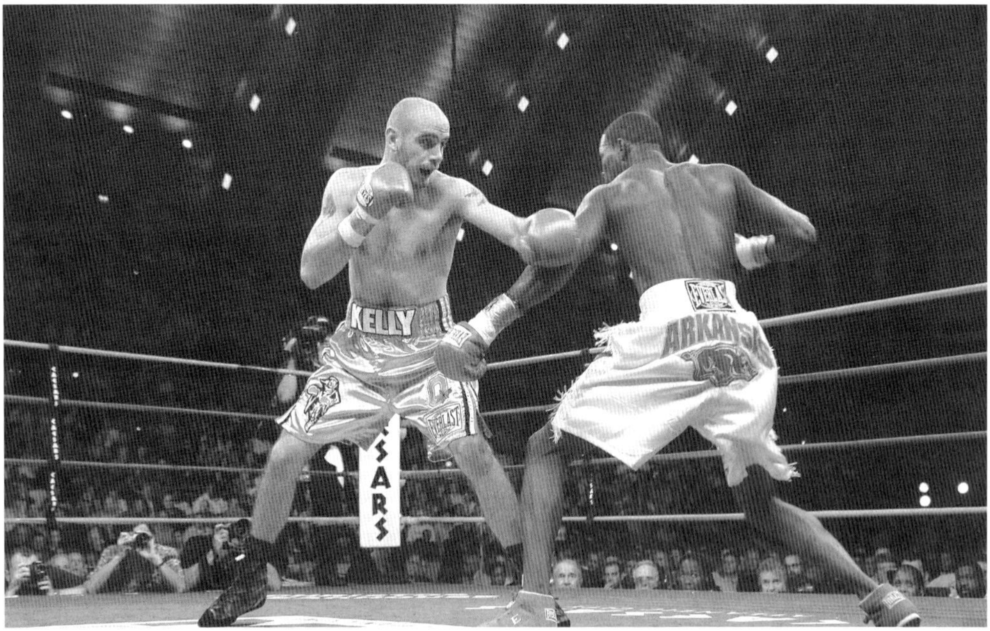

THE PRIDE OF YOUNGSTOWN. Kelly Pavlik, of Youngstown, Ohio, won the WBC and WBO middleweight titles with an upset victory over defending champion Jermain Taylor on September 29, 2007, at Convention Hall. Taylor floored Pavlik in round two and was leading on the scorecards before Pavlik caught the champion with a left hook in round seven. Pavlik followed up with a barrage of punches that compelled referee Steve Smoger to stop the fight. (Photograph by Ray Bailey.)

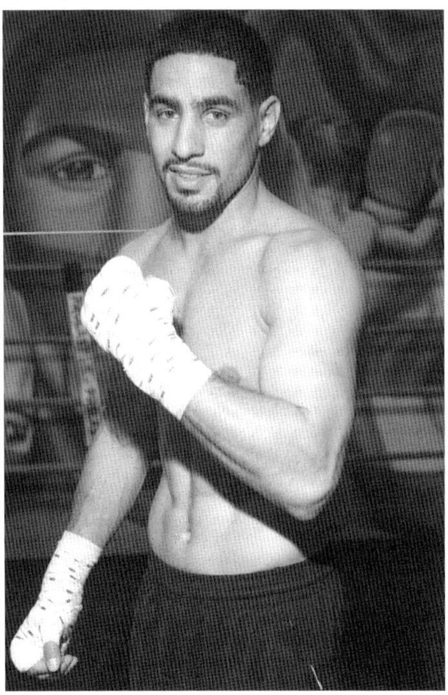

GARCIA DEBUTS. Multi-champion Danny Garcia made his professional debut on November 17, 2007, at the Borgata. Garcia scored three knockdowns and stopped Mike Denby in 68 seconds. He returned to AC for another knockout victory one year later and eventually won world titles at junior welterweight and welterweight. By the end of 2020, Garcia had a record of 36-3, with 21 KOs, and had participated in 10 world championship bouts. (Photograph by Darryl Cobb Jr.)

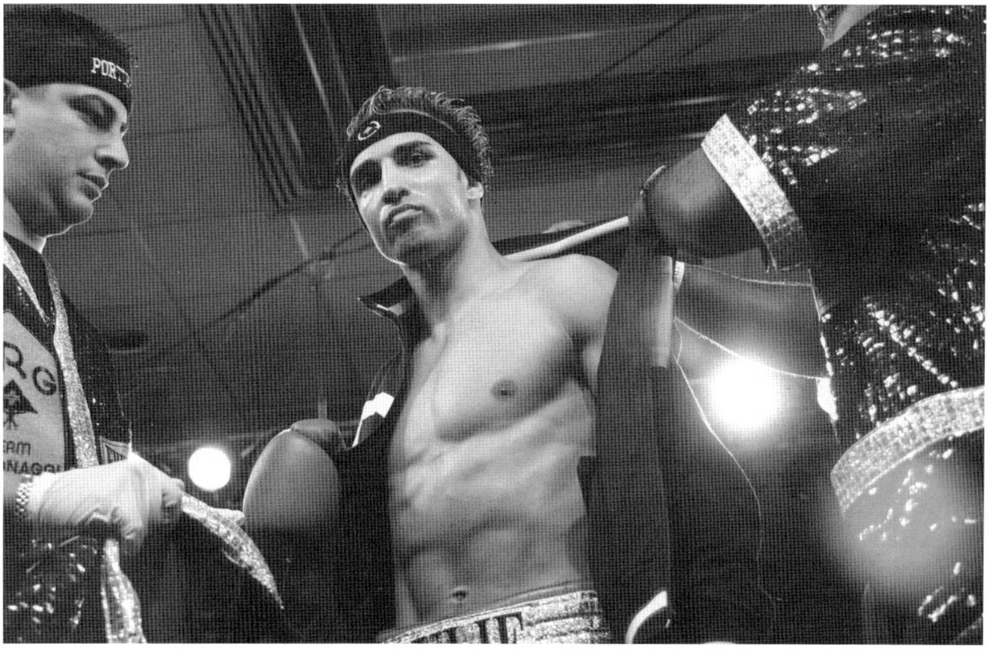

Magical Defense. Brooklyn native Paulie "Magic Man" Malignaggi came to Atlantic City twice during his career, including a 2008 defense of his IBF junior welterweight title against Hermann Ngoudjo at Bally's Park Place on January 5. Despite suffering a cut above his left eye in the fourth round, Malignaggi defeated the challenger via a 12-round unanimous decision. (Photograph by Ray Bailey.)

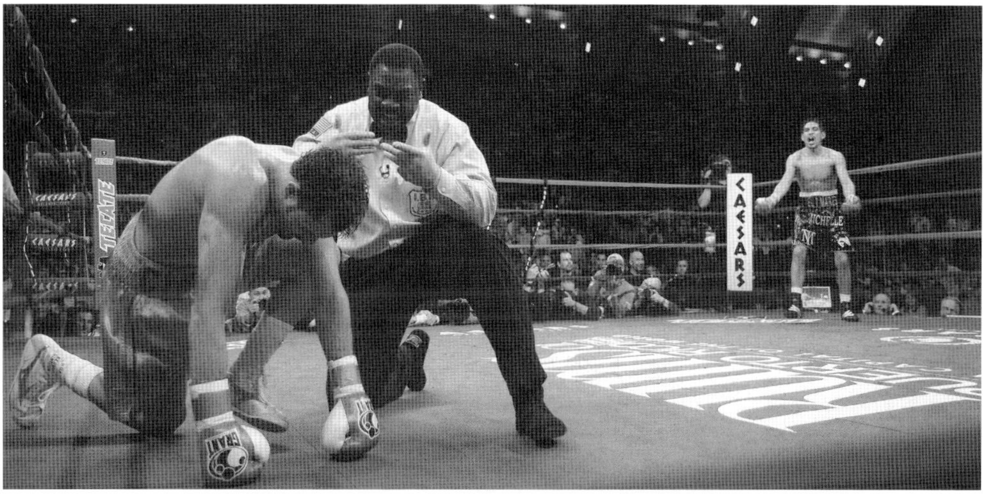

Perfect Boardwalk Record. Antonio Margarito won three title bouts at Convention Hall. First, he defended his WBO welterweight title for the fourth time with a 10th-round TKO over Sebastian Lujan on February 18, 2005. On December 2, 2006, Margarito won his seventh title defense by unanimous decision over Joshua Clottey. Finally, Margarito knocked out Kermit Cintron with a body shot (pictured) to win the IBF welterweight title on April 12, 2008. (Photograph by Ray Bailey.)

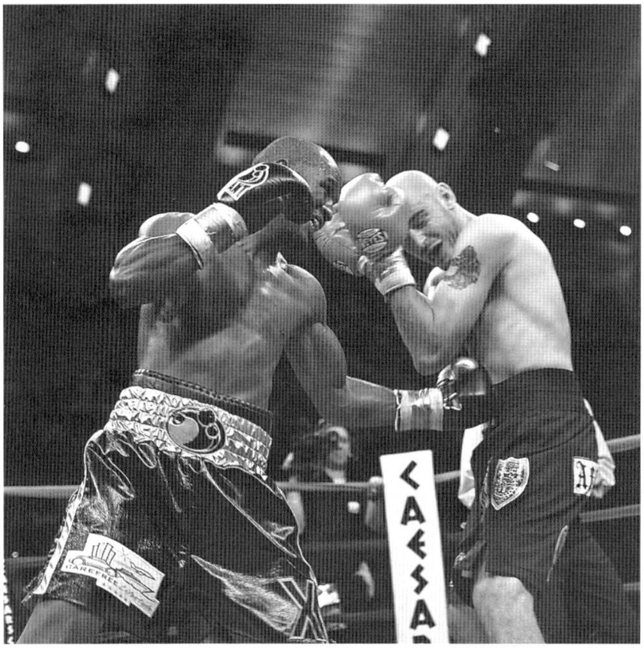

Big Boardwalk Upsets. Two of Bernard Hopkins's best career wins were major upsets at Convention Hall. On June 10, 2006, the 41-year-old Hopkins shocked much of the boxing world with an upset of IBO light heavyweight champion Antonio Tarver by a 12-round unanimous decision. Then on October 18, 2008, Hopkins did it again with a surprise 12-round unanimous decision victory over Kelly Pavlik in a super middleweight non-title bout. (Photograph by Ray Bailey.)

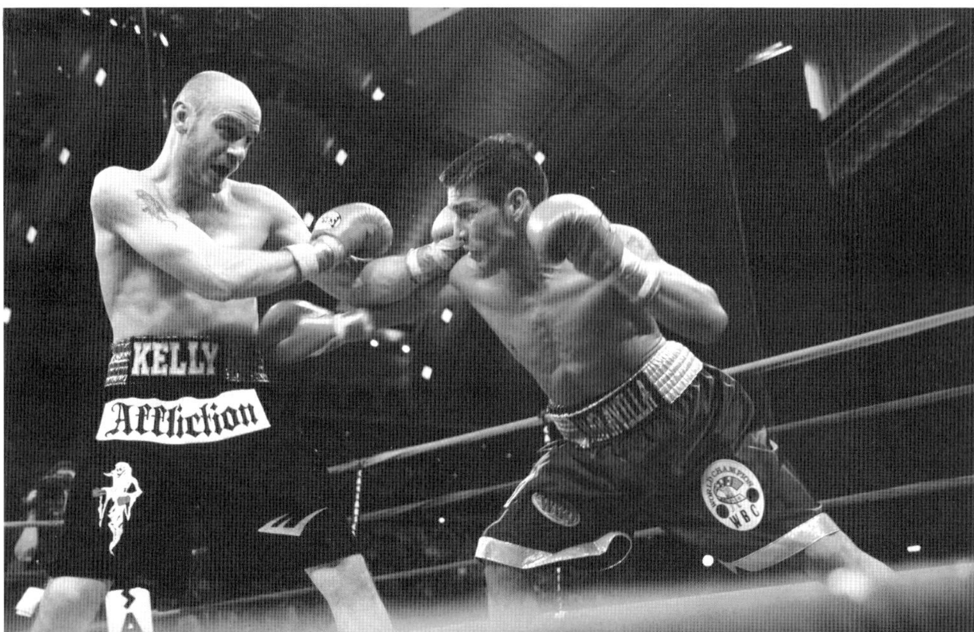

Martinez Wins Middleweight Crown. Sergio Martinez captured the middleweight championship on April 17, 2010, with a 12-round decision over Kelly Pavlik. Pavlik was making the fourth defense of his WBC, WBO, and *The Ring* magazine titles. The bout at Convention Hall was essentially even after eight rounds before Martinez rallied at the end of the fight to earn the victory. Martinez, who came off the floor in round seven, previously held the WBC junior middleweight title. (Photograph by Ray Bailey.)

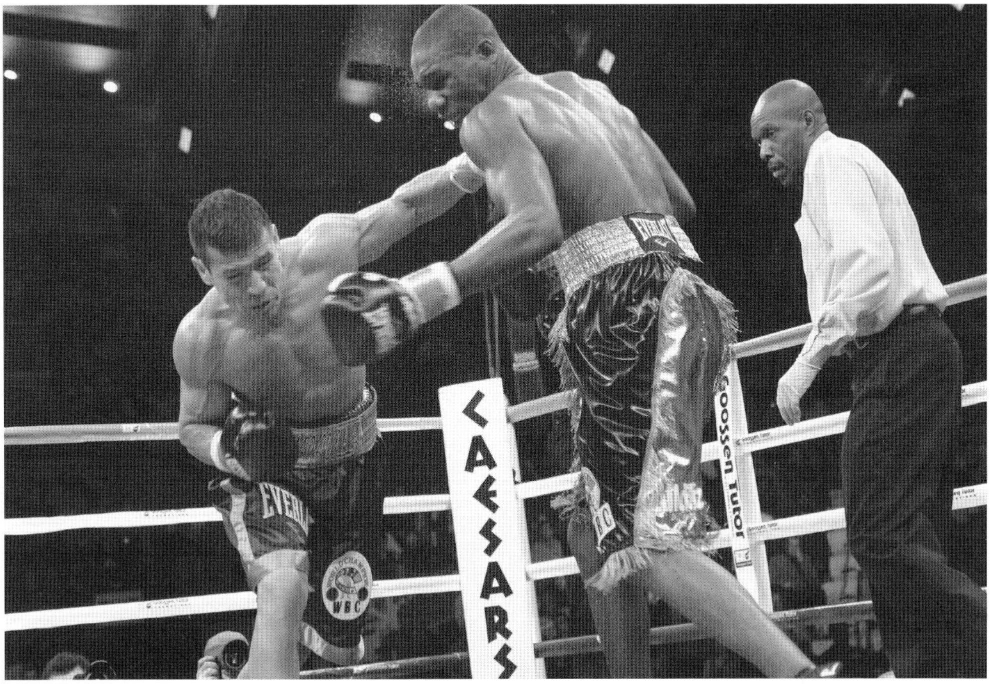

KILLER KO. In their first meeting, Paul Williams won an exciting decision over Sergio Martinez. However, in the rematch on November 20, 2010, at Convention Hall, Martinez (left) turned the tables with a crushing knockout in round two. Despite Williams's reputation as a puncher, it was Martinez who landed a devastating left that sent Williams crashing face-first onto the canvas. This was Martinez's first defense of his WBC, WBO, and *The Ring* magazine titles. (Photograph by Ray Bailey.)

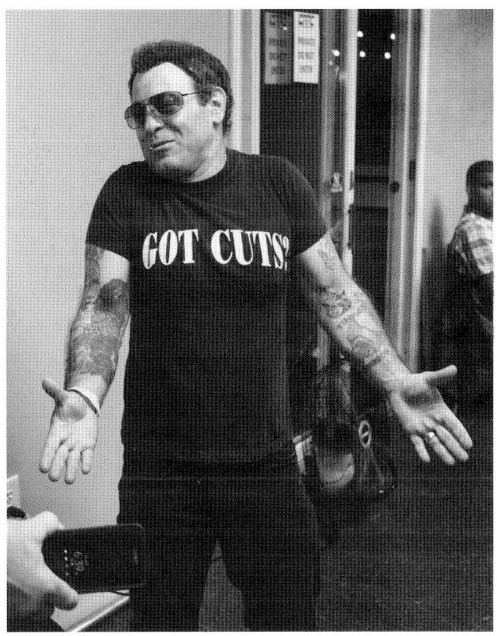

RENAISSANCE MAN. Joey Intrieri, also known as "Joey Eye," boxed in the 1990s but later made his mark as a cut man. Schooled by some of Philadelphia's best cornermen, Eye worked with numerous boxers through the years, from club fighters to champions. In addition, Eye held almost every other job in the business, including promoter, trainer, and gym proprietor. Joey also had a second career as an actor. (Photograph by Jano Cohen.)

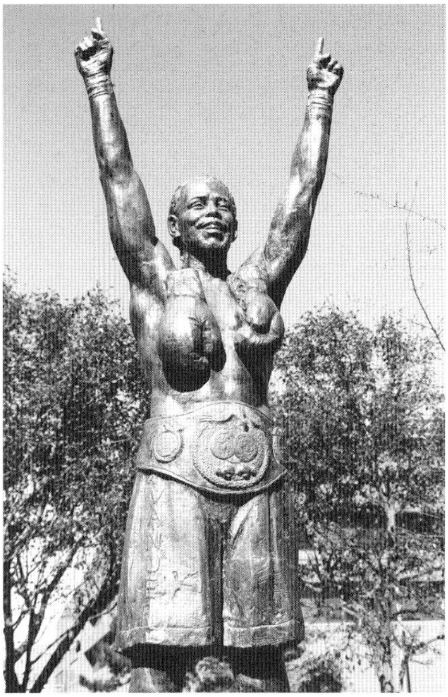

A HERO REMEMBERED. Few public figures are more beloved in Atlantic City than former IBF lightweight champion Leavander Johnson, whose life was tragically cut short by injuries sustained in a 2005 championship fight. In 2011, the city dedicated a statue by artist Brian Hanlon of a victorious Johnson in City Center Park at 1222 Atlantic Avenue. Johnson's record of 34-5-2, 26 KOs, and other career statistics are etched onto the base of the statue. (Photograph by John DiSanto.)

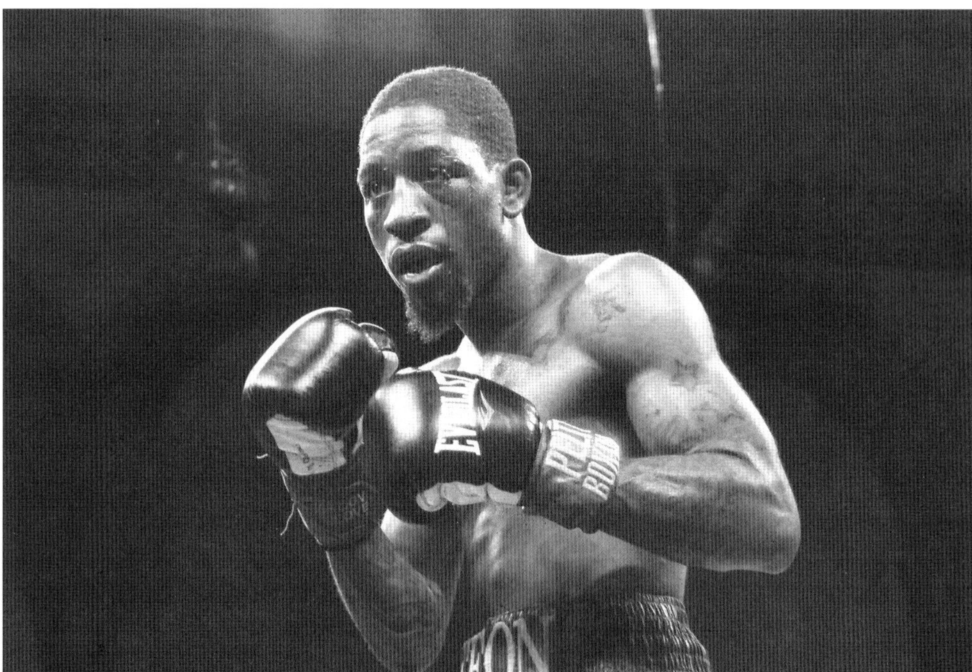

THE TWO TEONS. In his eight Atlantic City fights, junior featherweight Teon Kennedy often chose to brawl rather than use the slick skills that earned his nickname, "The Technician." However, regardless of which style he used, Kennedy was an entertaining fighter. His biggest win at the shore came on March 26, 2011, when he beat undefeated contender Jorge Diaz by decision to defend his USBA title at Convention Hall. (Photograph by Ray Bailey.)

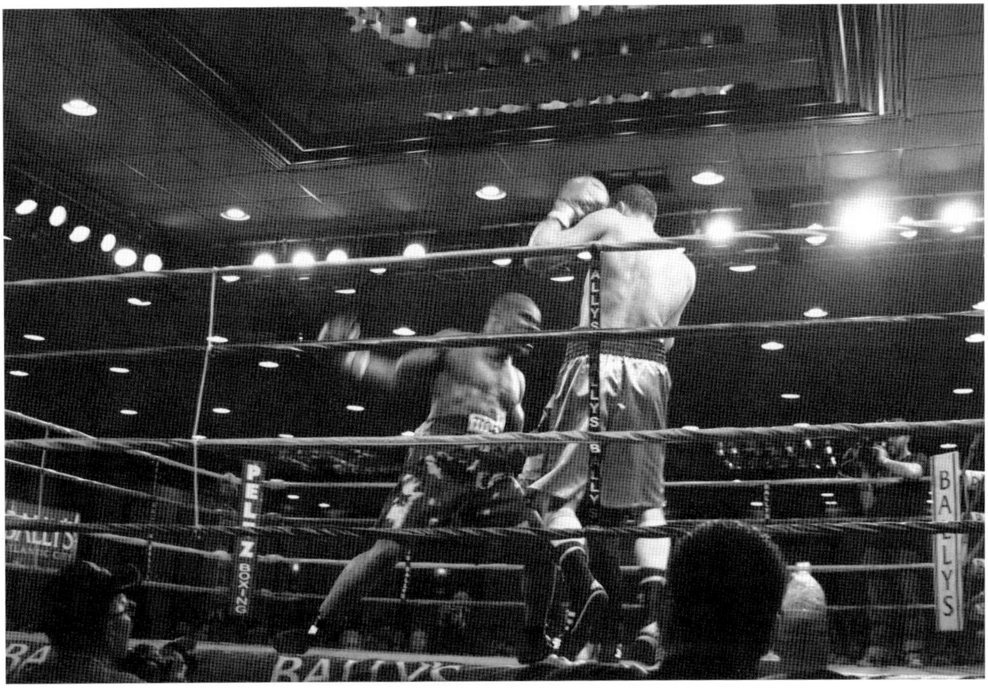

Colossal KO. USBA cruiserweight champion Garrett Wilson scored a last-minute knockout of Wildwood's Chuck Mussachio on November 19, 2011, at Bally's. After trailing throughout the entire fight, Wilson saved his title in the 12th round with a booming right hand that sent Mussachio crashing to the canvas for the 10-count. Wilson made five other starts at the shore, including wins over Omar Sheika and Andres Taylor. Mussachio appeared in AC 18 times. (Photograph by John DiSanto.)

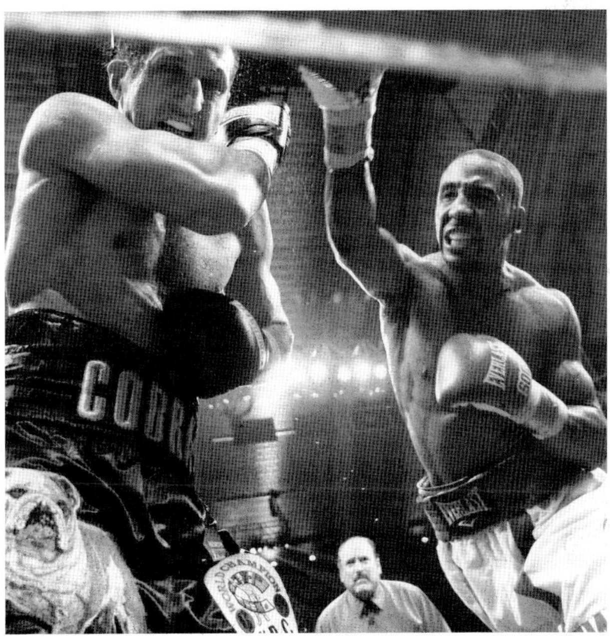

Ward Wins Tourney. After 10 preliminary bouts narrowed the tournament field down to the two best super middleweights in the world, Andre Ward (WBA champion) defeated Carl Froch (WBC champion) by unanimous decision to win the Super Six World Boxing Classic on December 17, 2011, at Convention Hall. Ward remained undefeated with the victory (25-0). He would eventually gain recognition as the world's best pound-for-pound fighter before retiring in 2017 with an undefeated record of 32-0. (Photograph by Ray Bailey.)

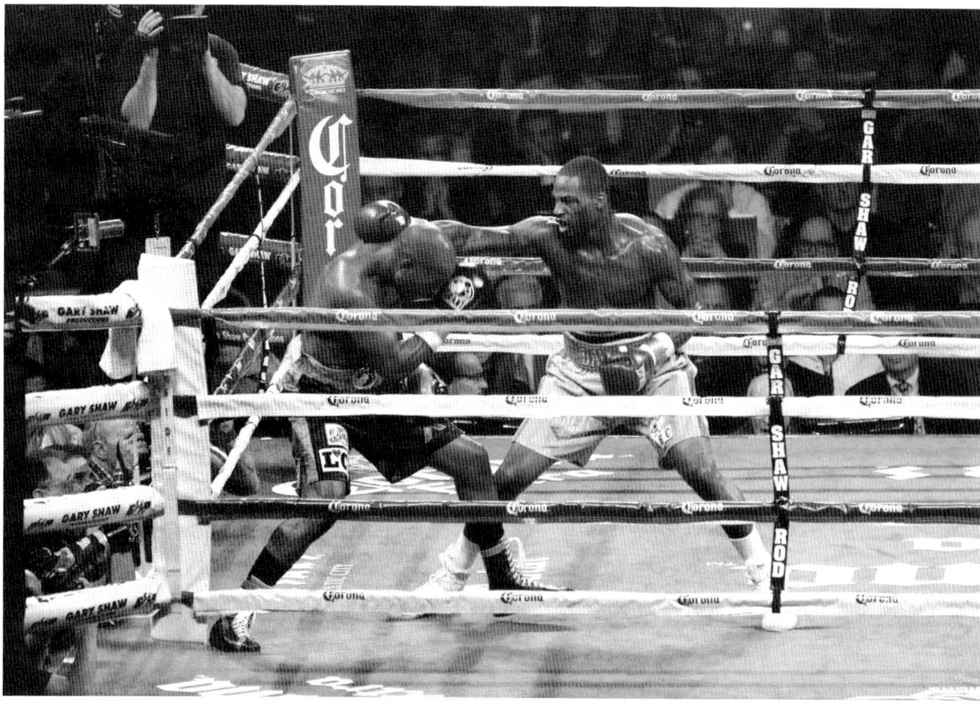

DAWSON DEFEATS HOPKINS. After their first meeting ended in a controversial no-contest, Chad Dawson (right) defeated Bernard Hopkins (left) by majority decision to win the WBC light heavyweight title on April 28, 2012, at Convention Hall. At the time, most assumed the 47-year-old Hopkins had finally reached the end of the line. However, the legend fought for nearly five more years and went on to capture more titles. (Photograph by Ray Bailey.)

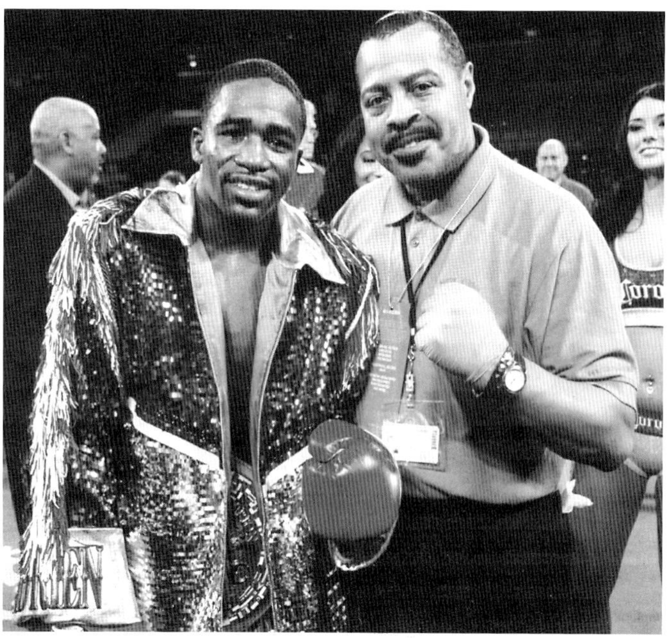

BRONER SHINES. Former WBO 130-pound champion Adrien Broner had two consecutive fights in Atlantic City. First, he moved up to lightweight and took the WBC title from Antonio DeMarco by eighth-round technical knockout on November 17, 2012, at Convention Hall. He returned to Convention Hall on February 16, 2013, to make his only defense of the lightweight title with a fifth-round technical knockout of Gavin Rees. (Photograph by Ray Bailey.)

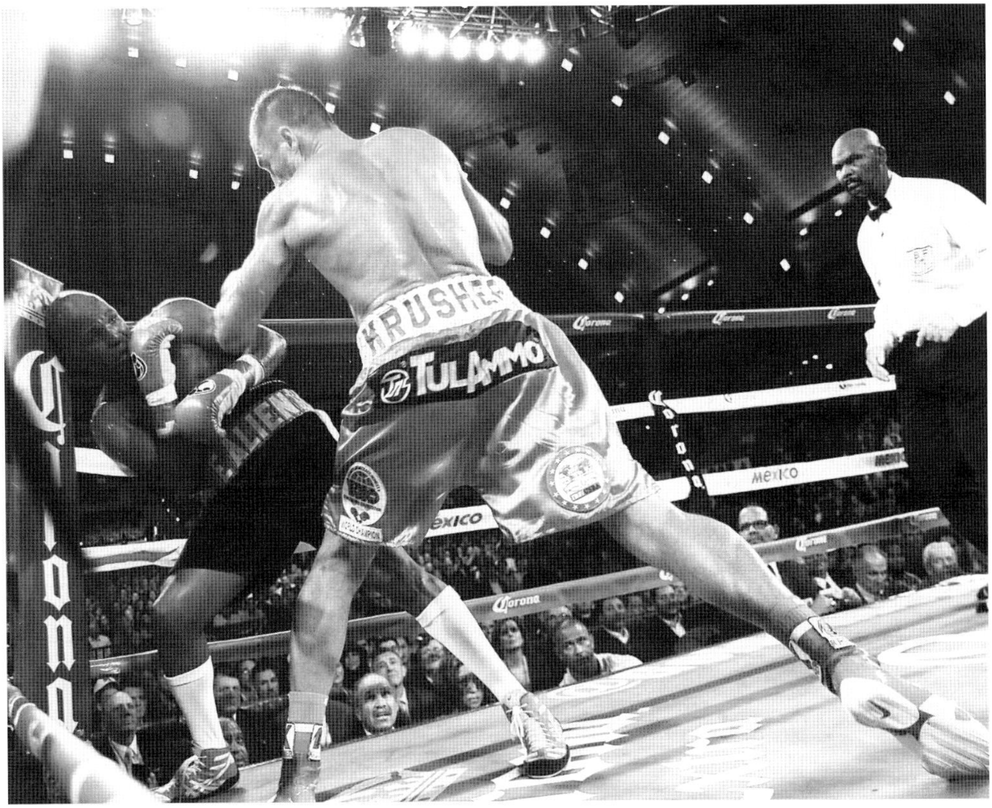

The End of an Era. In a light heavyweight championship unification bout, WBO champion Sergey Kovalev defeated WBA and IBF champion Bernard Hopkins by unanimous decision at Boardwalk Hall on November 8, 2014. Kovalev pressured and outworked Hopkins, who finally succumbed to Father Time, two months shy of his 50th birthday. This was the last of 19 appearances in Atlantic City for Hopkins. He retired after his next bout. (Photograph by Ray Bailey.)

Crowd-Pleaser. North Philly fighter Gabriel Rosado fought in Atlantic City five times, including his second shot at the middleweight championship on October 26, 2013, at Convention Hall. The crowd-pleasing "King Gabriel" gave WBO champion Peter "Kid Chocolate" Quillin plenty of trouble before being cut and stopped in round 10. Rosado defeated Saul Roman, Jamaal Davis, Latif Mundy, and Ayi Bruce in his other AC appearances. (Photograph by Ray Bailey.)

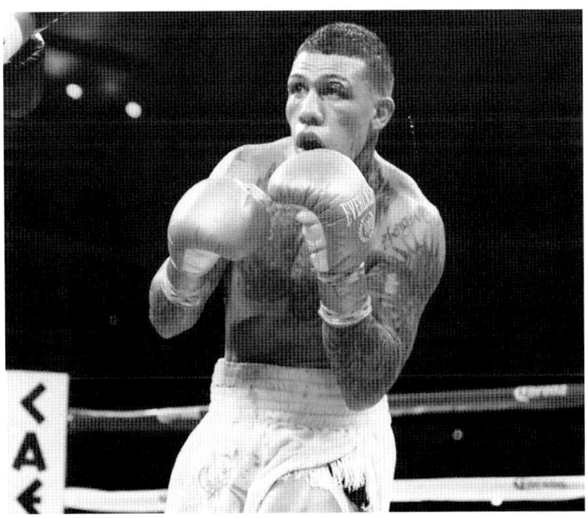

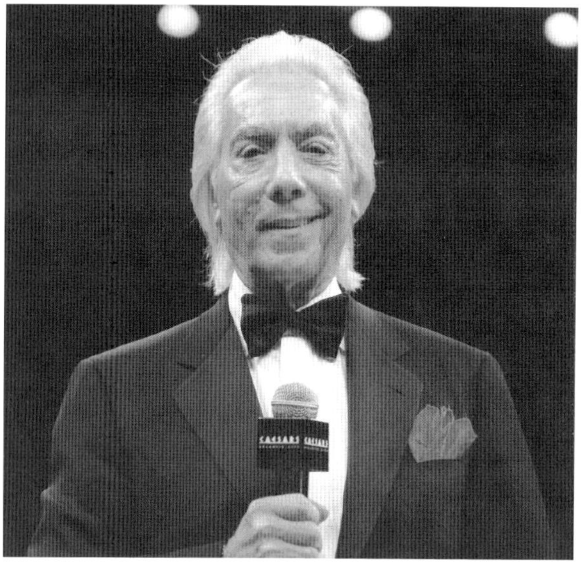

Boxing Emcee. In the modern era, Camden, New Jersey, native Nino Del Buono was Atlantic City boxing's busiest ring announcer. Del Buono worked numerous fight cards around the city and served as emcee for the Pennsylvania Boxing Hall of Fame, the Atlantic City Boxing Hall of Fame, and many other boxing-related events and functions. Retired from his family-owned bakery, Del Buono was also a film and stage actor. (Photograph by Ray Bailey.)

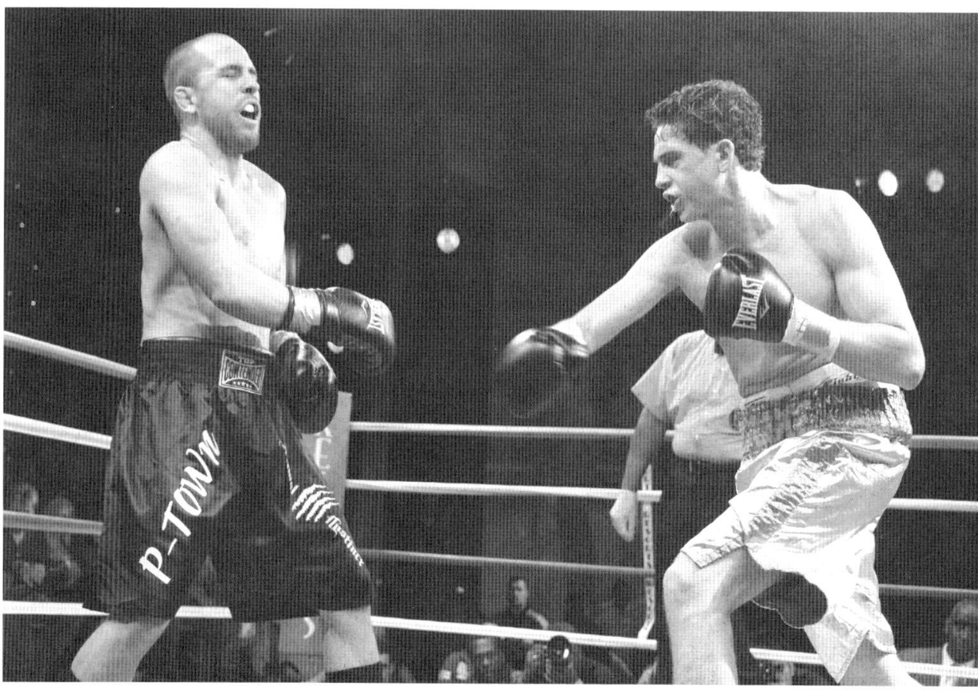

Boxer-Promoter Keeps AC Going. Millville's Thomas "Cornflake" LaManna's boxing career included 20 AC starts. However, his biggest contribution to the seaside fight scene was as a promoter. LaManna's Rising Star Promotions helped to keep the sport alive during the shore's 21st-century boxing slump. Rising Star staged shows at the Claridge and the Showboat, sometimes with LaManna (right) on the bill. Boxing historians believe Rising Star's fight card at the Showboat on February 24, 2018, was the first boxing show held on a casino floor, albeit inactive at the time. LaManna's mother, Debra LaManna, was Cornflake's business partner and copromoter. (Photograph by Ray Bailey.)

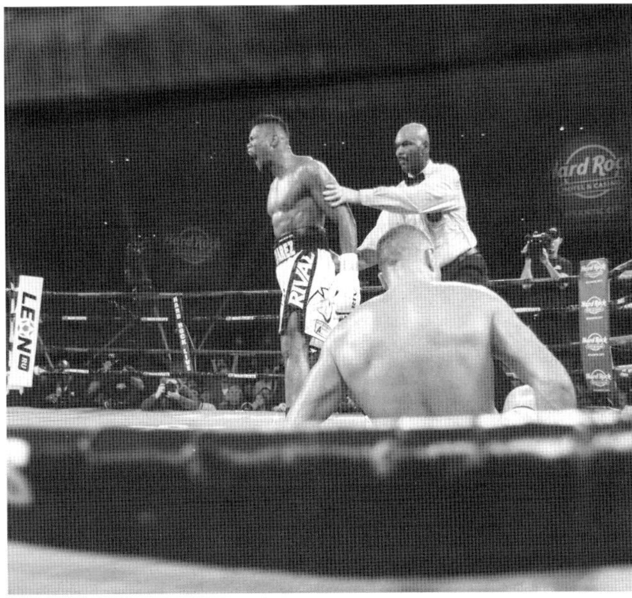

Krusher Gets Crushed. On August 4, 2018, WBO light heavyweight champion Sergey "Krusher" Kovalev held a comfortable lead on the scorecards halfway through his title defense against Eleider Alvarez at the Hard Rock. However, in round seven, Alvarez shocked the boxing world by knocking down Kovalev three times to take the title in a huge upset. Six months later in the rematch, Kovalev regained his crown by decision victory. (Photograph by Ray Bailey.)

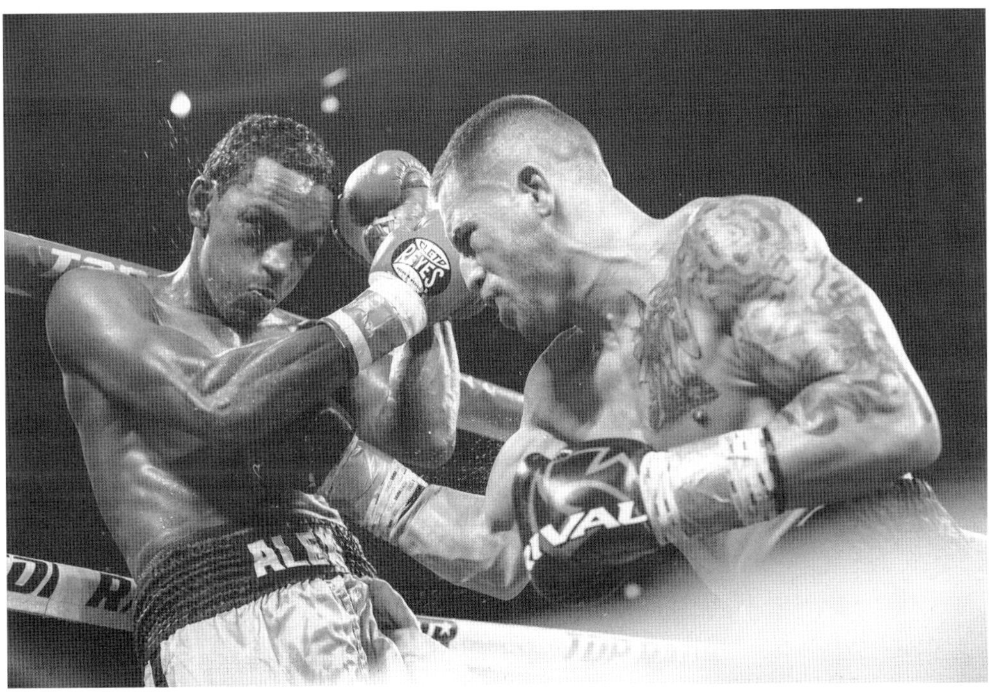

Lost Gem. One of the most grueling AC fights in recent history occurred on August 18, 2018, at Ocean Resort Casino. The nonstop slugfest between former WBA junior lightweight champion Jason Sosa (right) and Reynaldo Blanco was only witnessed by a small group of die-hard fans who stayed for the final bout of the night. Regardless, Sosa continued his comeback with a memorable eight-round unanimous decision victory. (Photograph by Darryl Cobb Jr.)

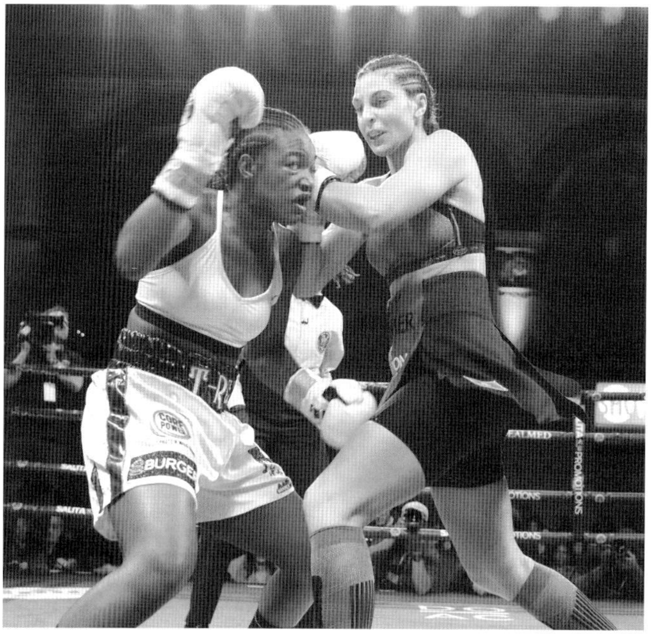

Females Unify Crown. On April 13, 2019, the two top female middleweights met in a unification bout at Convention Hall. Two-time Olympic Gold Medalist Claressa Shields, the WBA and IBF champion, and Christina Hammer, WBC and WBO champion, put all the titles on the line. After 10 rounds, Shields (left) emerged as an undisputed world champion, winning the bout by unanimous decision. The referee was Sparkle Lee, AC's premier female referee. (Photograph by Ray Bailey.)

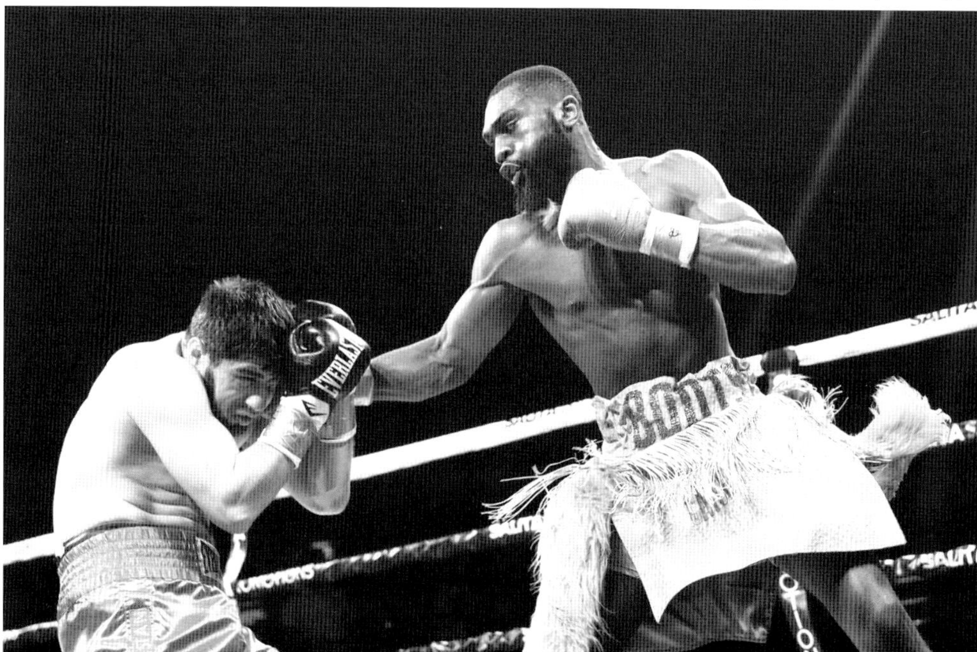

Hot Prospect. Fast-rising welterweight prospect Jaron "Boots" Ennis made two visits to Atlantic City as he rose in the rankings. The youngest member of the fighting Ennis family, which includes brothers Derek and Farah and father-trainer Bozy, stopped Mike Arnaoutis at the Showboat on June 1, 2018, and Bakhtiyar Eyubov at the Ocean Resort Casino on January 10, 2020 (pictured). By 2020, Boots boasted a record of 26-0, with 24 KOs. (Photograph by Darryl Cobb Jr.)

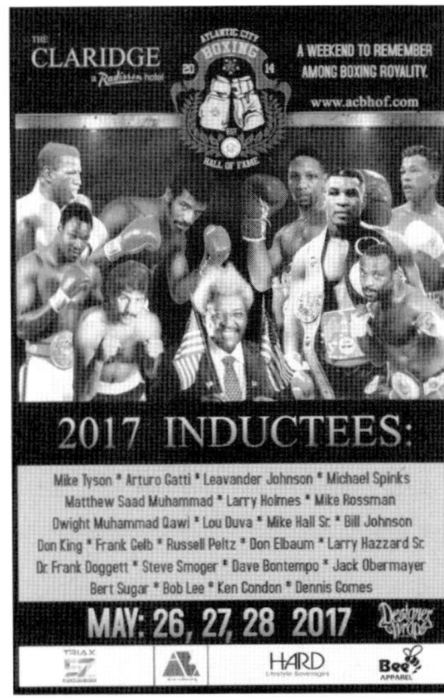

A Home for AC's Boxing History. The Atlantic City Boxing Hall of Fame, founded in 2014 by Ray McCline, is committed to bringing the city's rich boxing history to life through highly interactive ceremonies and exhibits over the course of its annual induction weekend. The 2017 inaugural induction class included many greats, including Mike Tyson, Arturo Gatti, Michael Spinks, Leavander Johnson, Lou Duva, Frank Gelb, Matthew Saad Muhammad, and others. (Author's collection.)

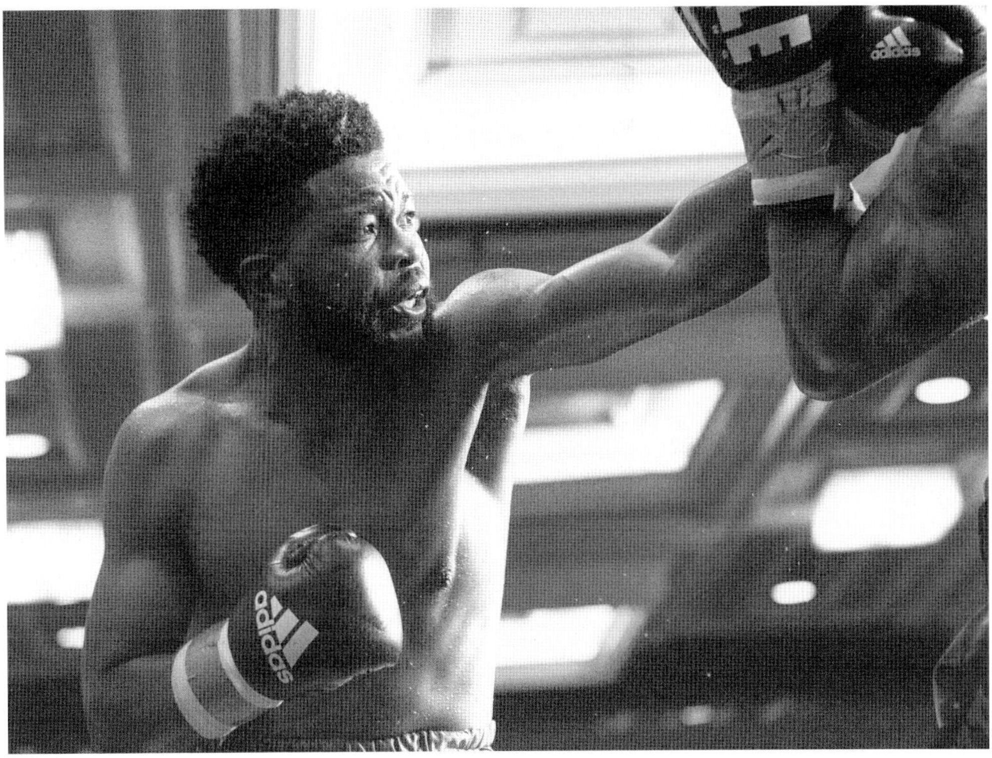

Other AC Boxers. The AC area produced numerous boxers who were not previously mentioned in this book. Whether Atlantic City natives or adopted sons, other fighters include Osnel Charles (pictured), Shamone Alvarez, John Brown, Joe Dorsey, Dick Dundee, Tilton Edgehill, Young Foster, Joe Hilsee, Bob Johnson, Bobby Jones, Nick Lucas, George Nelson, Eddie Palmer, Gabriel Pham, Billy Pimpus, Tiger Reed, Joey Reynolds, Jimmy Rhodes, Larry Russell, Al Walters, Ritz Walters, Ralph Ward, Vernon Williams, Harry Willis, and Anthony Young. (Photograph by Darryl Cobb Jr.)